Creative Machine Knitting

A voyage of discovery into colour, shape and stitches

Creative Machine Knitting

A voyage of discovery into colour, shape and stitches

Alison Dupernex

THE CROWOOD PRESS

First published in 2022 by
The Crowood Press Ltd
Ramsbury, Marlborough
Wiltshire SN8 2HR

enquiries@crowood.com

www.crowood.com

British Library Cataloguing-in-Publication Data
A catalogue record for this book is available from
the British Library.

ISBN 978 0 71984099 9

Cover design: Peggy Issenman

Typeset by Sharon Dainton Design
Printed and bound in India by Parksons Graphics

CONTENTS

ABBREVIATIONS

0	the punched hole or yarn in Feeder 2	MT	main tension
alt	alternate	MY	main yarn
beg	beginning	Ns	needles
cm	centimetres	NWP	non-working position
COL	carriage on left	P	purl
Col	colour	patt	pattern
cont	continue	PP	punchcard pattern
COR	carriage on right	PPL	punchcard pattern locked
dec	decrease	RC	row counter
dec	decreasing	rem	remaining
E wrap cast on		rep	repeat
	wind the yarn from the right in a clockwise direction	RH	right hand
E wrap braid cast on		sl st	slip stitch
	wind the yarn from the right in a clockwise direction and back in an anti-clockwise direction	st st	stocking stitch
		st	stitch
ff	fully fashioned	TD	tension dial
foll	following	tog	together
g	grams	UWP	upper working position
HP	holding position	WP	working position
inc	increase	WY	waste yarn
k	knit	X	the non-punched square on the punchcard, or the yarn in Feeder 1
MT + 1,2,3			
	main tension one, two, three sizes looser than the main tension		

ACKNOWLEDGEMENTS

I have thoroughly enjoyed the challenge of working on ideas which have been in my mind for years. Writing this book has been a voyage of discovery and a delight, but I have not done this alone and there is a wonderful team of friends and family without whose help I could not have done it.

My grateful thanks go to everyone at The Crowood Press for their advice and confidence in my work.

Huge thanks must also go to Anne Smith, the editor of *Machine Knitting Monthly*, whose patience and time working through my manuscript helped me enormously.

Chris Birch knitted some of the scarf samples with her usual expertise and good humour, so thank you.

The fabulous models who constantly dropped everything to make themselves available to try out various poses and wear my designs. Sharon McSwiney, Tim, Morag, Hazel, Mihika, Susie, Sam, Tom, plus Wulfie, Caspar and Cressida who required a lollipop for each photoshoot. Thanks also to Henry Arden for taking some of the images – perfect as always. Thank you to my husband Simon for producing the diagrams, and for proofreading the book.

Finally, thank you to the machine knitters worldwide who have offered encouragement and kind words regarding my work and practice. Either via email or Instagram. You cannot know how appreciated this is. Thank you all.

CHAPTER 1

AN INTRODUCTION TO DESIGN SOURCES

The aim of this book is to inspire you and open the door to a variety of design ideas that you may not have considered. The intention is for you to discover different combinations of stitch patterns and colours applied to garment shape, and then to be able to critically evaluate the overall integrity of the design concept that you have created. I hope the design ideas in this book will act as a springboard to give you confidence to try out your own customized versions, or send you off on a voyage of discovery.

The purpose of this book is not to encourage you to copy other designers' work, but to help you make use of the rich underlying principles that knitwear designers have been employing for hundreds of years – that is, the underlying grammar – in your own work. The book will not explain how to use your knitting machine, as there are many excellent books available that do this. It is assumed that, as a machine knitter, you already know the basics and can make a garment.

Ideas and inspiration are all around us, yet it is sometimes difficult to focus and hone in on one particular stimulus. Many designs will be a combination of several original ideas and elements, which all create a finished product. To help with this process you need to gather ideas and be open to inspiration wherever you are, and whatever you are doing, and you must not be afraid to accept that this process will lead to both success and failure.

CULTURE

All around the world countries have historic heritage patterns and designs that have stood the test of time, and are still being used as an inspiration and reinterpretation for contemporary designs. Regions within countries have used specific colour combinations and decorative symbols and have redesigned these, incorporating elements into their knitting, embroidery or weaving – in the UK you need only look at the differences in the classic fabric design heritage between England, Scotland and Wales, or the differences in typical design signifiers used by the Amish, the Native Americans and the descendants of the original Swedish immigrants in the USA state of Pennsylvania. Within each culture and sub-culture many of these classic design motifs are used repeatedly across a variety of crafts and skills, acknowledging that they have their origins deep within society.

Design, textile, costume, ethnographic and fashion museums such as the Victoria & Albert and the Fashion and Textile Museum, both in London, the Anna Wintour Costume Center at the Metropolitan Museum of Art in New York, the Musée de la Mode et du Textile and the Musée Galliera in Paris, and the Kyoto Costume Institute in Tokyo, hold a wealth of indigenous, ingenious, innovative and revelatory ideas – most of which can help to inspire your thoughts, and be reimagined when designing new knitted shapes or patterns. Proportions can be altered and colour combinations reimagined to create a unique and contemporary interpretation.

A wave of nostalgia and comfort is triggered in me by the sight of a Fairisle cardigan – a reminder of childhood perhaps. Although originally rather rough and scratchy to touch, the patterns were always uplifting with their joyful colour combinations. Yarn production has moved on considerably since the Prince of Wales was famously portrayed wearing a Fairisle top in the 1920s. Shetland wool is now easy care and soft to the touch, and the colour palette has been dramatically extended to include mixes reminiscent of the seas and heathery glens in the islands of the Inner and Outer Hebrides. Plaids, tartans and herringbone patterns all work well when placed alongside any Fairisle border or stripe.

The Kimono from Japan has influenced many Western designers for at least the past 150 years. Its unstructured, loose and relatively simple T-shape, together with its richly ornamented combination of geometric and naturalistic patterns, and bold but sympathetic colour combinations, continue to be a rich source of inspiration for designers – not only when studying shape, but also stitch pattern. An example of how this can be applied to contemporary design can be found in the Mulberry Blossom pattern.

You may find these other sources of classic design inspiring:

* Peruvian knitwear with its rainbow fluorescent colours knitted into stripes of animal motifs.
* Indian block-printed fabrics and sari

border colour combinations using an array of orange, terracotta, ochre and gold juxtaposed with emerald green, peacock blue and turquoise. If you place these colours in a stitch pattern on a ground of navy or deep red, the resulting knitted fabric will fizz and sing.

* Ancient Mexican motifs of stylized animals and birds, and the naturally dyed yarn colours of the large blanket ponchos.
* Scandinavian sweaters, with their pared back colours and the variety of motifs and border patterns that are easily adaptable for the knitting machine.
* Russia and other Eastern European countries such as Greece, Latvia, Romania and the Ukraine all have a national dress that embraces wonderful embroidered motifs and spirited colour combinations.
* Switzerland has its own traditional shapes and styles that exude individual character.

BOOKS AND PATTERNS

As well as considering textiles, another great resource to look into for inspiration are pattern books. These range from the 1856 masterpiece *The Grammar of Ornament* by Owen Jones, through to a wide selection of facsimile historical decorative pattern and cross-stitch books published both commercially and via museums, and to publications illustrating and explaining the major design influences of the twentieth and twenty-first centuries. These are all excellent sources of inspiration for a single motif or for an all-over pattern, as well as helping to decide on a choice of colours. Elements can be isolated and utilized, and a small stitch pattern can be adapted sensitively and extended into an elaborate border.

Lest we forget our own heritage, vintage hand-knitting patterns can be a

Vintage knitting pattern books.

valuable source of shape inspiration, with each decade of the twentieth and twenty-first centuries having its own distinct silhouette. For example, the 1930s created a distinct fitted shape with slightly puff sleeves and a stitch texture of lace and the use of cables as surface decoration, while the 1960s favoured the 'Sloppy Joe' loose V neck. All these shapes are readily adaptable for the knitting machine.

KEY CONSIDERATIONS AND ORIGINALITY

After reading this book, your aim should be to consider and adapt elements that appeal to you; then add your own design surprises to create an innovative and wearable garment with a unique character. It is not to be unoriginal, or to copy other designers' work verbatim.

When you discover a vintage or contemporary knitted garment, study the silhouette on the hanger or model. Consider the proportions – is it boxy, long, short, fitted or unstructured? Where is the main focus? Is it tied up with the stitch pattern, the relaxed shape, dropped shoulder, fitted sleeve or the high gathered sleeve? Look at the garment in detail and consider it from all angles – notice how it has been displayed and in what context. Thinking about all these different aspects will help you to broaden and deepen your own knowledge, and help you to understand

and eliminate details that don't spark any interest in you, whilst highlighting any ideas that can be adopted and adapted within your own practice. This process will stimulate new stitch textures, shapes and colour choices when next planning or adding to your own archive of design ideas.

Unless you are designing a garment to shock (and who doesn't do this sometimes), avoid extreme gimmicks such as wide, exaggerated shoulders or voluminous bell cuffs, as they date an item quickly and do not stand the test of time. Throwing every element into one design results in confusion, and does not produce a wearable garment for years to come.

Sweaters and cardigans in any fibres can be dressed up or down. A simple shaped garment will also create added value to other items in any wardrobe. For example, big thick cardigans can be worn as jackets outside. The simplest shapes work best for all figures and are more versatile when deciding stitch patterns and yarn choice.

There are also practical aspects to consider. For example, when and with what is the garment to be worn? Is it an occasion or everyday piece? Try to design for both, and make the garment adaptable as this is value for money and sustainable. Do not design just for 'best' wear or a few occasional outings as the item will spend most of its life residing in the back of a wardrobe and that is no life for a cardigan or sweater! The summer and winter seasons have merged and there is no such thing as day and evening wear which makes it essential that any design is truly versatile. The majority of clothing should be able to be worn all year round and in any setting, to create a sustainable value for any item of knitwear.

Always design a shape for the present that will stand the test of fashionable time.

CHAPTER 2

SUSTAINABLE OPTIONS FOR KNITWEAR DESIGNERS

When designing knitwear, we cannot ignore the fact that we are using a raw material and so should be mindful of our impact on our planet. In 1987, the United Nations Brundtland Commission defined sustainability as 'meeting the needs of the present without compromising the ability of future generations to meet their own needs'. Today, there are almost 140 developing countries in the world seeking ways of meeting their development needs whilst being mindful of the increasing threat of climate change. Sustainability is everyone's responsibility, not just that of our governments, and many of us are now realizing that this is a problem that needs addressing and at a quicker pace than in the past. According to the UN, the three pillars of sustainability are economic, social and environmental.

The **economic** pillar addresses the production of what we are making, and also looks at consumerism. We should not be making a profit out of any form of exploitative labour, either human or environmental. This also considers the financial benefits from a change in sustainable attitudes with the reduction of materials, energy and water. This will inevitably reduce our global footprint, and there is a direct beneficial correlation between sustainability and the economy.

The **social** pillar considers the people we are living with, our fellow human beings worldwide. To have a truly sustainable society we must develop and support education, security and leisure, and pass laws to ensure this in order to have a healthy society.

The **environmental** pillar considers how to protect and preserve our environment and natural resources. We must consider our impact on the environment, and make informed choices when we buy materials and consider how we run our businesses.

Each of these three pillars should work in harmony, and if we inform ourselves as to what is happening in our world, we will develop ideas and strategies to encourage change, which is both sustainable and beneficial to the environment.

DESIGN CONSIDERATIONS

The production, distribution and disposal phases of the clothing life cycle all create environmental impacts, but extending a garment's active life via design, maintenance and the reuse of clothing is an effective method of reducing our environmental sustainability impact. Decisions you make during the design and development process can significantly affect the extent to which the garments you create are sustainable. Product longevity is one of the key sustainability issues, which can play a part in minimizing the overall environmental impact of the finished garment. Ethical consumerism has resulted in a market for ethical fashion, defined as 'fashionable clothes that incorporate Fairtrade principles with sweatshop-free labour conditions while not harming the environment or workers, by using biodegradable and organic cotton'. Fairtrade clothing is a type of sustainable clothing defined as 'a trading partnership, based on dialogue, transparency and respect, that seeks greater equity in international trade, and the Fairtrade certification looks to provide an independent guarantee that disadvantaged producers in the developing world are getting a better deal'.

Clothing production is responsible for one of the major sustainability impacts on society and the environment, so sustainability is an important issue for the knitwear designer to consider. Due to a rise in the amount of clothing being purchased as 'Fast Fashion', the production and processing phases of the clothing life cycle are creating increasing environmental impacts. Post-purchase clothing care and maintenance also has a detrimental impact on the environment, and the product design and development process can affect a garment's sustainability during usage and eventual recycling or disposal.

FAST FASHION

The waste from fashion is a problem that has significantly increased due to the growth of 'Fast Fashion'. Fast Fashion garments are designed and produced within a relatively short timescale, thrive on frequently changing trends and consequent obsolescence, and are incompatible with the notion of sustainability, with over one million tonnes of clothes being discarded annually in the UK.

The problems inherent with Fast Fashion, and an increasing awareness of its negative sustainability impacts, have encouraged the development of the Slow Fashion movement, which respects resources and slows down the rate at which we consume them. Sustainable Slow Fashion has become prominent along with the desire for ethical consumerism, which has created demand from consumers for more sustainable goods, and considers various stakeholder needs, prioritizing quality over quantity as a more sustainable alternative to Fast Fashion.

SLOW FASHION

Perceptions that sustainable clothing is unfashionable have been overcome in recent years, with a growing awareness of Slow Fashion, and the launch of fashion exhibitions featuring sustainable clothing at international fashion weeks. In addition, a wider selection of sustainable clothing has become available on the UK market during the last decade with Marks & Spencer, H&M, Vivienne Westwood, People Tree and Linda Loudermilk all embracing the concept, so indicating a more widespread acceptance internationally of the sustainable clothing philosophy.

Sustainable clothing can fall into various categories, an example being garments made from organic cotton, which is produced without pesticides. Though it makes up only 0.04 per cent of the global cotton market, organic cotton is a yarn used frequently in the production of sustainable textiles and clothing. Clothing retailers such as Patagonia sell clothing made from organic cotton, as well as other sustainable fabrics including fleece manufactured from recycled bottles.

Sustainability is recognized as an important issue for clothing designers, with increasing demand from consumers for products that are environmentally and socially sustainable. Interest in sustainable clothing production and consumption is growing, but is difficult to always manage successfully, with some major fashion brands and retailers receiving negative publicity, and accusations that some of their products are manufactured in conditions that compromise social sustainability.

FAIRTRADE

Fairtrade is a system of certification that aims to ensure that a set of standards is met in the production and supply of a product or ingredient. For farmers and workers, Fairtrade means protected workers' rights, safer working conditions and fairer pay. For consumers it means high quality, ethically produced products.

For the knitwear designer Fairtrade encompasses questions such as the working conditions of people employed in the growing and production of the yarn, looking for evidence that the employees are making a living wage, that health and safety requirements are abided by, and where animals are involved, ensuring that they receive fair treatment, good living conditions and a cruelty-free environment.

Find out where your yarn originates from. If you have a favourite supplier, where and how do they source their yarn? Does your yarn have Fairtrade certification? If not, is your supplier Fairtrade compliant?

CONSUMER BEHAVIOUR AND SUSTAINABILITY

The rapid increase in the size of the sustainable clothing market implies that although customers are concerned about sustainability, their actions can suggest otherwise, since some consumers who profess to hold ethical views often do not transfer their intentions into ethical purchasing behaviours. Even environmentally aware customers make purchase decisions influenced primarily by economic and personal factors, as well as being based on sustainability, with many buying low-priced clothing from value retailers, despite being aware of the potential environmental impact of their actions, and the fact that this clothing is unlikely to be durable.

Customers also view the main sustainability issue related to clothing to be at the manufacturing stage. However, laundering clothes has a greater impact upon the environment than the initial production. Customers are, however, generally reluctant to wash clothing at low temperatures in case this compromises cleanliness.

Sustainable fashion requires us to rethink how we source our yarns and what we knit with them. It is impossible at the moment to be 100 per cent sustainable, but this should not prevent us from trying to do better. We must consider what we are producing with regard to the bigger picture – for instance:

* What is the expected life cycle of the garment that we are making?
* How do we intend to make it? Consider the design, and the source of the raw materials and their production.
* How will the finished item be transported or stored? How do you intend to market it, and finally sell it?
* How can the knitted fabric be used, reused, repaired, remade, and recycled or upcycled?

Changing consumer mindsets is never easy, as it requires a lot of awareness and resilience to make genuine progress towards sustainable consumption. Consumers can also find it hard to know when a garment is sustainable, and a number of consumers choose not to buy items labelled as sustainable, due to the fear of 'greenwashing' marketing campaigns.

A distinct location or origin can provide uniqueness, authenticity and meaning to a garment. There is, however, a disappointing homogeneity in branded fashion around the world – you see the same garments by the same designers for sale in London, Luxembourg, Lusaka, Lima, La Paz and Lisbon – however, the movement to buy local products can act as a countertrend to that sameness, and building a connection to a place with your designs can celebrate a unique culture that has meaning and relevance for both local and international customers.

In your designs you can try to reverse environmental damage by looking for organic or more environmentally friendly products, but a major challenge for the knitwear designer lies in the difficulty they have in effectively communicating their sustainability values and principles. This is because it is not enough to be sustainable, it is

Yarns.

also necessary to evidence this sustainability in the range of garments you produce, and in how you position your product range in the marketplace.

YARN TYPES AND SUSTAINABILITY

As a knitwear designer you have access to a wide range of yarns, from those derived from plants and animals, to those produced from mineral sources. In this section we will consider the sustainability of the different yarn types, so that you can be better informed as to the environmental impact of different yarn types.

The yarns that you use in your knitting start out as fibres. Textile fibres include natural fibres that are agricultural products from plants (for example cotton) or animals (for example wool), and manufactured fibres that are industrial products. Manufactured fibres can be further categorized into regenerated fibres that use natural polymers (for example

cellulose from wood or bamboo) as the starting material in fibre production, and synthetic fibres that are synthesized from small molecules (for example derived from oil or coal).

Plant-Based Fibres

The main component of plant fibres is cellulose, and plant fibres are generally considered by the consumer to be more environmentally friendly than synthetic fibres. This is because the growth of plants results in sequestration of CO_2 from the atmosphere, natural plant cultivation consumes less energy than the production of synthetic polymers and fibres, natural plant fibres are produced from renewable resources, and at the end of their lifecycle they are biodegradable.

Cotton: Cotton is the most common natural fibre used for clothing. It is a cellulose fibre that grows in a ball around the seeds of the cotton plant (gossypium), and has soft and fluffy

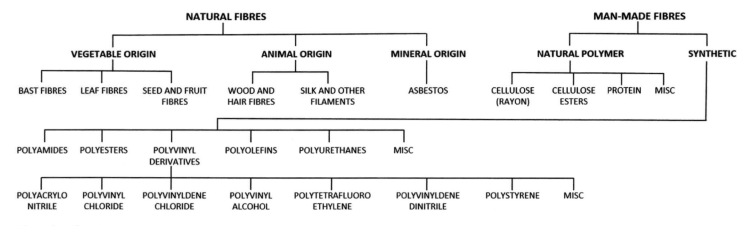

Fibre classifications.

staple fibres.

Jute: Jute is a type of bast (the phloem or inner bark surrounding the stem) fibre composed of cellulose, lignin and pectin. It is extracted from the stem of the jute plant.

Linen: Linen fibres are extracted from flax plants and contain about 70 per cent cellulose.

Hemp: Hemp is a bast fibre extracted from the stalk of hemp plants that grow well in soils that are well drained, rich in nitrogen and non-acidic.

Animal-Based Fibres

Animal fibres are based on proteins, generally keratin, or sericin and fibroin. Keratin-based fibres include sheep wool, alpaca, angora, cashmere, camel and mohair. Other keratin-based animal fibres include fur and human hair. Silk consists of two main proteins, sericin and fibroin, fibroin being the structural centre of the silk, and sericin the sticky material surrounding it.

Wool: Wool is the hair from a sheep or lamb, and is a 100 per cent natural fibre. It is normally obtained through shearing. Lambswool, Merino, Shetland, Donegal and Icelandic Lopi

are all sheep or lamb-based yarns. Tibetan fur refers to the white wool of the Tibetan lamb.

Cashmere and mohair: Cashmere and mohair are the hair of goats and are 100 per cent natural fibres. Mohair comes from the Angora goat, and cashmere from the Cashmere goat. Pashmina is a fine variant of spun cashmere.

Angora: Angora hair or fibre is the downy coat produced by the Angora rabbit, and is a 100 per cent natural fibre. Most breeds of Angora rabbit moult, with their natural growth cycle about every four months, and it is normally this moulted fibre that is used in yarn production.

Other animal hair fibres: The camel family includes camel, alpaca, llama and vicuna, and the wool is obtained by shearing. Chiengora wool is a yarn obtained from dog hair. Shahtoosh is made from the hair of the Tibetan antelope (Chiru). As the Chiru is an endangered species under CITES, the possession and sale of shahtoosh is illegal in most countries.

Silk: Silk is a natural protein fibre produced by certain insect larvae to form cocoons. The best known silk is obtained from the cocoons of the

larvae of the mulberry silkworm, Bombyx Mori.

Regenerated Fibres

Regenerated fibres are man-made fibres produced from a natural source, with plant-derived cellulose being the most common building block. The production of regenerated fibres is energy intensive.

Viscose rayon (modal): Viscose rayon is the first manufactured fibre, having been patented in England by Sir Joseph Swan in 1892. It is produced from natural cellulose materials such as tree trunks, bamboo and plant stalks. Modal is a type of rayon made from reconstituted beech tree cellulose, which is stronger, lighter and more breathable than viscose rayon. Viscose rayon/ modal is soft to the touch, drapes well, and is breathable, moisture absorbent and biodegradable.

Lyocell (Tencel/ SeaCell): To develop a more environmentally friendly regenerated cellulose fibre to replace viscose rayon, the UK firm Courtaulds developed lyocell (trade mark Tencel) commercially in the 1990s. Lyocell production is judged to be more eco-friendly than the method used for viscose rayon or modal, as it uses an organic solution in its production rather than the sodium hydroxide used in making viscose rayon/ modal. SeaCell is a type of lyocell that is based on dried algae seaweed rather than on plant material.

Synthetic Fibres

Synthetic fibres are synthesized from small molecules derived from oil or coal. They are manufactured by the extrusion of liquid through fine holes in a spinneret, the liquid jets then being drawn, stretched and hardened to form a continuous filament, or spun/staple yarns, with the required characteristics. The production of synthetic fibres is energy intensive.

Polyester: Polyester is a long-chain synthetic polymer and is the most commonly used fibre, accounting for 55 per cent of all fibre consumption worldwide. It can be used on its own, or blended with other fibres such as cotton, silk or wool.

Nylon: Nylon is a long-chain synthetic polyamide developed by DuPont in the 1920s, and was the first commercially successful synthetic fibre. Nylon is now mostly found blended with other fibres such as cotton, polyester or spandex.

Acrylic (modacrylic): DuPont created acrylic fibre in 1941 under the name Orlon. It is a long-chain synthetic polymer manufactured initially as a filament, then cut into short staple lengths similar to wool hairs, which are then spun into yarn. It has good durability and wear resistance, strong resistance to sunlight, resistance to all biological and many chemical agents such as diluted acids and alkalis and organic solvents, and resistance to oxidation.

Modacrylic fibres are synthetic co-polymers that were first produced in 1949 by the Union Carbide Corporation. Modacrylic fibres have similar properties to acrylic fibres, but in addition are flame retardant and non-combustible.

Spandex (elastane/lycra): Spandex was developed commercially by DuPont in 1959 and is a long-chain synthetic polymer based on polyurethane. It is lightweight, abrasion resistant, soft, smooth, supple and highly elastic – it can be stretched repetitively to over 500 per cent of its original length and still recover its original length.

The production of both regenerated and synthetic fibres is an energy-intensive process.

CONCLUSIONS

The major environmental issues associated with the production of knitted garments are:

* **Energy** use in laundry, the production of primary yarns especially for man-made fibres, and in yarn manufacturing of natural fibres.
* **The use of toxic chemicals** that may harm human health and the environment – in particular in conventional cotton production.
* **The release of chemicals** in waste water – especially in wet pre-treatment, dyeing, finishing and laundry – which may harm water-based life.
* **Solid waste** arising from yarn manufacturing of natural and other fibres, and the making up and disposal of products at the end of their life.

Interest in the environment among consumers has been growing in recent years, and more people are becoming aware of green alternatives to regular products. It is, however, difficult to see whether, for example, a cotton garment has been made from conventional or organic cotton, or dyed with non-toxic or harmful dye stuffs, just by looking at it. Eco labels are helpful guidelines, but there is a confusing array of 'eco' labelling schemes, not all of which certificate to an internationally recognized standard.

There are barriers to changing to a more sustainable future, and changes in the sourcing, production, use and reuse of clothing to reduce environmental impact and promote social equity will only occur if driven by consumer choice. In order to create change, you would need to consider adopting many of the following good practices:

Buy second-hand clothing and textiles where possible: The idea of taking used clothing to a charity shop, clothing bank or second-hand dress agency is well established in the UK, and around 30 per cent of clothing is recycled in this way in the UK. If not fit to be reworn or reused, then dispose of used clothing and textiles through recycling businesses that will extract and recycle the yarn or fibres.

Buy fewer, more durable garments and textile products: There is a clear environmental disadvantage to Fast Fashion – the most sustainable management of clothing and textiles products would be to use them until the end of their 'natural' life. However, Fast Fashion assumes a rapid turnover of clothing that is discarded long before the item has reached the end of its useful life.

Lease clothes: Lease clothes are clothes that would otherwise not be worn to the end of their natural life. Initially the idea of leasing clothing rather than purchasing it seems unattractive to many consumers, however, leasing is already common practice for formal and evening wear, where the clothes are worn for a specific short-term purpose such as a wedding.

Repair clothes: Repairing extends the useful life of clothing and textile products. However, the practice of repairing clothes has declined, influenced by two factors. The first is price deflation in the global clothing market, leading to customers viewing clothes as disposable items. The second is the decline in sewing and darning skills, which has contributed towards the frequent disposal of clothes that could have been repaired relatively easily. Clothing supplied through leasing arrangements is regularly repaired, so adding to sustainability.

Be energy conscious: When buying new clothes, choose those made using the least energy and producing the lowest toxic emissions, made by workers paid a credible living wage with reasonable employment rights and conditions. It is not always obvious which alternative uses least energy – a recent study estimated that it took 109MJ of energy to make the material, manufacture, transport, use and clean, and dispose of a cotton T-shirt, whereas a viscose blouse consumes 44MJ of energy to make the material, manufacture, transport, use and clean, and dispose of it – the dominant impact between the two garments being the washing of the cotton T-shirt.

Wash clothes less often: Also wash them at lower temperatures using eco-detergents, hang-dry them, and avoid ironing where possible.

Swap yarn with another knitter: Everyone has yarn they haven't used for months, years even. Pass it to another knitter and swop with another yarn that inspires – and of course use it!

Buy second-hand or end-of-range

Cashmere yarns.

yarn: Buy second-hand yarn – there is lots available. Many yarn buyers buy too much or have simply not used it, so be prepared to buy second hand. Very often you can source small cones of yarn in a variety of textures and qualities direct from mills that have them left over from a run. This will encourage your designing skills to create a piece using this yarn. It can be mixed in with other colours and lengths to make an interesting marled yarn.

Buy local: The transportation of yarn and machinery causes large amounts of CO_2. This can be minimized by buying locally. It is worth looking up local yarn spinners or suppliers. Question if the yarn is completely local, as there are some mixes that incorporate other yarns that are not spun locally but are imported. Sometimes it is just not possible to obtain the quantity and quality you require, but this should not prevent us from trying.

Minimalism: Only buy the yarn you need. Do not stockpile and continue to buy yarn when you have an attic or

work room that is already overflowing.

Buy organic: When buying yarn ask if it is free from pesticides. How was it produced? For example, there are many wool spinners in the UK, so did they use local wool, and if so, from what breed of sheep? They will be able to tell you where it was sourced. Organically produced yarns tend to have a smaller carbon footprint than those produced with chemical assistance. Some companies trumpet the 'organic' label but this can be misleading and is not a guarantee of any sort of quality. For example, most organic cotton uses large amounts of water in its production.

Use eco-friendly yarns: A sustainable yarn is one that is biodegradable and has been produced and spun using a non-toxic method. Textiles release fibres to the environment during production, use, and at end-of-life disposal. Natural fibres are bio-degradable, however there is a growing risk of ecological and human health issues associated with the release of non-biodegradable microfibres and nanofibres from yarns containing man-made fibres.

Use natural dyes: The raw materials are all either mineral or vegetable. Traceability and production should all be sustainable and transparent. The dying process is also important when considering sustainability. When yarn is dyed, how long does it take? Ideally under an hour. Does the process use cold water, and again, how much water? Is the water recycled? Is the dye colourfast to a standard? Are all the materials used tested and traceable to meet the standards of the environmental management? And is fair labour used in all processes?

You may not get the answers to all or any of these questions, but we must start to think about and reflect on the impact environmentally of our practice. It is difficult when there is so much malpractice in the world to be overwhelmed and not bother to try and make our own small changes but singly, we can make a difference and many people all making little changes can make a huge difference.

My knitting sweater with needle-hook damaged holes.

HOW TO REDUCE WASTE, REUSE AND UPCYCLE

The Japanese philosophy of *wabi-sabi* has its roots in Zen Buddhism, and is a world view centred on the acceptance of transience and imperfection, and of appreciating beauty that is imperfect, impermanent and incomplete. It is worth celebrating and acknowledging this sentiment in practice. If a piece of knitted fabric is damaged by a pulled thread, wear and tear or moth, this tells the story of the garment and its life so far. It is its patina, if you like, and this can have a beauty all of its own.

Repairing and mending sets up a rhythm and creates a meditative frame

of mind, and instils a respect for the fabric and its history. Every piece of clothing is worthy of repair, and the knitted fabric lends itself to repair – either invisibly or with a glorious contrasting celebratory patch over a hole or threadbare area.

Repairing and reusing has always been a skill employed within my family. Patchwork quilts were stitched from various blouses and skirts, and socks were darned. Worn-out jumpers and cardigans were unpicked and the good yarn wound into skeins, washed, and weighted with a milk bottle to straighten the yarn when drying, and reknitted. It is no longer acceptable to discard clothing through boredom and lack of wear. Choose carefully and own what you need.

I love the idea of knitting small Fairisle patches and sewing them over the top of a hole. The underside of the repair and the surrounding loose threads can then be darned to anchor them firmly in place. When knitting the patch use a tighter tension than normal

to keep the fabric firm. The repair is celebrated and becomes a design feature in itself.

Patched sweater showing repair.

CHAPTER 3

DESIGN BASICS

To successfully design an exciting and wearable knitted garment, your head, heart and hands must all work in unison. Design means change and trying something new, having an idea and working through it using your previous experiences and your current inspiration. Design means fresh problem solving, and questioning what has gone before.

To be a successful designer you need a receptive and open mind. The design process is both challenging and invigorating as it encompasses positive and constructive ideas – 'same old, same old' is abandoned, and the imagination comes into play as the spark of an original idea is explored and developed. Our design criteria have to adapt constantly to changing attitudes, your own preferences and outside influences.

As the creative process takes place your vision is turned into reality, albeit working within the constraints of the materials and technology you have to hand. However, these constraints themselves can also be liberating, as too much choice can be mesmerizing and you become like rabbits caught in headlights wondering which avenue to explore, rooted to the spot and exploring none. A simple idea for a design can be worked on, and layers that are added regarding shape, texture, colour, materials and function are all explored and made into a tangible piece of work that expresses the choices made, and reflects our ideals and experiences.

EXPERIMENTATION

To design is to create – it is not a repetition of previous ideas but the creation of an original piece of work. One catalyst for this can be the materials that we have available. Experimentation is the key: without copying what has gone before, use the materials in their simplest sense and play. Get to know them, the feel of them without stitch pattern or embellishments, and see what can be achieved.

When the character and possibilities of the materials have been realized, add pattern and texture, so building up both your aesthetic knowledge and a better understanding of their technical limitations.

* Will the materials respond to geometric stitch patterns, or is it better to use natural flowing forms and shapes?
* Do you need a sharper edge and a precise block of colour? If so, a marled variegated colour and random

The machine at work.

thickness will not work, but instead use a sleek, fine, flat yarn and colour, both of which will respond well to the pattern you are designing.

You are creating a fabric of value, which is then transferred into a piece of clothing or interior textile – therefore from conception to completion you are part of the catalyst, so you do need to consider where or who or what the fabric is for.

RECOGNIZING THE MARKET

Personal statements are all very well, but it is not practical for most designers to take weeks to make one piece, as you would not be able to recoup the costs of producing the garment with the selling price achievable in the market place. Financial constraints are unimportant if you are designing and knitting solely for pleasure and have unlimited funds at your disposal, but

how much something costs to make, where you can sell it, what it can be sold for, and what margin you achieve are all critical factors to consider when running a business. When designing, consider whether you are adding cost or adding value – if the cost of adding a design tweak exceeds the value to your customer, then is it worthwhile?

It is unrealistic to work without any idea of specification and market, and it is a discipline that must be mastered, so it is true to say that the market is an element of the catalyst. Over the years some exceptional design students whom I have known have doggedly maintained a mantra of perfectionism, and will spend days and weeks creating a garment that is unsaleable, meaning that the creative design process has failed, and the garment produced is a personal statement rather than a business opportunity. Sadly, over the months they become disillusioned – but blaming the market is not acceptable, as the fault lies with the student not understanding, and failing

to learn how to make the designs work in industry and the wider world. A knowledge of what the market wants and needs is important, as is how this can be produced to a cost without sacrificing quality and creativity. This applies to a sole trader as well as to a factory designer.

You must be adaptable when considering design, colour, proportion, shape and texture. Wonderful new and innovative yarns are being spun all the time, but a single colour, non fancy yarn may sell better. That is not to say that you only design what the public wants, because to an extent the designer has to create the demand, and then be able to supply that demand at an affordable price and with a realistic margin.

New ideas are always welcome and you must learn to trust your creativity and build on it. There is little point in copying what others are doing, as they are already doing it better and there is little or no room for creativity – aspects of outside influences will transfer into your work, but not as a slavish copy.

It is much easier to have worked and experimented and developed your own idea, as it will have your signature in terms of colour, shape and style, so building your portfolio as an original designer. The customer has a choice, either to be receptive to a new design, or to reject it. Designers and the public need each other – this is a healthy relationship, with information flowing both ways.

FASHION AND FUNCTION

Designing beyond an initial idea and use of materials in an original way can invigorate your world. To make something practical as well as beautiful is the ideal aim, and how you use the materials that you have to express yourself can be a truly creative

Fairisle knitting with wool using dried hydrangea colours.

experience, out of which comes self-confidence, excitement and knowledge.

Not so long ago knitted items were out of fashion and were thought of as 'fuddy duddy' – however, this is no longer the case, with actors such as Russell Crowe, Ewan McGregor, Meryl Streep, Julia Roberts and Scarlett Johansson, also novelist Margaret Atwood, musician Ronnie Wood, and Olympic athlete Tom Daley all being keen to be photographed knitting.

Our relationship with design and colour changes constantly. At certain times of our lives, especially in a work setting, we may need to conform to a certain look and accept certain sartorial standards – there is a 'correct' way to dress that must be adhered to, the constraints of which can easily spill over into our private lives and affect our confidence as to what styles, shapes, designs and colours really suit us. Many people find it easier to conform to the pervading fashion, as they don't know what suits them best – it is what they feel happiest and most at ease wearing, when anything else destroys confidence and comfort.

We like to express to the outside world which social group we belong to, or aspire to belong to. The line, shape and colour of clothing will relate all this information concerning your social status to an onlooker in a second. When designing it is possible to play with this idea, and juxtapose florescent colours with an otherwise dark and austere tweed suit, and mix traditional Fairisle patterns with florals. With today's fashion it can be much more acceptable to wear something that is exciting and creative, although there will always be work situations that require a particular uniformity of look.

QUESTIONS AND CHOICES

Knitting is a truly democratic art, as everyone can design something. Imagination is the only boundary and this can be developed by you getting to know the materials and their limitations. With limitation can come liberation, and with a knowledge as to what can be achieved it is impossible not to put something of yourself into the design, a colour, or feeling, which makes any original design truly personal, and the joy is expressing this and sharing your idea and the process in a visual way.

Designing through knitting makes you responsible for your own actions. You are creating and making decisions and selecting choices, being critical of your actions and making spontaneous adjustments, so acquiring more knowledge and experience. When the fog begins to lift and the journey of the completed item is done you get a sense of achievement and pride, only for this to be replaced by a new idea and another experiment, which you will explore with an open mind.

It is vital to experiment with your materials and knitting machine, as trial and error is the key to progress and good design. What will work? What is possible? This knowledge will inform and encourage good technique and inspire your creativity and spontaneity, because your design process is built on a firm foundation.

Every design that uses a material, shape and colour will have limitations. For example, when thinking about fibre – what is its thickness? How elastic is it when knitted up? Will a change of stitch choice enhance or constrict this process? What is the interaction of adjacent colours? And does the overall aspect require a choice change? Knowing the answer to these questions will be liberating, and you will be free to express your ideas and execute them

speedily, with you and your inspiration driving the process, rather than the process constricting you and becoming trite and frustrating. Always have an open mind when working on new ideas, and keep on experimenting!

Designing is expressing ourselves and allowing others to see what excites and makes us passionate. The results are there for all to see, and this will transfer to your audience – a social activity in fact!

USING YOUR SENSES

You need all your senses to be used to design happily – it is possible to hear and feel when the machine has dropped a stitch or is not working smoothly, so you need to get to know your machine and listen to it, and to the different sounds it makes. Different yarns make different sounds as they slide and glide through the yarn brake, so you can be aware of knots in the yarn before they become a hole. Feel the yarn as it knits, create a balanced rhythm and steady your breathing – work with an open mind, and keep referring to the materials being used and be responsive to them, react to them, and be flexible and prepared to change your method or idea as required.

GOOD PRACTICES

With practice, you will gain knowledge and confidence, and this will increase your flexibility, so concentrate on what you don't know rather than on aspects you are familiar with, as this will broaden and enlighten the work. Accept what you do know and build on it – try other stitches and shapes, and educate yourself constantly through the senses. Does it feel right? Is it fit for the intended purpose? And did you enjoy the processes of making it? And if not, why not?

Keep asking questions of yourself and your work. It is not always necessary to have a finished piece of work in mind, as experimentation and revisiting a known technique or method, utilizing a new or untried yarn or stitch or machine, can be actively investigated and creative problems solved through a process of refinement. This will build up a knowledge that can sit in the back of your mind for years in gestation, but will prove invaluable one day on a new design project. Life will always be challenging, and it is your response to these challenges that makes you the person you are.

Challenges are opportunities in the making, and finding solutions to those challenges through knitting can allow you to identify a new and creative design project. The rhythm within knitting, the carriage sliding back and forth, and the geometry within the stitch patterns, such as the honeycomb repeat, offset, climbing its way up the knitted fabric – the rhythm links your head, heart and hands in a positive way, and the order, sequences and your coordination become the essence of knitting.

The rhythm of our work finds cohesion in good design, whereby the completed design is a narrative of our thought processes – it articulates the continued discoveries, and is a tangible expression of the mind in motion. The journey and process is as important as the final piece. The act of machine knitting is like dancing, holding up the yarn with the left hand while pulling the carriage back and forth in a steady flow of movement. Each pull and push has a purpose as it builds on the previous movement. Each row is dynamic, and a taut length of yarn is transformed into an elastic fabric that expresses your own individuality and creates a historical document of your process and practice: rhythm and motion, rhythm and repetition, row after row, creating a dynamic design. By focusing on this steady rhythm, the breath is steadied and it takes on the rhythm of the movement: changing the yarn and the colours, allowing them to thread gently through the fingers creating a soft movement of fluidity and an even tension. The slight changes and variations within the texture and structure of the fabric are witness to the handmade aspect of the design.

Designing a knitted fabric, as with any creative work, is a journey of discovery and of respect for the materials and the process. To those who make, it is obvious that the process hones their observational and problem-solving skills. Your knowledge of yourself and your environment are both improved, and constantly reflecting on decisions made and refining them is not an inward-looking exercise – so always be aware of other new ideas, fashions, trends, innovations and inventions from around the world, and consider how they can inspire your designs.

Being curious from first-hand experience is a good way to learn. Very often I will make a minimum of three colourways for a scarf design, and over the years I will revisit the design using a different colour palette or a slight stitch variation, and knit another series with a different character to the original design.

On a more practical note, a golden rule that I always follow is that if in doubt about sizing, knit a size up. Unless you are a size zero model, a tightly fitted garment can look skimpy and uncomfortable as it does not allow the fabric to drape as intended, and a stretched stitch pattern looks ugly.

If you are knitting for a person with a large frame, consider designing a soft, unstructured garment that falls and drapes from the shoulders, and look to use quiet, cold base colours such as greys, blues, shades of purple and mid green. If you are knitting for a person with a small frame, they can be made to appear larger when your design incorporates hot reds, yellows, pinks, oranges and lighter pastel tones.

HARMONY

Bold stitch pattern choice and colour sense can make an extraordinary overall design and create an almost lyrical image. When creating a design, colour and pattern are visual stimuli that can inspire on their own many complex emotions that very often cannot be easily expressed in words.

Many designers are influenced by synaesthesia, which is a union of the senses in which a sensory stimulus associated with one sense automatically triggers another unsuppressible sensory experience in a (usually) different sense. It is a useful aid in better understanding how the creative design process works – how our mental processing to achieve the final design can be so efficient, given the profusion of our mentally stored information and the wide variety of issues and decisions that we must overcome, each of which require highly specific and different thought processes to arrive at a solution. Synaesthesia can be explained for the knitwear designer as a breakdown in the barriers that keep information from being shared between different parts of the brain, the conscious and subconscious, and the different senses.

To achieve harmony in your design, consider the use of colour and pattern, or alternate small or large patterns and colours, which will set up a rhythmic overall pattern. Experiment with using softer colours and shapes, and juxtapose them with sharp bright or dark intense colours and patterns. Look to combine the muted with the fiery to create interest and change of visual texture.

Large simple shapes can create a bold silhouette, while smaller shapes can organically twist and undulate, creating a vibrant sense of rhythm. It is amazing what can be achieved with a little stitch and change of colour.

Complimentary colours such as blue and orange can be alternated, for example within a traditional Fairisle pattern, to achieve a harmonious combination. A bright, primary, smooth red yarn can be juxtaposed with a lightly textured pastel blue, mauve and vanilla yarn. The overall pattern can then be sharpened up by using either white or black for a row or two.

Pink, aqua, lilac, marine blue, navy, purple and white with a splash of yellow ochre work well as colour combinations over a Fairisle design, to mimic the colours and ebb and flow of the sea with the landscape in the background.

Try new ideas constantly and improvise, as this can encourage further experimentation, originality and innovation. If you normally work with muted shades, try deep resonant harmonies such as sonorous red, blue and green using a bold stitch pattern.

It can be a useful exercise to take a photograph of your work in black and white, as this reduces colour to greys and highlights texture, and new, unseen patterns can emerge. A piece of knitted fabric that uses several types of yarn such as mohair, angora, silk and wool is reduced to a landscape scene, and experiments such as this will enhance your knowledge of the character of your yarns and stitch patterns. Try this with a cable.

Always view the piece you are working on as a whole. As the design progresses, keep pinning it up on a board or model, and stand back and look out of the corner of your eye, or try turning it upside down, to uncover any imbalances. Does a colour or pattern dominate? Can a colour be altered? Another shaped panel added or the length extended? Does it harmonize, and blend to give an exciting and interesting complete fabric? The decisions made on texture, colour and stitch pattern are all combined in harmony or discord to make a well-designed textile.

BLENDING YARNS

Creating and blending together yarns to make your own colours and textures adds originality, individuality and depth to your designs. For example, if your inspiration is a seascape of brilliant, shimmering water and distant cloudy skies, several shades of blue can be mixed to create the perfect scene.

Look at the painting *Une Baignade, Asnières* by Georges Seurat, and study the way in which he broke down large areas of a scene into dots of colour. Use this idea to blend three or four ends of fine yarn together, using similar shades to create a grey green, blue green, mint green or olive green. Knit a few rows and add another colour, and remove a colour or texture of yarn. When a variety of textures and colours are blended they react with other yarn colours around them, creating a varying interesting texture and depth.

A variety of yarns can be bought commercially that consist of blended shades. Some Shetland wool yarns have several colours within a thread, creating wonderful subtle mixes of heathery woodland; they also have lovely names, which inspire the imagination: sandalwood, sunglow, sunrise, thistledown and fog.

Other yarns are dip dyed, also known as space dyed, or section dyed. This is when short lengths of the yarn are dyed different colours at intervals throughout the yarn, either repeated in a sequence or more randomly, depending on the

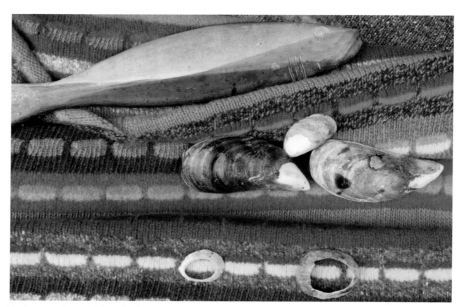

Variegated and blended yarns.

required outcome. Where one colour meets another during the dying process natural seepage occurs and the colour value alters, creating another shade or tone of colour. Be aware that when using these yarns the colour can 'pool' when knitted – that is, a particular colour congregates over several rows and creates a star-burst effect which can shift the balance of the desired pattern. To avoid this, and achieve an even colour distribution, use the end from one small cone and knit a few rows, then use an end from another cone and work a few more rows, and repeat.

Some yarn has a variegated effect throughout but uses only one strand of cream and another of blue, and this is twisted together. The overall effect is even, yet with an attractive mottled character. If two contrasting strands are used and they are not twisted together but pulled through the yarn brake together, a short stripe is created as one colour comes to the fore and the other falls behind it; this process reverses as the knitting takes place. This way of knitting is dynamic, as you cannot predict the actual outcome and the overall effect can be more attractively random.

Try adding yarns with slubs, which are thick and thin lengths, either at regular or irregular intervals to create a depth of textural interest. Or try blending yarns with nepps, which is a tiny fleck of contrasting colour and texture twisted into the fibre during the spinning process. Flecks can be added in a variety of colours and this creates a real depth and interest, particularly when designing and knitting a garment using the Fairisle technique. Mirroring the colour of some of the tiny nepps present in the main yarn used in Feeder One, and using them in Feeder Two, enhances and adds a consistency to the colours chosen and compliments the

Blended yarn coats.

other shades.

Experiment by using yarns of different weights and consistency and blending them together. For example, use several fine yarns dyed in a similar blue. The character of each yarn will be very different due to the variety of dye take-up. Some will be even and consistent, while others will be patchy and mottled. Add mohair and angora for textural interest. Sometimes the pattern lies in the yarns themselves and not in clever intricate stitch patterns. Always attempt to allow the character and personality of each yarn to balance and complement the others used in the blending process.

Every garment or item made using

the blended yarn with no stitch pattern creates a different overall pattern. It is totally fascinating how the colours flow and create a gentle movement. I have made hundreds of coats using blended yarn and I never tire of the colour combinations and the surprises and subtleties that appear.

Create your own colours by mixing threads together. It is possible to create hazy, indistinct soft contours that bleed and melt together and set up an impressionist, atmospheric landscape, seeming to float across the knitted fabric rather than be anchored in a stitch pattern. Variations of one basic colour can be made – a basic grey thread can be added to others to make slate grey, blue grey, beige grey, green grey, purple grey and so on, each having its own characteristic and subtle shading. When mixed or added in stripes the results can be mesmerizing.

When you have blended a yarn, it is vital to knit a tension swatch at least 15 x 15cm, then wash, press and measure the usual 10 x 10cm. That way you will build up your knowledge regarding which yarns work well together, and how they interact when washed.

Always label the swatches with vital information such as yarn mix and tension in stitches and rows, because when you refer back to the piece you will know what you did, and will be able to refine your design and to safely recreate the original design.

It is also useful to note your thoughts regarding stitch patterns, as each change in pattern will alter the colour value and overall effect. Certain colours and textures will dominate while others recede, or if you are using several different textural stitch patterns by changing stitch types.

You can experiment with interesting and unique blending ideas, which can be used and further developed. Some delicate stitch patterns can be overwhelmed and may disappear when using certain yarns and colours. For example, cable knits on the whole work better using lighter colours, which create a slight shadow and enhance the surface texture. If you use a busy, variegated and fluffy yarn then the cable effect is lost in a chaos of colour and confusing texture.

YARN COUNT

Yarn counts are the measure of the grist or thickness of a yarn and relate to the length of yarn required to achieve a certain weight. Historically these varied considerably with many differing regional and fibre counts, so I will go through three of the most commonly used standards.

An **Nm count** (*Numéro metrique*) of 1 is where a single strand of unplied yarn that is 1,000m long weighs 1kg. If the yarn is plied with another, this is shown as 'count/plies', so a yarn with an Nm count of 6/2 is one that has two strands of yarn each with a count of 6, plied together with a 'resultant' count of 3 (6 divided by 2). 1,000m of each of those three 'resultant' strands weighs 1kg – so 1kg of Nm 6/2 is 3,000m long. The higher the 'resultant' number, the finer the yarn.

The **Tex** count is the weight in grams of 1,000m of yarn. For example, a yarn count of 28 Tex means there are 28 grams of yarn per 1,000m of that specific yarn

The normal **UK standard** found on the inside of cones of yarn is given in Table 3.1.

Table 3.1: UK standard yarn weights

Yarn count	Approximate thickness
2/36s	Fine 1 Ply
2/34s	Fine 1 Ply
2/32s	1 Ply
2/30s	1 Ply
2/28s	1.5 Ply
2/24s	2 Ply
2/20s	2 Ply
2/14s	3 Ply
2/10s	Fine 4 Ply
2/8s	4 Ply

CHAPTER 4

CLASSIC JACKETS AND CARDIGANS

A cardigan is a knitted open-fronted garment designed to fit the upper part of the body, with either a button or zip fastening; it is traditionally made out of wool. It differs from a knitted pullover or sweater, in that neither of these garments open in front, but must be pulled over the head to be worn.

HISTORY AND POPULAR CULTURE

The cardigan was named after James Brudenell, the 7th Earl of Cardigan, a British Army major general who led the infamous Charge of the Light Brigade at the Battle of Balaclava during the Crimean War. It is modelled after the knitted wool waistcoat that British officers wore in that conflict. The fame that Lord Cardigan achieved due to the popularizing of the legend of the Charge of the Light Brigade led to the rise in demand for the cardigan and knitted wool waistcoat: they were deemed a useful addition to the country's wardrobe, and so began to be made commercially.

In 1883 Coco Chanel (née Gabrielle) was born, and it is to Chanel that we owe the modern woman's cardigan because she hated how 'tight-necked men's sweaters messed up her hair when she pulled them over her head'. Once Chanel picked up the design, its future was assured. Chanel was designing more practical clothing for

women and making sweater shirts, and was looking for inspiration in men's costume such as sailor suits, fisherman's sweaters and riding sweaters. It is said that she cut up an old sweater and sewed a ribbon round the collar, and that became the famous Chanel cardigan. Her cardigans were tailored, neat and fitted, and in 1915 she dressed the aristocratic women who were helping out as volunteer nurses during World War I. A more androgynous and egalitarian style was created, which was easier and more practical to wear. Sadly, the price that Chanel charged for her cardigans kept them out of reach of most people.

Over time, cardigans were being produced commercially for the mass market. The bolero style, a short and close-fitting jacket, was ideal for the 1960s ski slopes or a trip to the opera! After World War II, a revolution in fashion meant that women no longer wanted to wear girdles and create an hour-glass waist, and by the late 1940s, American varsity students were wearing 'Sloppy Joes' – a buttoned, long, baggy cardigan with sleeves pushed up to the elbows, also called a Natch varsity cardigan. The Sloppy Joes made a return in the 1960s. Many were knitted in fluffy mohair, while Bridget Bardot famously wore a cardigan unbuttoned over a striped shirt.

In the 1990s the librarian style became popular, neat and demure, to be replaced by the loose, grand-dad

style so loved by punks and hippies. Droopy pockets and holes were part of the design, as seen worn by the Dude in *The Big Lebowski*, contrasting with the more formal and close-fitting fluff-cuffed cardigan as worn by Alicia Silverstone in *Clueless*. The cardigan can still instigate controversy, as when Michelle Obama greeted Queen Elizabeth at Buckingham Palace in 2009, and there was low-level grumbling that this was not suitable attire!

The 2020s cardigan is seen as cosy and comfy when pulled on over pyjamas for duvet days, or brightly coloured and patchwork when worn by the likes of singer/songwriter Harry Styles. Taylor Swift is a fan and sings: 'When I felt like I was an old cardigan under someone's bed you put me on and said I was your favourite.' To accompany her album a retro varsity-style cardigan uniting cables and silver stars was produced.

STYLE AND CONSTRUCTION

Cardigans can create a feeling of protection when wrapped around the body, and big cosy cardigans can become a best friend. Their versatility is unique as they can be tailored and smart as an office jacket, yet with a change of colour and style can be crafted into a genuinely useful piece of clothing that will last for decades. They are ideal for the British climate, which can produce all four seasons in one twelve-hour period. They are kind to our shape, as they drop from the shoulders and gently drape over the lumps and bumps, disguising what we would rather not have on show. Patterns and yarns have become more sophisticated and stylish, with the result that it is now possible to make many of the best and most loved cardigans at home.

The single colour cardigans in this chapter are all based on classic shapes, easy to wear and update by choice of colour and length, sleeve width or stitch edging. The edgings can be either hand knitted and picked up on the machine, or the back and front of the garment can be cast on with WY and the edgings added later, the stitches being picked up on to needles from the WY. Garter-stitch edgings are textured and can be knitted with a garter bar. Moss-stitch edgings can be either hand knitted, or machine knitted by dropping stitches and reforming. For variety, any of the edgings can be made deeper for turned-back cuffs and a collar to make a garment feel cosy and warm.

Adding another fine yarn to the MY can add subtle changes to the stitch. I have added a cotton chenille to the Donegal soft wool, and hand knitted a moss-stitch edging. This makes for a crunchy, textured feel, especially when mixed with the alchemy of colours spun into Shetland yarn and the brightly coloured nepps within the Donegal wool. Just adding a fine single colour grey to a variegated wool can make a delicate change, as shown in the Round-Neck Short Cardigan. The choice is yours to make.

LONG ULTRAMARINE CARDIGAN WITH COLLAR

Although knitted using one colour, these are by no means plain cardigans. They have moss-stitch edgings, turn-back cuffs and a cosy collar. The front, back and sleeve cardigan pieces have been knitted in stocking stitch. The cuffs and bottom border are picked up and hand knitted using a moss stitch. If you prefer, you can machine knit the moss-stitch edging by dropping each alternate stitch and reforming, offsetting this process on the subsequent rows.

Ultramarine Cardigan.

Materials

650g of Knoll Soft Donegal 5527
Roe
7 buttons
A pair of 2.25mm 13 UK knitting
needles

Measurements

To fit chest 100–104cm
Length to shoulder 80cm
Sleeve length 46cm

Tension

28 sts and 40 rows = 10cm
MT 8

Machines

Suitable for standard gauge
punchcard and electronic machines

Method

POCKET LININGS (MAKE TWO)

Bring forward 30 sts to WP, cast on with
WY, change to MC, k 88 rows, k off on
to WY.

BACK

Using WY, cast on 200 sts, k a few rows
and change to MC. Dec 1 st ff at each
of every seventh row until 140 sts
remain. Cont to knit without shaping
RC 220.

Armhole Shaping

Dec 1 st ff at the beginning of the next
10 rows, 130 sts remain.
  K until RC 314.

Shoulder Shaping

At the end of each alt row place into HP
15 Ns four times and 14 Ns twice. K the
two shoulders and the centre neck 42
sts on to three separate ends of WY.

Bottom Edging

Pick up the sts from WY and work 3cm
moss stitch. Cast off loosely.

LEFT FRONT

WY cast on 90sts and change to MC.
K until RC 140 at the same time.
Dec 1 st ff at the side edge at beg of
every 10th row until 70 sts remain.

Place Pocket

Bring 30 sts from the right to HP, pick
up the sts from the pocket lining right
side facing on to the next 30sts and
bring the remaining sts to HP. K 1 row
across the pocket sts and k on to WY.
K off the machine, pick up the other
end of the pocket lining, remove the
WY and cont to k across all sts until RC
220.
  Rep armhole shaping as for back.
Cont to k without shaping until RC
290.

Shape Neck

Cast off 10 sts on the neck edge. K 1
row dec 1 st every alt row on the neck
edge until 44 sts rem.
  Cont RC 314, shape shoulder as
back.
With the right side of the back piece
facing, pick up the left shoulder sts k 1
row T10 and latch off.
  Pick up the sts from WY and work
3cm moss stitch. Cast off loosely.

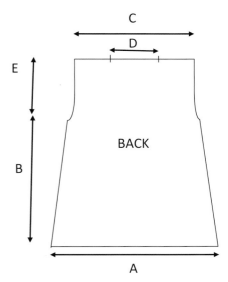

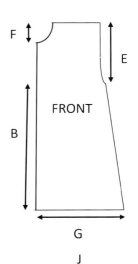

		Long	Short
A		76cm	74cm
B		61cm	35cm
C		56cm	61cm
D		22cm	23cm
E		25.5cm	25.5cm
F		8cm	11cm
G		38.5cm	41cm
H		36cm	40cm
I		51.5cm	52.5cm
J		52cm	51cm

Diagram for Long and Short Cardigans.

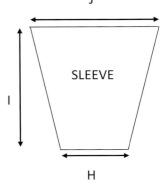

RIGHT FRONT

Rep as for left front, reversing all shaping.

SLEEVES

Wrong side facing and with the shoulder seam on the centre needle, pick up 150 sts from the armhole of the front and back pieces.

Dec each end of every sixth row until 100 sts remain; cont to k without shaping RC 186. Remove from machine on to WY and pick up the sts on to the knitting needle. Work 7cm moss stitch and cast off.

Rep for second sleeve.

BUTTON BAND

Left Band

Cast on 12 sts and work in moss stitch for the length of the front up to the neck shaping, place sts on holder.

Right Band

As for left band but placing 7 buttonholes evenly, the first being 15cm from the bottom and the final one 6cm from the neck shaping.

COLLAR

Sew button bands to fronts and pick up sts around the neck to include both band sts. Work 10cm moss stitch and cast off loosely.

POCKET TOPS

Pick up the sts from the pockets and work 3cm moss stitch. Cast off loosely. Sew up pockets and side seams. Add buttons to band. Wash and press.

STONE SHORT CARDIGAN

Note: This is a larger size than the Long Ultramarine Cardigan with Collar.

The edgings on the Stone Short Cardigan were hand knitted using moss stitch, and a fine thread of grey cashmere was added to the main yarn to create a texture and subtle colour change. Once again this can be worked by hand with knitting needles or on the machine by reforming the stitches.

Stone Short Cardigan showing two yarns used for the edgings.

Materials

560g of Knoll Soft Donegal 5521 Ramour
Optional 100g of a fine grey yarn
5 buttons
A pair of 2.50mm 13 UK knitting needles

Measurements

To fit chest 100–108cm
Length to shoulder 60cm
Sleeve length 43cm

Tension

28 sts and 40 rows = 10cm
MT 8

Machines

Suitable for standard gauge punchcard and electronic gauge machines.

See the 'Diagram for Long and Short Cardigans' in the pattern for the Long Ultramarine Cardigan with Collar for measurements

Method

All cuffs, edgings and button bands are made using the same method as the Long Ultramarine Cardigan with Collar (previous pattern).

POCKET LINING (MAKE TWO)

Using WY, cast on 30 sts, change to MC and k 60 rows, k on to WY.

BACK

Cast on 182 sts using WY and k a few rows; change to MC RC000, k 6 rows and dec ff each end of every sixth row until 150 sts rem. Cont to RC 130.

Armhole Shaping

Dec 1 st ff at beg of every row 10 times; 140 sts rem.

Cont to work without shaping to RC 230.

Shape Shoulders

Bring 18 NS to HP at the end of the next two rows.

And 15 NS on the next four rows; 48 sts remain.

K the two shoulders and the neck sts on to three sections of WY.

Complete the bottom edging as the Long Ultramarine Cardigan with Collar (previous pattern).

LEFT FRONT

Using WY cast on 91 sts, k a few rows, change to MC, work 40 rows at the same time dec 1 st ff on the right side every sixth row.

Place Pocket

As the Long Ultramarine Cardigan with Collar (previous pattern).

Cont to dec on side edge 75 sts rem. Cont without shaping to RC 130.

Armhole Shaping

Dec 1 st ff at right edge five times, 70 sts rem.

Cont without shaping until RC 200.

Cast off 10 sts, k 1 row then dec ff 1 st on the neck edge until 48 sts rem, cont until RC 230.

Shape shoulder as back.

Complete bottom edging as for the Long Ultramarine Cardigan with Collar (previous pattern).

RIGHT FRONT

Work as for left front reversing all shaping.

SLEEVE

Pick up 160 sts from the front and back armhole and MC dec 1 st ff each end of every 6th row until 100 sts remain.

Cont to RC 180 and k on to WY or work the edging required.

BUTTON BANDS

Complete as for Long Ultramarine Cardigan with Collar (previous pattern) but placing 5 buttonholes on the right band.

Any of these shapes can be adapted for a Fairisle version by working a tension square and reassessing the rows and stitches required.

TURQUOISE ROUND NECK CARDIGAN

A classic shaped cardigan that can be long or short. First of all, decide which edging method you are going to follow. Cast on using waste yarn and change to main yarn and machine knit the back, fronts and sleeves and then pick up the stitches from the waste yarn and work the required moss stitch, or garter stitch. Alternatively, work the edgings and then pick up the stitches on to the machine to knit the main pieces.

If you decide to make a thicker textured edging by mixing two yarns together, the former method is the best as you will need to decrease the number of stitches required for the edging. As a general rule, for the first method pick up three stitches and then knit two together until all stitches have been picked up. Continue to knit the edging as required.

Method

BACK
Note: The edgings are hand knitted in moss stitch and then picked up on to the machine.

Materials
675g of Knoll Soft Donegal wool
5572 Vichy
6 buttons
A pair of 2.25mm 13 UK knitting needles

Measurements
To fit chest 92–102cm

Tension
28 sts and 40 rows = 10cm
MT 8

Machines
Suitable for all standard gauge punchcard and electronic machines

Turquoise Round Neck Cardigan.

Using UK 13, 2.25mm needles cast on 180 sts and k in moss stitch for 3cm; leave the end 10 sts on a holding pin. Pick up 160 sts on to the machine and continue in k using MY, or for the alternative method cast on 160 sts using WY k a few rows, change to MY and continue as instructed.
RC 000 k 20 rows.

Inc 1 st at each end of the next and every alt until 182 sts.
K 6 rows.

Dec 1 st ff at each end of the next and foll 6th row until 140 sts remain.
Continue to RC 200.

Armhole Shaping
Dec 1 st ff at the beg of the next and foll alt rows until 130 sts remain.
Cont to RC 300.

Shape Shoulder
Place 14 Ns into HP on the outside edge on the next and foll 3 rows.

And 12 Ns twice. K sts on to WY in three sections, the two 40 st shoulders and centre 50 sts and remove from machine.

Finish Side Edging
Using knitting needles pick up 10 sts from the st holder and k 20 rows moss stitch; at the same time dec 1 st on the right every alt row until 0 sts remain.

Rep for the other side reversing shaping.

POCKET LININGS (MAKE 2)
Cast on 30 sts with WY, k a few rows, change to MY and k 80 rows, remove from machine with WY.

RIGHT FRONT

Using 13 UK, 2.25mm knitting needles cast on 104 sts and k moss-stitch edging for 4cm.

Leave 10 sts on the right and 14 sts on the left on st holders 80 sts WP or cast on using WY k a few rows, change to MY and cont as instructed.

RC 000 cont to k with MY 20 rows, inc 1 st at the right on the next and foll alt rows until 11 sts have been inc 91 sts.

K 6 rows dec 1 st ff on the next and foll 6th row until 70 sts remain at the same time on RC 100 place pocket 30 Ns from the front edge. Right side of lining facing pick up the sts from one end of the waste yarn, k 1 row across these sts only and cast off. Pick up the sts from the rem end of the lining on to the empty needles and cont to k to RC 200.

Armhole Shaping

Right side dec 1 st ff on the next and foll alt rows until 5 sts have been dec, 65 sts remain.

Cont to RC 260.

Shape Neck

Cast off 10 sts on the neck edge and k 1 row dec 1 st ff on the next and foll alt rows 15 sts have been dec.

Cont to RC 300.

Shape shoulder as back.

Join shoulder sts to back by picking up the corresponding sts from the back with RS facing k 1 row MT+2 and latch off.

Complete side edging as back.

LEFT FRONT

Rep as for right front reversing all shaping.

SLEEVES (MAKE 2)

Pick up 150 sts between the armhole shaping with the centre shoulder seam at the centre of the machine.

RC 000 k 6 rows dec 1 st ff at each

end of the next row and the foll 6th row until 100 sts remain.

Cont to k to RC 186.

K the edging by either transferring to knitting needles and completing 5cm in moss stitch or any of the alternative methods.

Cast off.

BUTTON BANDS

Left Band

Pick up rem 14 sts from the st holder and work the length of the front using moss stitch. Place sts on holding needle.

Attach to front edge.

Right Band

K as for left band placing 5 buttonholes up the front. **Note:** A sixth buttonhole is placed in the collar. Attach to front edge.

Pick up sts around the neck and the left front band. Cont to work in patt placing a buttonhole 2.5cm from the edge; cont to work a further 2.5cm and cast off.

MAKING UP

Sew side seams, sew in ends. Sew pocket bags and edging in place. Add buttons. Wash and press lightly.

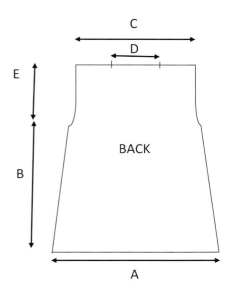

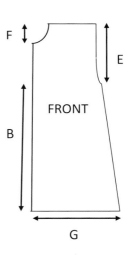

	Long	Short
A	67cm	68cm
B	54.5cm	40cm
C	52.5cm	59cm
D	20cm	22.5cm
E	27cm	25.5cm
F	13cm	13cm
G	40.5cm	42cm
H	32cm	34cm
I	51.5cm	48cm
J	54cm	54cm

Diagram for Round Neck Cardigan.

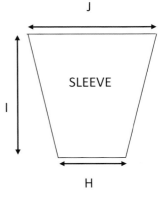

SHORT VERSION SAND CARDIGAN

With very little alteration the long cardigan can be adapted to a shorter and a larger version. The edgings are hand knitted with moss stitch and a fine cream thread of cashmere added to the main yarn to create a textural interest.

Method

BACK

Cast on 180 sts and work the edging as before. Place 10 sts either side on to holding pins.

RC 000 k 20 rows and inc each end of every alt row until 172 sts k 4 rows.

Shape Sides

Dec 1 st ff each end of the next row and every foll 4th row until 150 sts rem.

Cont to RC 150.

Materials
600g of Knoll Soft Donegal wool 5508 Foyle
Optional 100g fine cashmere yarn when knitting the edgings
A pair of 2.25mm 13 UK knitting needles
5 buttons

Measurements
Around chest 122cm
Length to shoulder 66cm
Sleeve length 43cm

Tension
28 sts and 40 rows = 10cm
MT 8

Machines
Suitable for all standard gauge punchcard and electronic machines

See diagram for Round Neck Cardigan (previous pattern)

Short version, Sand Cardigan with Shiver Scarf.

Armhole Shaping
Foll instructions for the long length 140 sts.

Work to RC 250 shoulder shaping, place 15 Ns into HP on the next 6 rows. Remove the two shoulders 45 sts and the centre neck 50 sts from the machine on 3 sections of WY.

RIGHT AND LEFT FRONT
Make two pocket linings as for Round Neck Cardigan (previous pattern).
Foll the instructions as the long version but casting on 85 sts.

And placing the pocket on RC 80, 30 sts from the front edge.

Foll instructions as appropriate for short back to RC 210.

Shape Front Neck
Cast off 12 sts, k 1 row and dec ff on the next and foll alt rows until 45 sts remain.

Shape shoulder as back. (Do not knit off the machine on WY.)
Join back shoulder to front by picking up the corresponding appropriate sts, k 1 row MT+2 k 1 row and latch off.

SLEEVES

With right side facing, pick up 154 sts from the armhole shaping with the shoulder seam in the centre 0.

RC 000 k 6 rows dec 1 st ff at each end of the next and foll 6th rows until 100 sts remain.

Cont to RC 176.

Work the required edging and cast off.

BUTTON BANDS

Left Band

Pick up sts from holder and k the required length.

Right Band

K as for left band placing four buttonholes up the front. Note a fifth buttonhole is placed in the collar.

Attach the bands to the front edge. Pick up sts around the neck and the left front band. Cont to work in patt, placing a buttonhole 2.5cm from the edge and cont to work a further 2.5cm and cast off.

MAKING UP

Sew side seams, sew in ends. Sew pocket bags and edging in place. Add buttons. Wash and press lightly.

SHORT AND LONG PEPLUM JACKETS

The fronts, backs and sleeves of the jacket are knitted in stocking stitch using main yarn unless specified.

The jackets are versatile; the whole style of them can be altered depending on which border and cuff technique you choose. The image shows a fitted jacket knitted with Knoll Soft Donegal Wool and the edgings are worked with the wool and chenille combined and knitted by hand using a moss stitch first row knit one , purl one, repeat to end, second row, purl one, knit one repeat to end. Repeat these two rows. This results in a crunchy, almost rustic textured finish. Because two yarns are combined the overall weight of the main yarn will be thicker so some stitches from the main body of the garment will need to be decreased as the edging will be wavy. I usually pick up four stitches and then knit two stitches together, as this results in a flatter fabric. If only one thread of the main yarn is being used the result is more delicate and intricate.

Alternatively, a garter stitch can be used either by working with a garter bar on the machine, or knitting by hand.

SHORT PEPLUM JACKET

Method

LOWER BACK PANELS (KNIT TWO – FAR LEFT AND RIGHT)

Using WY, cast on 54 sts, k a few rows. Change to MY RC 000.

K 3 rows, start to shape sides, dec 1 st ff at each end of the next and every 4th row until 30 sts remain.

K 2 rows RC 50. Release from the machine on WY.

CENTRE PANELS (KNIT 2)

Using WY, cast on 44 sts, k a few rows. Change to MY, k 3 rows.

Shape sides, dec 1 st ff at each end of the next and every 4th row until 20 sts remain.

K 2 rows RC 50; using WY release the machine.

Materials
500g of Knoll Soft Donegal 5503 Forbes
150g chenille in similar shade to MY
5 buttons
A pair of 2.25mm 13 UK knitting needles

Measurements
To fit bust 92–102cm
Length to shoulder 60.75cm
Sleeve length 45cm

Tension
28 sts and 40 rows = 10 cm, measured over stocking stitch
Approx MT 8

Machines
Suitable for all standard gauge punchcard machines

Front view of the Short Peplum Jacket.

Back view of the Short Peplum Jacket.

UPPER BACK

Push 100 Ns to WP. Starting on the left, with wrong side facing, pick up the 30 sts from one of the lower back panels, the two centre panels and finally the last lower back panel.

RC 000 using MT – 4 and MY, k 20 rows.

RC 000 using MT k 1 row.

Shape sides by inc 1 st ff at each end of every foll alt row until 144 sts.

K 18 rows. RC 62.

Shape Armholes

Cast off 10 sts at beg of next 2 rows. Dec 1 st ff at each end of the next row and every foll alt row until 100 sts remain.

K 80 rows.

RC 167, place a marker each side of centre 44 sts.

Using WY, release from the machine.

RIGHT FRONT

Push 70 Ns to WP at right of centre. Using WY, k a few rows.

RC 000 MT, change to MY, k 1 row. Shape sides by dec 1 st ff at the right edge of the next and every foll alt row until 50 sts remain. K 10 rows RC 000 MT – 4 k 20 rows.

RC 000 MT, k 1 row, shape side by inc 1 st ff at the right edge on the next row and every foll alt row until 72 sts. RC 62.

Shape Armhole

Cast off 10 sts at beg of the next row. K 1 row dec 1 st ff on the armhole edge of the next and every foll alt row until 50 sts remain. K 42 rows RC 129.

Shape Neck

Cast off 8 sts at beg of next row. Dec 1 st ff at the neck edge of next row and every foll alt row until 28 sts remain. K 10 rows. RC 167.

Join Right Shoulder

With right side facing, replace 28 sts from the back shoulder on to the corresponding Ns. Using MT+1, K 1 row and latch off.

LEFT FRONT

Repeat as for right front, reversing all shapings.

SLEEVES

Cast on 70 sts using WY and k a few rows.

Change to MY RC 000 K 5 rows. Shape sides by inc 1 st ff at each end of the next row and every 6th row until 120 sts. K 8 rows. RC 158.

Shape Sleeve Top

Cast off 10 sts at beg of the next 2 rows. Dec 1 st ff at each end of the next and every foll alt row until 36 sts remain, then on every foll row until 30 sts remain.

RC 226 cast off.

CUFFS

See notes on borders and cuffs.

Using hand knitting needles with MY and chenille, pick up and k in moss stitch for 20 rows. 6cm. Cast off keeping st patt correct.

LOWER BACK BORDER

Join panels together using mattress stitch. Using hand knitting needles, and MY and chenille combined, pick up 196 sts from lower edge and k 10 rows.

Cast off.

LOWER FRONT BORDERS

Pick up 70 sts and work 10 rows in moss stitch and cast off.

BUTTON BAND

Using knitting needles, MY and chenille together, cast on 10 sts. Work in moss stitch until band measures the same as the front edge. Leave sts on holder. Sew band in position. Mark the position for 5 buttons, making sure that one button is placed 2cm from the top and another where the tight waist rows are knitted and the remaining evenly spaced.

BUTTONHOLE BAND

Work as for button band making buttonholes over 2 sts as markers are reached. When the band has been completed leave sts on needle and sew in place.

COLLAR

Cast off 5 sts at the beginning of the button band and continue to keep patt correct, work across the rest of the band sts. Pick up around neck shaping, and across back and down the front neck 90 sts and across the button band. Cast off 5 sts at beg of the next row and cont to work 38 rows 10cm moss stitch.

Cast off loosely.

MAKING UP

Set in sleeves. Join side and sleeve seams. Sew on buttons.

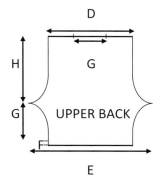

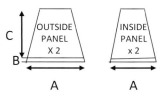

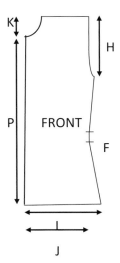

A	19.25cm Outside Panel 15.5cm Inside Panel
B	2.5cm
C	12.5cm
D	35.5cm
E	51.25cm
F	4cm
G	15.5cm
H	26.25cm
I	25cm
J	17.75cm
K	9.5cm
L	55cm
M	39.5cm
N	17cm
O	42.5cm
P	51.25cm

Diagram for the Short Peplum Jacket.

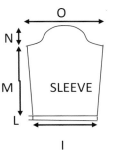

LONG PEPLUM JACKET

Method

The basic pattern for the upper back, fronts and sleeves remains the same as the shorter version.

LOWER BACK PANELS (FAR LEFT AND RIGHT)

Cast on 50 sts using WY, k a few rows. RC 000 change to MY, k 20 rows and dec 1 st ff at each end of the next and foll 12 rows until 30 sts remain.
   Cont to k until RC 132 remove from machine on to WY.

CENTRE PANELS (KNIT 2)

Cast on 50 sts using WY, k a few rows. RC 00 change to MY, k 20 rows dec 1 st ff at each end of the next and foll 10th row until 28 sts rem. Cont to RC 132 and remove from machine on to WY.

Materials
500g of Knoll Soft Donegal wool 5538 Fitzgerald
150g chenille in similar shade to MY
7 buttons
A pair of 2.25mm 13 UK knitting needles

Measurements
To fit bust 92–102cm
Length to shoulder 76cm
Sleeve length 45cm

Tension
28 sts and 40 rows = 10cm measured over stocking stitch
Approx MT 8

Machines
Suitable for standard gauge punchcard and electronic machines

Long Peplum Jacket from the front.

Long Peplum Jacket from the back.

UPPER BACK

Bring forward 116 Ns to WP and pick up the two outside and centre panels. MT – 3 k 20 rows.

RC 000 MT inc 1 st ff at each end of every 3rd row until 140 sts. Cont without shaping to RC 52.

Armhole Shaping

Cast off 10 sts at beg of the next 2 rows, dec ff 1 st at beg of each row until 110 sts remain.
**Cont to k RC 98.

Shape Shoulder

Place 15 sts opposite the carriage into HP for the next 4 rows (wrapping the yarn around the end needle to avoid a hole).

Remove the sts from the machine on to WY in three separate sections. 30 sts for each shoulder and the centre 50 sts for the back neck.

RIGHT FRONT

Cast on 78 sts using WY at the right side of the centre of the machine. Change to MY, k 6 rows.
Right side shaping, dec 1 st ff on the next every foll 6th row until 58 sts remain, cont to RC 132.

Release from the machine with WY. Cont as right side of back until ** k to RC 70.

Neck Shaping

Cast off 10 sts at the neck edge and cont to dec ff 1 st on the neck edge every alt row until 30 sts remain.

RC 98 shape shoulder as back. With right side of back piece facing, pick up the shoulder sts on to the corresponding Ns and k 1 row MT+2 and latch off.

LEFT FRONT

As for right front reversing all shaping.

SLEEVES

K two following the shorter version instructions.

BORDERS AND BANDS

Follow instructions for shorter version but with 7 buttonholes evenly spaced.

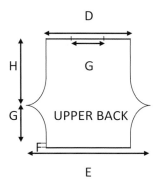

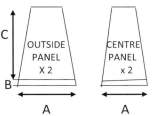

A	20.5cm Outside Panel	20cm Centre Panel
B	2.5cm	
C	31cm	
D	42cm	
E	55.5cm	
F	4cm	
G	14cm	
H	26cm	
I	31cm	
J	21cm	
K	11cm	
L	6cm	
M	38.5cm	
N	20cm	
O	40cm	
P	25cm	

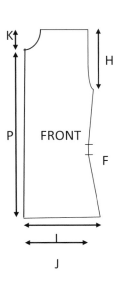

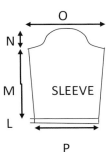

Diagram for the Long Peplum Jacket.

Method

Decide what edgings you are going to use. Either use the garter bar to knit a garter-stitch edging, or drop and manually knit stitches for a moss-stitch edging, or hand knit the edging adding a chenille thread to add texture and interest. If you use the last method, fewer stitches will be needed due to using two yarns together, and the chenille is bulky. Using a textured yarn along with the main yarn also makes a feature of the neckline. The V neckline is wide and framed by the rugged edging, which complements the country feel and style of this jacket.

It is also possible to knit the main pieces by casting on using waste yarn and then picking up the bottom edge stitches and knitting the edging down from the top.

Materials
400g of Knoll Soft Donegal wool
5524 Abbert
100g of chenille
6 buttons
A pair of 2.25mm 13 UK knitting needles

Measurements
Small: Chest 100cm, length 56cm, sleeve length 55cm

Medium: Chest 108cm, length 58cm, sleeve length 56cm

Large: Chest 112cm, length 59cm, sleeve length 56cm

Tension
32 sts and 40 rows = 10cm

Machines
Suitable for all standard gauge punchcard and electronic machines

Claret Cardigan.

Moss-stitch chart X0X0XOXOXOXO and reform the stitches, and reverse this stitch pattern for the following row.

BACK
Cast on 138, 150, 162 sts and k the edging patt chosen for 3cm. RC 000 change to MY k 5 rows. Dec ff on the next and foll 7th rows until 124, 140, 152 sts.

K 10 rows. Inc 1 st ff at side seam edge on the next and foll 9th row until 140, 154, 168 sts.

Cont to k to RC 138.

Shape Armholes
Cast off 7, 8, 9 sts at beg of next 2 rows.

Dec 1 st ff at each end of next 5, 7, 9 rows and then on foll alt rows until 109, 115, 123 sts remain.

Cont to k to RC 226, 234, 238.

Shape Shoulder
Place into HP 11, 12, 13 Ns at beg of each row 4 times and 11, 11, 12 Ns twice.

Remove from the machine on to WY in three separate sections, two shoulders and one centre neck.

RIGHT FRONT

Cast on 66, 74, 82 sts and work your chosen edging for 3cm.

Change to MY RC 000 k 5 rows. Dec on the side edge on the next and every foll 7th row until 62, 69, 76 sts. K 10 rows. Inc on the next and every foll 9th row until 70, 77, 84 sts.

K 12 rows RC 126.

Start to Shape Front Edge

Dec on front edge of next and every foll alt row 4 times 66, 73, 80 sts. Dec 1 st on the foll 4th row.

K 1 row RC 138.

Shape Armhole

Cont to keep shaping correct on the front edge by dec 1 st every 4th row. On the armhole edge cast off 7, 8, 9 sts at beg of row.

Dec 1 st at armhole edge on the next 5, 7, 9 st rows and then on alt rows until 44, 46, 50 sts.

Cont to dec on the front edge until 39, 41, 44 sts rem.

Dec on foll 6th rows until 33, 35, 38 sts. Cont to k without shaping until RC 225, 233, 237.

Shape shoulder by placing 11, 12, 13 Ns into HP on the next and foll alt row.

K 1 row. Place all Ns in HP.

Join shoulder by picking up the corresponding sts from the back. K 1 row MT + 2 and latch off.

LEFT FRONT

Rep as for right front reversing all shaping.

SLEEVES

Cast on 68 sts, 74 sts, 78 sts and work the edging patt chosen for 3cm RC 000.

Change to MY, k 5 rows, shape sides inc 1 st at each end of the next and every foll 6th, 6th, 4th rows until 90, 112, 84 sts.

Cont to inc on the next and every foll 8th, 8th, 6th row until 110, 120, 128 sts.

RC 160.

Shape Top

Cast off 7, 8, 9 sts at beg of next 2 rows. Dec 1 st at each end of the next row and foll 4th until 84, 92, 96 sts, then on every foll alt row until 66, 72, 80 sts, then on every row until 48, 54, 62 sts rem. Cast off.

RIGHT BUTTONBAND

Cast on 172, 176, 182 sts and cont in patt; work 6 buttonholes after 2cm, cont to patt for a further 2cm. Cast off 115 sts.

Shape Lapel

Cast off 6 sts at beg of every foll alt row until all sts have been cast off.

LEFT BAND

Work as for right band omitting the buttonholes.

COLLAR

Cast on 142, 152, 162 sts, work in patt for 7.5cm. Dec 1 st at each end of every row until 122, 132, 142 sts. Cast off 6 sts at beg of the next 12 rows. Cast off rem sts.

MAKING UP

Sew in sleeves. Sew side seams. Pick up back neck and pick up corresponding sts from collar, k 1 row MT+2 and latch off. Sew rest of collar in place. Sew on buttons.

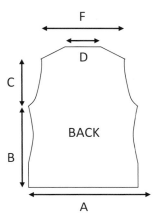

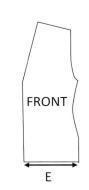

	Small	Medium	Large
A	49.5cm	54cm	59.5cm
B	34cm	34cm	34cm
C	22cm	24cm	25cm
D	15cm	16cm	17cm
E	24cm	27cm	30cm
F	38.75cm	41cm	44cm
G	24.25cm	26cm	28cm
H	40cm	40cm	40cm
I	3cm	3cm	3cm
J	12cm	13cm	13cm
K	39cm	43cm	46cm

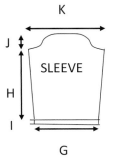

Diagram for Claret Cardigan.

SHORT BOXY KLEIN BLUE CARDIGAN

This cardigan is based on a close-fitted, short matador cardigan. The bottom border is knitted in garter stitch, which can be achieved either by using a garter bar, or by hand knitting and picking up on the machine.

Method

BACK

Cast on 104, 116 sts and k in garter st 5cm, 30 rows.

Cont in st st inc each end of the next and every foll 4th row until 124, 136 sts.

Cont without shaping RC 68.

Shape Armholes

RC 000 dec 1 st at beg of each row until 106, 118 sts RC 17. Mark with a contrasting thread.

Materials
380g of Todd & Duncan Lamaine Lambswool Klein Blue 2/14s 3 ply yarn. The yarn is doubled to make the cardigan

5 buttons

A pair of 2.25mm 13 UK knitting needles

Measurements
Size 1: Across chest 43cm, length to shoulder 43cm, sleeve length 49.5cm

Size 2: Across chest 46cm, length to shoulder 47cm, sleeve length 53cm

Tension
29 sts and 41 rows = 10cm, measured over stocking stitch
MT 8

Machines
Suitable for all standard gauge punchcard and electronic machines

Klein Blue Cardigan.

Cont without shaping RC 46, 54. Inc 1 st at each end of the next and every foll alt 8th rows until 116, 128sts. Cont to RC 84, 92.

Shape Shoulders
K centre sts on to WY, 50, 54 and remove from machine.

Work one shoulder at a time.

Place 7, 8 Ns at the outside edge to HP on the next and every foll alt row until 28, 32 Ns are in HP, at the same time dec 1 st on neck edge every row 5 times.

Remove from machine on to WY. Rep for other shoulder.

LEFT FRONT
Cast on 74, 80 sts and work 30 rows garter st.

Place the first 25 sts on to a holding needle.

RC 000.

K in st st RC, 64, 68.

RC 000.

Shape Armhole
Dec 1 st on the next row armhole edge and foll alt rows until 40, 46 sts rem RC 17.

Mark with a contrasting thread, cont to k without shaping until RC 46, 54. Inc 1 st on the armhole edge on the next and the 4 foll 8th rows.

Work to RC 68, 72.

Shape Neck
Cast off 6, 8 sts on the neck edge.

Dec 1 st every row on neck edge until 28, 32 sts rem.
Cont to RC 84, 92.

Shoulder Shaping
Place 7, 8 outside Ns into HP on alt rows until all sts are in HP.

Join Shoulder to Back
With right side of back facing pick up the corresponding sts on to the Ns, k 1 row MT+2 and latch off.

RIGHT FRONT
Rep as for left front reversing all shaping.

SLEEVES (MAKE 2)
Pick up the armhole sts between the markers on to the machine, 90, 96 with the shoulder seam at the centre.
RC 000. K 1 row. Inc at the beg of each row until 108, 114 sts.
K 6 rows.
Dec 1 st at each end of every 6th row until 70, 74 sts rem, cont to RC 182,

remove from the machine, WY and hand knit garter st border 30 rows.

LEFT FRONT BAND
Pick 25 sts and work the length of the front, leave sts on a holder.

RIGHT BUTTONBAND
Mark the four button placements, the fifth is worked after the neck edge has been picked up.
Pick up the 25 sts from the holding needle and knit the length of the front working the buttonholes over 2 sts in the centre of the band.
Sew the bands on to the fronts and pick up sts around the front neck, across the back and down the rem neck shaping; work in garter st for 5cm placing the final buttonhole in the collar.

MAKING UP
Join side and sleeve seams. Sew on buttons.

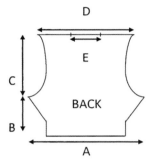

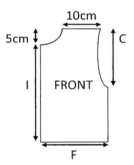

	Size 1	Size 2	Fairisle
A	39cm	46cm	42cm
B	23cm	27cm	28cm
C	20cm	22cm	21cm
D	42cm	46cm	44.5cm
E	24cm	28cm	26.5cm
F	23cm	26.5cm	26cm
G	22cm	24cm	22cm
H	49cm	53cm	51.5cm
I	38cm	42cm	40cm

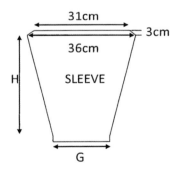

Diagram for Klein Boxy Cardigan and the Fairisle version.

SEA MIST FAIRISLE CARDIGAN

The Short Boxy Klein Blue Cardigan (previous pattern) can easily be adapted to make a fitted Fairisle cardigan using Knoll Soft Donegal. The colours and stitch patterns are inspired by sea mist. The traditional Fairisle patterns are knitted in soft muted colours, and the pattern is lost in areas as if in the mist, only to reappear in a few bright aqua stitches. Shades of grey, pale blues and aqua are used with small busy patterns to encourage the pattern to disappear and reappear. A selection of small three- to seven-row Fairisle stitch patterns was used.

Three rows of stocking stitch are worked between each stitch pattern.

The garter-stitch edgings are a combination of two ends of yarn, a pale grey cashmere and a slightly darker wool and silk. This creates a depth and texture to the surface of the stitch which is already enhanced as the character of the garter stitch is one of a rippled, corrugated tactile fabric.

The fronts and back of the cardigan was lengthened so the armhole shaping began on RC 80; all other shaping remained the same. For the sleeve, pick up 96, 103 stitches between the markers and increase to 114, 118 stitches.

All other instructions remain the same.

Materials
450g of MY Knoll Soft Donegal 5580 Silver Mist

Smaller amounts of 5519 Moy (Aqua), 5548 Malone (Pale Blue), 5580 Foyle (Beige), 5507 Swilly (Cream), 5564 Peacock (Turquoise), 5509 Greese (Grey), 5511 Unshin (Charcoal), 5582 Purple Heart (Mid Purple), 5521 Ramour (Mid Grey)

5 buttons

Measurements
Across chest 45.5cm
Length to shoulder 54cm
Sleeve length 48.5 cm

Tension
31 sts and 37 rows = 10cm measured over Fairisle patt
Approx MT 8

The cardigan pictured was knitted in the larger size

Sea Mist Fairisle Cardigan.

CHAPTER 5

FAIRISLE KNITTING

Fair Isle is an island in northern Scotland that lies 24 miles to the south of the Shetland isles, and is the most remote inhabited island in the United Kingdom. It is made out of Devonian sandstone and is only 3 miles long by 1 mile wide. It has little by way of natural resources, but is surrounded by rich fishing grounds. The main form of agriculture is crofting, with each croft having a few acres of arable land and the right to graze sheep on the scattald, or common grazing. In 1954 Fair Isle was taken over by the National Trust for Scotland, and tourism was encouraged.

A BRIEF HISTORY OF FAIRISLE KNITTING

Fairisle knitting is a stranded knitting technique where there are two colours in a row. A book of knitting patterns and instructions was published in the 1970s and distributed widely. In fact it is now irrelevant whether the item has actually been knitted on Fair Isle or not, as the term is now generic and refers to the knitting technique rather than the place of manufacture.

Fair Isle was first populated around 6,000 years ago, and evidence of some of its earliest inhabitants is still visible today in the form of Neolithic land divisions, Bronze Age *burnt mounds*, and an Iron Age fort. Later the island became an important location for Viking and Norse settlers, and the Vikings conquered the island and ruled from Norway around 876 to 1379. Its

Fairisle jackets on a boat.

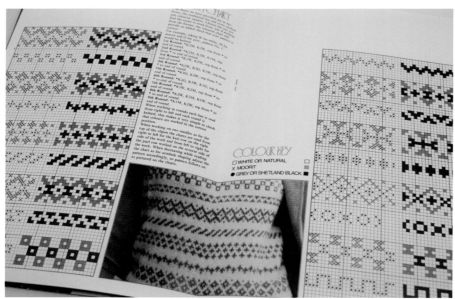

Original Fairisle patterns produced by the National Trust for Scotland and published in the 1970s.

close proximity to Scotland meant that trading and cultural influences can be traced from around 1200, and this came to the fore when in 1468 Orkney and Shetland were mortgaged to pay the balance of the dowry of Margaret of Denmark when she married King James the Third of Scotland.

Knitting was being practised by 1500, the warm fabric created being ideal for the weather conditions; also the presence of sheep meant that wool was freely available. In 1564 Fair Isle was documented as a producer of hand-knitted thick stockings; however, this did not last long, and by the Victorian era these were being machine knitted.

There are many theories and much conjecture as to the first examples of the brightly coloured stranded knitting on the island of Fair Isle. In 1588 the Spanish Armada flagship *El Gran Griffon* was shipwrecked in the cove of Stroms Hellier, and the 300 surviving sailors spent six weeks living with the islanders. Folklore has it that the islanders saw examples of colourful knitting being worn by the Spanish sailors, which they copied. This is a lovely tale, but there is no real evidence to substantiate this claim, even though it is still being written about as a fact both online and in print. There is no doubt that the islanders were sea faring and travelled throughout the known world, so it is highly likely that some of the patterns came via their travels – there are examples of woven cloth from the Baltic region, Estonia, Lithuania and Russia using similar designs and motifs.

The Baltic states used the stranded knitting technique for all-over patterns, and their traditional embroidery patterns can be seen mirrored in knitted Fairisle designs. Estonia has ancient examples of knitted mitten, glove and stocking patterns in museums, so it is reasonable to surmise that some of the patterns arrived via sea routes.

There are hundreds of different Fairisle knitting patterns, and they reflect, and were influenced by, designs seen in sampler embroideries and pattern charts that were sold in booklets throughout the Victorian era. They bear more than a passing resemblance to the cross-stitch and lace techniques practised across Europe, and many patterns use symmetrical and geometric embroidery motifs to design crosses, diamonds, stars, hearts and stylized flowers.

On Fair Isle there is no mention of any brightly coloured patterned textiles on the island before 1850, so this is the most likely date that Fairisle knitting was first practised. The skill spread to the Shetland Islands due to their close trading proximity, and the range and variety of patterns were added to and expanded upon. This also ties in with the earliest examples of Fairisle knitting in Shetland using commercial vegetable dyes, such as madder for red, indigo for blue or ragwort for gold. The local natural dyes were limited and subtle, even though the patterns knitted were varied, the main colours used being bands of red, white, dark blue and brown with splashes of gold. There are also examples of knitting design sheets being sold in Lerwick, Shetland, in the 1920s, where the design inspiration was taken from lace curtains, pottery and even floor linoleum.

Shetland islanders continued to knit their wonderful bright distinctive patterns, and every other cottage was producing its own versions and developing its own colour variations, albeit subject to the limitations imposed by the technology and the available yarn colours. The islanders used to barter the garments made, but the hours spent working on an item meant that the pay was poor – however, perhaps it was better than nothing. Fairisle knitting was not limited to the production of a complete garment – there are old examples of Fairisle patterns added as a border on a plain bag or glove cuff. Gradually, as more designs were created, they started to be written out on scraps of paper and shared between families.

The first synthetic dye, mauveine, was invented in 1856 by William Henry Perkin, and was an aniline dye derived from coal tar. The mauveine dye was quickly followed by a variety of shades of purples and magentas, yellows, blues and pinks, with these colours being much more intense than any available from the traditional natural dyes – and so they became very fashionable. However, by 1910 much of the yarn was still home dyed, with just a few lengths of synthetic dyed yarn to add bright colour and to produce a more distinctive eye-catching result.

A major turning point came in 1921. The Prince of Wales was famously presented with a jersey by a firm of Lerwick drapers to wear whilst playing golf, and Fairisle-designed knitwear saw its popularity soar: its future was more or less assured. It was a perfect fashion for the Art Deco period, and the bright-coloured patterns teamed with garish plaid plus fours were a 'must have' item of clothing on the golf course.

The work was now in demand and merchants were selling all the stock the crofters could make, but the pay was still poor. However, this changed during World War II when the island's strategic importance saw servicemen stationed there. The servicemen ordered their sweaters direct from the knitters, who were at last paid a realistic rate for their work. The knitters were also able to be more creative with their colours and patterns, as a contingent of servicemen from Norway brought with them designs from their own country, such as large stars and sprigs, and these became incorporated into Fairisle

designs. To keep up with demand the hand-frame knitting machine was being used in homes. The famous and distinctive yoked sweater was introduced, which created a perfect amalgamation of a hand-knitted yoke and a machine-knitted front, back, sleeves and ribs.

However, fashion is fickle, and the sweaters and cardigans later fell out of fashion as there were no new designs – so sweaters were considered dated, and the woollen yarn considered itchy by consumers used to the soft feel of synthetic yarns and machine-washable merino wool. There is a lesson here for designers – you have to adapt to survive in a design-led marketplace.

The 1970s saw the arrival of the oil boom in Scotland, which paid very high wages not seen before in the Scottish islands. Knitting was still taught in schools in the 1960s, and wool production was slowly rising, which meant that when the fashion returned for Fairisle knits, the Shetlanders were well placed to start up small businesses to fill orders. Domestic knitting machines were used in the home, and knitters were self-employed as outworkers, based on a piece rate. Factories were also started up using electronic machines. Today, hand and machine knitting is thriving on the islands, boosted by excellent design and internet communication, allowing customers to buy patterns and designs online throughout the world. Yarn spinners have increased their range of colours and also sell worldwide.

Shetland Wool Week runs annually and creates a tourism boost, and attracts makers and buyers alike. Also, Fairisle knitters continue to adapt and customize their designs to a variety of influences, so attracting new customers from emerging markets whilst retaining customers for more traditional designs.

FAIRISLE STITCH PATTERNS

It is not always possible to pinpoint the origin of a particular stitch pattern, as many countries have similar motifs. However, several of the more popular patterns are simple to knit and therefore easy for you to copy and customize. For example, the star motif can be seen in Greek embroidery, beaded work by the American Indians, and in Scandinavian countries where it resembles a snowflake.

Many of the patterns reflect other similar ones, in that they are mainly geometric and symmetrical, with the emphasis on diagonal rather than vertical lines – many are worked over an odd number of rows, and the centre of the motif is a single row in contrasting colours, and a mirror image for the rows knitted below and above.

Many of the designs were not written out formally but were committed to memory or pieced together from scraps of paper, and the knitters would create their own patterns by building up and assembling ideas from previous patterns. Having a symmetrical motif makes this easier to commit to memory.

It is interesting to discover that many motifs can be used both horizontally and vertically. Many of the patterns are peerie (small) and relatively easy to adapt for a knitting machine, either a twenty-four stitch repeat punchcard or electronic. The main rule is to avoid strands (floats) that carry over more than seven stitches.

One feature of a Fairisle stitch pattern is that, with a few exceptions, each motif is complete, with the same colours used to begin and end a pattern, with a change of colour emphasis on the middle row. On a practical note, horizontal lines produce a more elastic knitted fabric, and strong vertical lines tend to tighten the

Fairisle sketchbook.

finished work.

When working on a design the information you need to know is how many rows complete a pattern, and how many stitches are required for a repeat. It helps the design process if you group patterns together of similar repeat and row count, and look for a smaller pattern to juxtapose with a larger one. To find out what the stitch repeat is, you count along the stitch pattern from one pattern to the next. You need to work the pattern so that the main motif is placed in the centre. For example, when using an OXO

border pattern the lozenge shape is better in the centre as the other motifs are joining devices and the weight of the design is with the lozenge. It also makes it easier when calculating adding or taking away stitches to match up side seams and so on. Joining devices can be altered to make the pattern repeat longer or shorter. The example in the photo shows a star motif extended with a joining X to create an OXO pattern and a more interesting design than simply a row of stars.

It is very easy to design your own patterns by repeating motifs and

adding small joining peerie motifs.

Peerie (small) patterns: These are completed in 5–7 rows with repeats of 2–6 stitches across the row. They are useful patterns when changing the background colour without a hard line.

Border patterns: These are completed in 9–15 rows. Deeper borders will often alternate between narrower ones, and there are hundreds of variations with no pattern being repeated. Choose patterns that work in harmony together and flow easily from one to another. They can also be adapted to make all-over patterns.

Fairisle patterns: These are completed in 15–17 rows, mainly made of six- to eight-sided lozenge shapes linked with a cross; some can be elaborate. These are called OXO patterns.

Large Fairisle patterns are completed in 17–19 rows.

Large stars: These are completed in 21–31 rows. It is worth noting that the larger the motif, the less flexible it becomes when designing due to placing and combining with other patterns. They are usually enclosed top and bottom with a peerie (small) or border pattern. There are many examples to be found and documented from Norwegian Selbu mittens.

All-over patterns: There is a huge variety of these, and many of the Fairisle patterns can be adapted to all-over patterns. Many are based on diagonal and geometric variations, of the star or of the diamond. Diced patterns also lend themselves to this format.

Seeding: These are small patterns used for filling in. Many variations can be found on the palm of mittens and

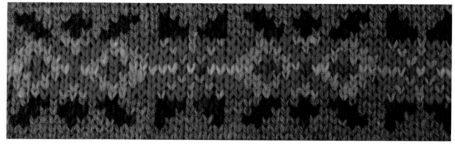

The star extended with a joining X.

gloves, and a variety of excellent examples can be found on Norwegian sweaters, often placed after a large Fairisle motif is worked.

Peaks and waves: Peaks are a way of grading the colours used from light to dark. They are not a true diamond shape as the two centre rows are the same. Waves shade the background but in a softer, less dramatic way. Usually four colours are used, and a bright border pattern is placed into the centre.

Examples of colour grading are navy blue, medium blue, light blue and white. It is desirable if the border pattern placed in the centre of the wave has a stitch repeat that is divisible by four, as it will then line up with the tip of wave. Whatever border pattern is chosen should also line up in the same way for the peaks.

Variations and Stitch Patterns from Norway

There are many examples of the Louse (or Lice or Spider) stitch pattern from Norway, beginning around the 1850s. There is no definitive date as to when it was first made, but Annemor Sundbo states in her book Setesdal Sweaters that a sweater using this stitch pattern was gifted as a wedding present in 1836. The design is called Setesdal after the Setesdal valley of southern Norway, a UNESCO heritage site.

The Louse pattern and variations became the most widely worked pattern in Norway, and was incorporated into a distinctive national sweater that has stood the test of time. The Louse pattern is placed between two more intricate pattern borders. The overall shape resembles the British fisherman gansey, but instead of being worked in one colour and a textured stitch, the pattern is knitted using two colours and the Fairisle technique, with

the Scandinavian version having a deep plain lower border. Both of these attractive designs have endured over the years with little or no changes. It is the traditional use of the stitches and this format that makes them so distinctive.

Very often the decorative cuffs and front neck opening were made from fabric and embroidered. The sweaters produced in this way were all slightly different, as every knitter customized the design and created their own variations, but the overall look and style remained distinctive. In some sweaters the deep plain band at the base of the design was to be tucked into the trousers, so intricate, bulkier stitch patterns were not required or seen. More recently, the fashion is not to tuck this band in and it has become part of the visual style.

The reason that the precise history of the Setesdal sweater lacks a lot of corroborating evidence is that many examples were either moth-eaten or worn out, and were then taken to be recycled in the shoddy factories. Local people sold their rags to the factory for a relatively high price, and during World War I there was a shortage of wool and every Norwegian had to supply rags to be processed. Even in the 1980s old woollen garments were not thought to have any value and were ripped up and the wool strands used to stuff mattresses and sleeping bags. Many exquisite examples of the sweaters and their stitch designs were therefore lost to the national heritage archive.

The two-colour stitch patterns used in the Setesdal sweaters are easily adapted for use on the knitting machine. From the early 1900s knitting machines were imported into Scandinavia, and many of the sweaters were knitted this way. The design has been adapted over the years, and other

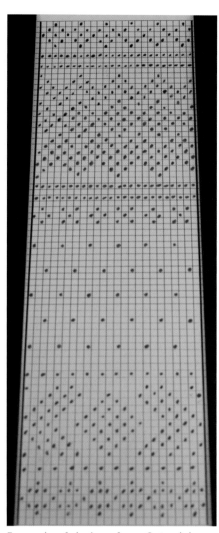

Example of designs from Setesdal sweaters.

motifs and colours have been added. It is now plain to see the similarities between many of the Fairisle and Shetland stitch patterns, and it is fascinating to study how each culture and knitter, through use of colour, spacing and shape, has customized and creatively adapted a basic pattern to their own design.

The distinctive Norwegian Setesdal style of sweater became fashionable in the 1920s with the opening up of international travel, glamorous skiing trips, and being worn by royalty. They are still made in quantity and bought by locals and tourists alike. The following are examples of patterns that have been adapted to fit the twenty-four stitch repeat of the punchcard knitting machine. There are endless varieties of Fairisle stitch patterns, and the similarities with Scandinavian examples are obvious. The Norwegian and some other Scandinavian stitch patterns do appear to have names, so I have used them where appropriate.

The information needed when deciding which pattern to use is: what is the stitch repeat, and the row count.

Peerie Pattern

The following are all examples of peerie patterns, from top to bottom numbered 1 to 12:

1. Rep 8 sts RC 5. These small patterns both resemble a coffee bean.
2. Rep 6 sts RC 5.
3. Rep 4 sts RC 4.
4. Rep 6 sts RC 6.
5. Rep 4 sts RC 3.
6. Rep 6 sts RC 5.
7. Rep 6 sts RC 5.
8. Rep 4 sts RC 5.
9. Rep 4 sts RC 7.
10. Rep 12 sts RC 4.
11. Hearts rep 6 sts RC 7.
12. Rep 12 sts RC 8.

Border Patterns

Border patterns usually have a 9 to 15 row count. Here they are numbered 1 to 6 from top to bottom:

1. Rep 6 sts RC 10.
2. Rep 12 sts RC 15.
3. Rep 12 sts RC 10.
4. Rep 12 sts RC 9.
5. Rep 12 sts RC 13.
6. Rep 12 sts RC 11.

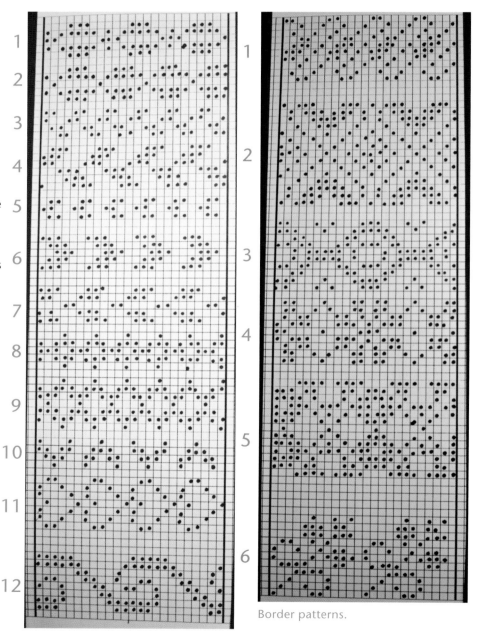

Peerie patterns.

Border patterns.

Joining Patterns

The following are examples of joining patterns, for use when designing your own variations. They are numbered 1 to 3 from top to bottom:

1. Rep 15 sts RC 11.
2. Showing two variations: Rep 7 sts RC 11.
3. Three different small joining patterns: Rep 5 sts, 5 sts, and 3 sts RC 9.

Medallion Pattern

Examples of a Medallion pattern progressing to a larger pattern with joining devices, numbered 1 to 4 top to bottom:

1. A Medallion that becomes the first motif in an OXO pattern: Rep 13 sts RC 13.

2. Add a peerie top and bottom, and a joining border pattern at the side: Rep 24 sts RC 23.
3. Single motif: Rep 13 sts RC 13.
4. Joining pattern added to complete the design: Rep 24 sts RC 13.

Spruce Twig and Star Pattern

Spruce Twig and Star examples are numbered 1 to 5 top to bottom. Note how the individual sections of the small stars resemble hearts.

1. The Spruce Twigs are an excellent motif and resemble pine needles – ideal when knitting a skiing hat. Here are two variations: Rep 9 sts and 9 sts RC 8.
2. The Star, which is also known as the less attractive 'spit ball' in Norway as it resembles a reindeer's spit on the snowy ground: Rep 8 sts RC 7.
3. Star: Rep 12 sts RC 11.
4. Star: Rep 12 sts RC 11.
5. Star: Rep 12 sts RC 9.

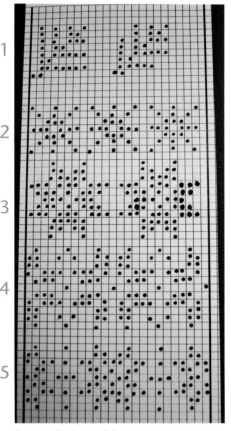

Joining patterns.

Medallion pattern progressing to a larger pattern with joining devices.

Spruce Twig and Star.

Louse and Spider, and Star Patterns

The following are both Woodlouse and Spider examples, numbered 1 to 4 top to bottom:

1. Basic Louse/Spider: Rep 11 sts RC 11.
2. Endless and all-over Louse/Spider pattern: Rep 12 sts RC 12.
3. Border variation: Rep 12 sts RC 11.
4. Variation: Rep 12 sts RC 9.

Louse and Spider variations create an Argyll pattern with the motifs overlapping and swinging back and forth creating a real sense of movement. Numbered 1 to 3 top to bottom:

1. Border: Rep 12 sts RC 11.
2. All-over variation: Rep 12 sts RC 10.
3. All-over pattern: Rep 12 sts RC 20.

Ram's Horn Pattern

Large and bold Ram's Horn patterns, numbered 1 to 3 top to bottom.

1. Ram's Horn border: Rep 24 sts RC 16.
2. Deep border with Ram's Horn and Roses: Rep 24 sts RC 31.
3. Ram's Horn variation: Rep 24 sts RC 23.

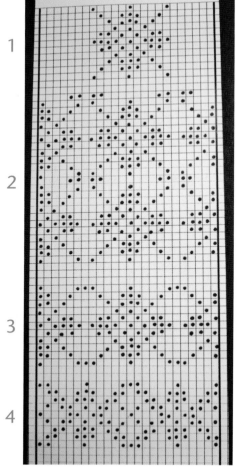

Louse and Spider patterns.

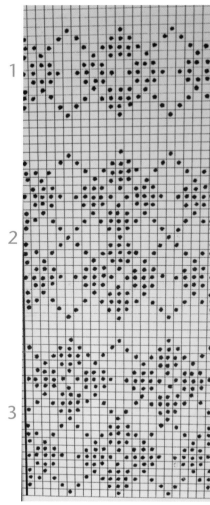

Louse and Spider variations.

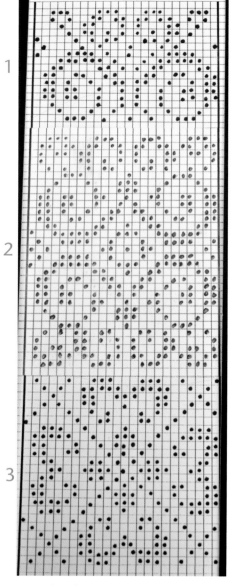

Large Ram's Horn patterns.

Goat's Horn and Hearts Pattern

Examples of Goat's Horn and Hearts patterns, numbered 1 to 2 top to bottom. Patterns can be built up using two or three motifs incorporated within a design.

1. Goat's Horn and Hearts: Rep 24 sts RC 23.
2. Goat's Horn and Rose: Rep 24 sts RC 23.

Ox-Horn Pattern

Ox Horn and Twigs – some designs have larger branches: Rep 24 sts RC 23.

Rose Variation Patterns

The Ram's Horn can be adapted into a Rose design, and there are many

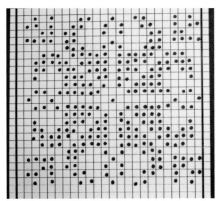

Ox Horn large pattern.

variations of this. For example:

1. Rep 24 sts RC 23.
2. Rep 24 sts RC 23.
3. Rep 24 sts RC 21.

Rose and Rose Petal Patterns

Examples of Rose and Rose Petal patterns, numbered 1 to 3 top to bottom:

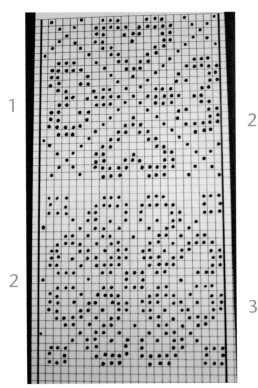

Goat's Horn and Hearts patterns.

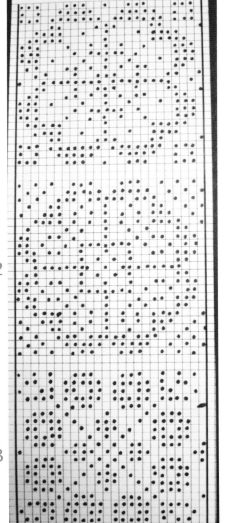

Rose variation patterns.

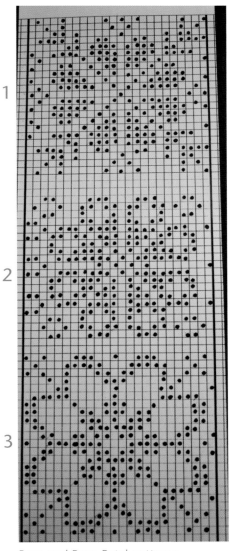

Rose and Rose-Petal patterns.

1. Eight-Petal Roses: Rep 24 sts RC 23.
2. Variation of an Eight-Petal Rose: Rep 24 sts RC 19.
3. Rose and Snowflakes: Rep 24sts RC 23.

Star Patterns

Examples of Star patterns, numbered 1 to 2 top to bottom:

1. Large Single Star and Roundels: Rep 24 sts RC 23.
2. Stars within a Rose: Rep 24 sts RC 23.

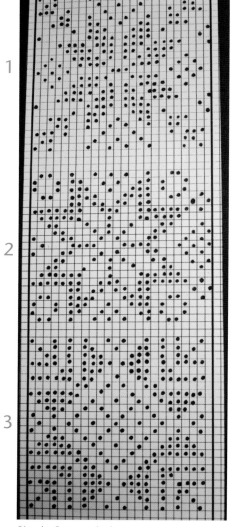

Star patterns.

Single Star variations, numbered 1 to 3 top to bottom:

1. Rep 24 sts RC 23.
2. Rep 24 sts RC 21.
3. Rep 24 sts RC 23.

Single Star variation patterns.

Examples of Single Stars with Branches, numbered 1 to 3 top to bottom:

1. Star with Branches: Rep 24 sts RC 23.
2. Star with space between the points: Rep 24 sts RC 23.
3. Star variation: Rep 24 sts RC 23.

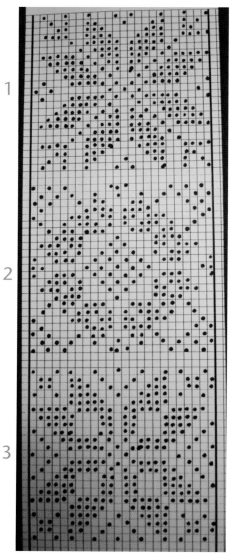

Single Star with Branches patterns.

Hearts Pattern

Examples of Hearts patterns, numbered 1 to 3 top to bottom:

1. Hearts: Rep 20 sts RC 19. This motif requires a joining pattern device.
2. Reverse Hearts: Rep 24 sts RC 23.
3. Border with peerie pattern top and bottom: Rep 12 sts RC 21.

Spanish Pattern

This resembles an embroidered Spanish pattern that has been adapted for the knitting machine: Rep 6 sts RC 17.

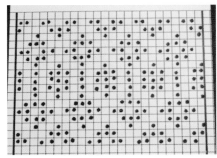

Spanish pattern.

Pattern Variations

The following three pattern variations have a very different feel to the previous ones and have a geometric look. I have used the second pattern many times and it can be seen worked into the Paisley waistcoat, a rich and interesting stitch pattern.

1. Lozenge: Rep 24 sts RC 17.
2. Deep Border using Ram's Horn and Hearts motif: Rep 12 sts RC 25.
3. Spanish Embroidery pattern: Rep 24 sts RC 29

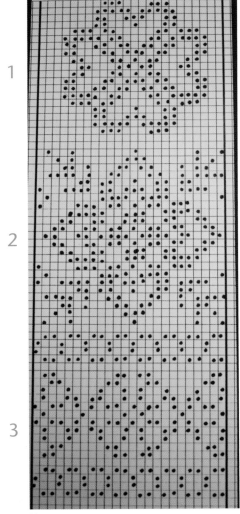

Hearts patterns.

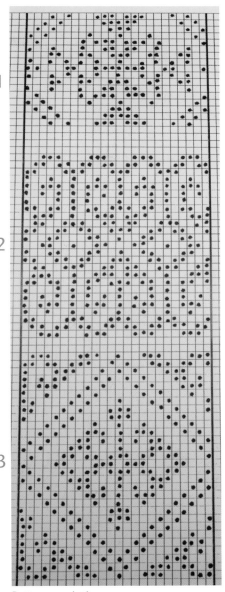

Pattern variations.

All-Over Patterns

All-over patterns, numbered 1 to 3 top to bottom. It is also useful to have not only the stitch repeat but also the row repeat.

1. Floral Scallop: Rep 24 sts RC 20.
2. Star and Moon endless pattern: Rep 12 sts RC 12.
3. Woodlouse: Rep 4 sts RC 10.

Fairisle Knots Patterns

Examples of Fairisle knots patterns, numbered 1 to 3 top to bottom:

1. Simple knot used as a motif: RC 13. This design would require joining to the left and right side if used as a border.
2. Interlaced border: Rep 8 sts RC 15.
3. Vertical twist: Rep 8 sts RC 19.

All the above patterns are works in progress and can be used as a border pattern or adapted and mixed with other floral or geometric patterns. It would be an interesting exercise to pick one particular pattern and knit it using a variety of colourways and joining patterns to extend your knowledge and add to your archive of ideas. An example of the vertical twist cable can be seen in the Paisley waistcoat.

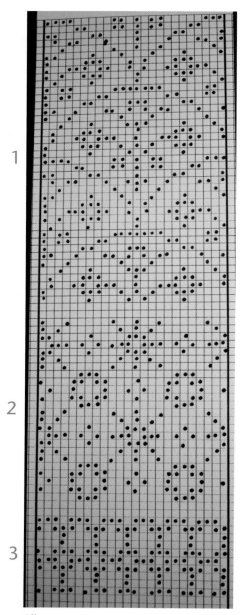

All-over patterns.

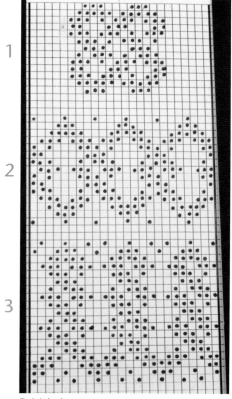

Fairisle knots.

DESIGNING WITH FAIRISLE

Traditional Fairisle and cable patterns can be worn in the summer or winter, and are equally desirable when knitted in wool or cotton. They are true classics, and their versatility extends to various shapes of cardigans, sweaters, hats and scarves. Elements can be used as borders, and any of the stitch patterns can be mixed with plain colours or all-over patterns. Mixing stitch patterns can add a striking contrast – for example, traditional Fairisle patterns always respond when juxtaposed with plaids, tartans, checks, stripes, herringbone tweeds or paisley patterns, creating a contrasting visual texture.

When designing and considering colour choice, start with one of the base colours such as navy, brown or maroon, and then add your contrasting colours, considering all options from soft pastel shades to bright primary colours. Every base colour will have a variety of shades that will add depth and interest while complimenting the contrast colours – for example:

* When working with **navy** as the base colour, try adding pale blue, cream, grey, pale pink or pale yellow with small amounts of bright blue as contrast colours.
* For a rich dark **red**, add shades of ochre, navy, soft mid blues, cream and even light brown.
* For **grey**, try adding cream, red, shades of cinnamon and ochre, or lavender to warm up the cool colours.
* Strong contrasting colours are required to enhance **beige**, so try using cream, dark brown, mid green, with small amounts of gold, terracotta and apricot.

When choosing yarn, natural and regenerated fibres are generally

Traditional Fairisle stitch patterns.

superior to synthetic fibres, as they are more comfortable to wear and drape better on the body. Over time with wash and wear they will take on a patina that enhances their texture and feel, while synthetic fibres tend to become flat and flaccid, and more prone to pilling.

Traditional panel Fairisle design Shetland jumpers were designed geometrically with one panel placed down the middle of the front and back and two identical panels either side. This is not absolutely necessary, as with careful choice of colour and pattern the design can still look balanced and flow. Calculations can be made so the pattern is lined up perfectly on the shoulder from front to back if this is an effect you want to achieve.

For cardigans and jumpers knitted from bottom to top it is possible through choice of pattern and tension to match the pattern perfectly across the side seams and shoulders; however, this does require careful calculation beforehand. Peerie and border patterns

are easier to match. Larger patterns can be half matched using the row and stitch repeat information, and by keeping the colour match across the row to give an illusion of matching. You will know the approximate width required, and it is possible to add a few extra stitches without unduly altering the overall size and fit of the garment. Or simply choose another stitch pattern with a slightly smaller repeat. Most repeats are in even numbers.

The stitch pattern will remain distinct if the contrast between the background yarn in Feeder 1 and the colour in Feeder 2 is kept at a constant tone whenever colour changes are made. The centre row should be emphasized using a dark or light colour. If the required result is for a less distinct stitch pattern, you need to narrow the tonal choice of colours and the pattern will appear and disappear. This can work well, as can be seen on the Sea Mist Cardigan.

Archive colour schemes for traditional Fairisle show items knitted using red and white following on with borders of blue and gold. Interestingly, some colour changing was random and not in line with the pattern chart. In general, examples show a symmetrical colour scheme, which is then repeated in reverse after a centre contrasting row.

When studying vintage Fairisle sweaters it is interesting to note that sleeves were originally knitted short, so as to keep dry and clean. Separate cuffs were worn over the top when working at sea.

MAKING A SKETCH BOOK

The sketchbook peerie patterns pictured here used peerie and border patterns, and the colour scheme was based on the climate crisis with cool blues and greens moving into hot reds, pinks and yellows. I have found it very useful whenever I see or use another

stitch pattern to first knit a small section. It may not be a perfect finished pattern, possibly having extra stitches or rows, but I think of it as a working 'drawing', which can be perfected later. I group my designs in colours so they are easier to find and place when designing. Some patterns that I have knitted in this way have not been used yet, but they are there when I need them. Practice on working out colourways really focuses your mind, and explores which combinations of patterns and colours will complement each other, and work best in your finished design. I call these samples my *sketch book*, and they are an aide-memoire of ideas and work to refer back to and constantly update.

I cast on a hundred stitches and work through stitch patterns for approximately six hundred rows and cast off. If you want to add more at a later date you can pick up the stitches and knit on another few stitch patterns.

Fairisle Stitch Pattern 1, chart. Worked over 3 rows, 4 sts rep.

A

B

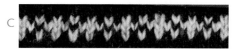
C

Fairisle Stitch Pattern 1, knitted examples A, B, C.

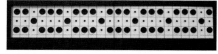

Fairisle Stitch Pattern 2, chart. Worked over 3 rows, 4 sts rep.

A

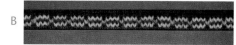
B

C

Fairisle Stitch Pattern 2, examples A, B, C.

Sketchbook peerie patterns

Stitch sketchbook.

Fairisle Stitch Pattern 3, Chart. Worked over 4 rows, 4 sts rep, colour change rows 2, 2.

A

B

C

Fairisle Stitch Pattern 3, examples A, B, C.

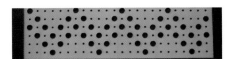

Fairisle Stitch Pattern 5, chart. Worked over 6 rows, 6 sts rep, colour change rows 2, 2, 2.

A

B

C

Fairisle Stitch Pattern 5, examples A, B, C.

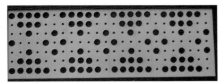

Fairisle Stitch Pattern 7, chart. Worked over 7 rows, 6 sts rep, colour change rows 2, 3, 2 or 3, 1, 3.

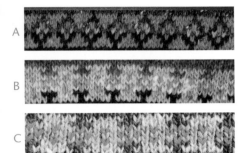

A

B

C

Fairisle Stitch Pattern 7, examples A, B, C.

Fairisle Stitch Pattern 4, chart. Worked over 5 rows, 3 sts rep, colour change rows 2, 1, 2.

A

B

C

Fairisle Stitch Pattern 4, examples A, B, C.

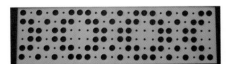

Fairisle Stitch Pattern 6, chart. Worked over 6 rows, 8 sts rep, colour change rows 2, 2, 2.

A

B

C

Fairisle Stitch Pattern 6, examples A, B, C.

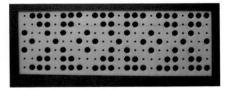

Fairisle Stitch Pattern 8, chart. Worked over 7 rows, 8 sts rep, colour change rows 3, 1, 3.

A

B

C

Fairisle Stitch Pattern 8, examples A, B, C.

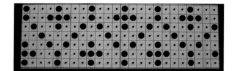

Fairisle Stitch Pattern 9, chart. Worked over 7 rows, 8 sts rep.

A

B

C

Fairisle Stitch Pattern 9, examples A, B, C.

Fairisle Stitch Pattern 10, chart. Worked over 8 rows, 8 sts rep, colour change rows 2, 4, 2 or 3, 2, 3.

A
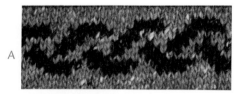

B

C
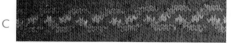

Fairisle Stitch Pattern 10, examples A, B, C.

Fairisle Stitch Pattern 11, chart. Worked over 9 rows, 4 sts rep, colour change rows 3, 3, 3.

A

B

C
Fairisle Stitch Pattern 11, examples A, B, C.

Fairisle Stitch Pattern 12, chart. Worked over 9 rows, 4 sts rep, colour change rows 3, 3, 3.

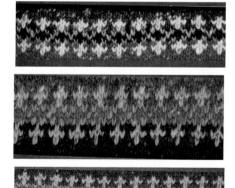

Fairisle Stitch Pattern 12, examples A, B, C.

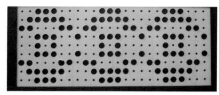

Fairisle Stitch Pattern 13, chart. Worked over 9 rows, 8 sts rep, colour change rows 3, 3, 3.

A
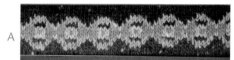

B

C
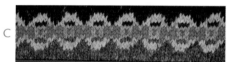

Fairisle Stitch Pattern 13, examples A, B, C.

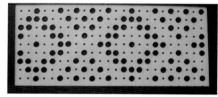

Fairisle Stitch Pattern 14, chart. Worked over 9 rows, 12 sts rep, colour change rows 2, 2, 1, 2, 2.

A

B

C

Fairisle Stitch Pattern 14, examples A, B, C.

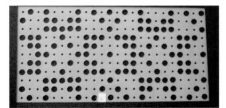

Fairisle Stitch Pattern 15, chart. Worked over 11 rows, 12 sts rep, colour change rows 2, 3, 1, 3, 2.

Fairisle Stitch Pattern 17, chart. Worked over 11 rows, 8 sts rep, colour change rows 3, 2, 1, 2, 3.

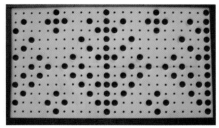

Fairisle Stitch Pattern 18, chart. Worked over 12 rows, 12 sts rep, colour change rows 3, 3, 3, 3.

A

B

C

Fairisle Stitch Pattern 15, examples A, B, C.

A

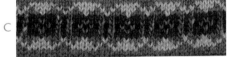

B

C

Fairisle Stitch Pattern 17, examples A, B, C.

A

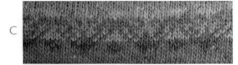

B

C

Fairisle Stitch Pattern 18, examples A, B, C.

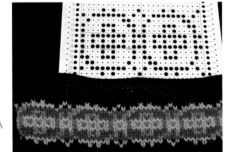

A

Fairisle Stitch Pattern 16, chart and example A. Worked over 13 rows, 12 sts rep, colour change rows 2, 3, 3, 3, 2.

B

C

Fairisle Stitch Pattern 16, examples B, C.

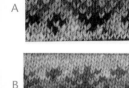

Fairisle Stitch Pattern 19, chart. Worked over 13 rows, 8 sts rep, colour change rows 2, 3, 3, 3, 2.

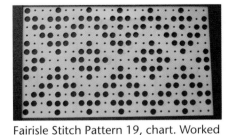

A

B

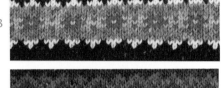

C

Fairisle Stitch Pattern 19, examples A, B, C.

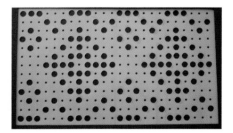

Fairisle Stitch Pattern 20, chart. Worked over 13 rows, 12 sts rep, colour change rows 3, 3, 1, 3, 3.

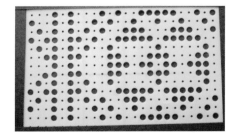

Fairisle Stitch Pattern 21, chart. Worked over 13 rows, 24 sts rep, colour change rows 3, 3, 1, 3, 3.

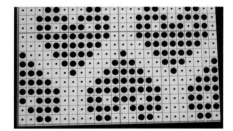

Fairisle Stitch Pattern 23, chart. Worked over 13 rows, 12 sts rep, colour change rows 3, 3, 1, 3, 3.

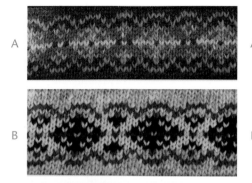

Fairisle Stitch Pattern 20, examples A, B, C.

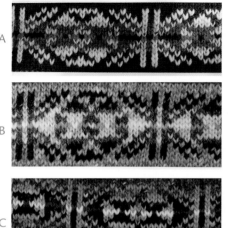

Fairisle Stitch Pattern 21, examples A, B, C.

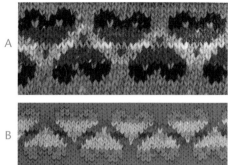
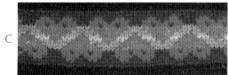

Fairisle Stitch Pattern 23, examples A, B, C.

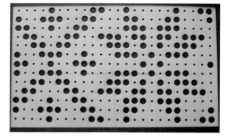

Fairisle Stitch Pattern 22, chart. Worked over 13 rows, 24 sts rep, colour change rows 3, 3, 1, 3, 3.

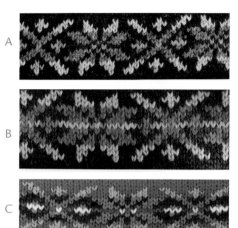

Fairisle Stitch Pattern 22, examples A, B, C.

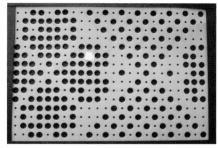

Fairisle Stitch Pattern 24, chart. Worked over 15 rows, 24 sts rep, colour change rows 4, 3, 1, 3, 4.

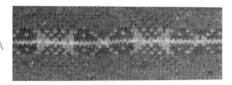

A

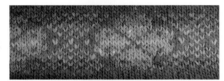

B

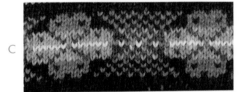

C

Fairisle Stitch Pattern 24, examples A, B, C.

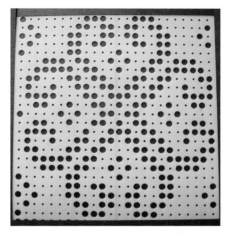

Fairisle Stitch Pattern 25, chart. Worked over 23 rows, 24 sts rep, colour change rows 3, 3, 3, 5, 3, 3, 3.

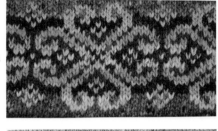

A

B

C

Fairisle Stitch Pattern 25, examples A, B, C.

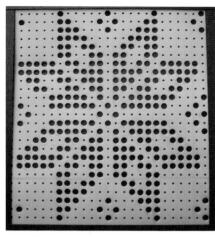

Fairisle Stitch Pattern 26, chart. Worked over 25 rows, 24 sts rep, colour change rows 4, 4, 4, 1, 4, 4, 4.

A

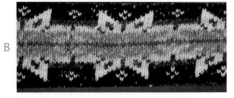

B

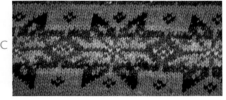

C

Fairisle Stitch Pattern 26, examples A, B, C.

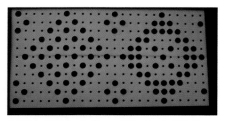

Fairisle Stitch Pattern 27, chart. Worked over 11 rows, 24 sts rep and colour change rows 2, 3, 1, 3, 2 or 3, 2, 1, 2, 3. This pattern fits well between the Wave or Diamond Peak patterns.

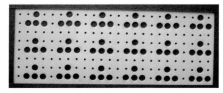

Fairisle Stitch Pattern 28, chart, Wave Pattern. Worked over 10 rows, rep 4 sts. See Table 5.1 for pattern sequencing.

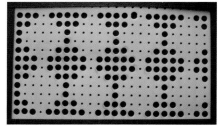

Fairisle Stitch Pattern 29, chart, Diamond Peak. Worked over 12 rows, stitch rep 6 sts. See Table 5.2 for pattern sequencing.

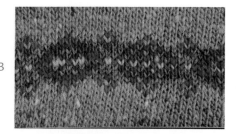

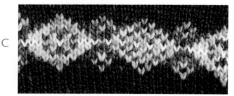

Fairisle Stitch Pattern 27, Examples A, B, C.

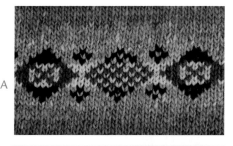

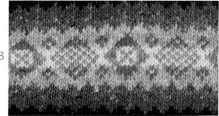

Fairisle Stitch Pattern 28 with Pattern 27 placed in the middle. Examples A, B.

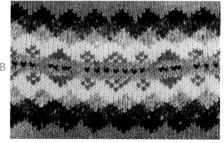

Fairisle Stitch Pattern 29 with Pattern 27 worked in the middle A, B.

Table 5.1: Chart 28 Wave Pattern Sequence using four colours 1, 2, 3, 4

Rows	Stitch Pattern	Pattern Setting	Feeder 1	Feeder 2
1		Knit	1	
2	28	Fairisle	2	1
1	28	Knit	2	
2	28	Fairisle	3	2
1	28	Knit	3	
2	28	Fairisle	4	3
1		Knit	4	

Table 5.2: Chart 29 Diamond Peak Pattern Sequence five colours 1, 2, 3, 4, 5

Rows	Stitch Pattern	Pattern Setting	Feeder 1	Feeder 2
3	29	Fairisle	1	2
3	29	Fairisle	1	3
3	29	Fairisle	4	3
3	29	Fairisle	4	5

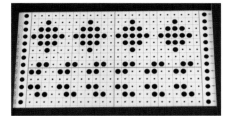

Fairisle Stitch Pattern 30, chart. Worked over 17 rows, the first 6 rows are repeated after the diamond motif. Stitch rep 12 sts.

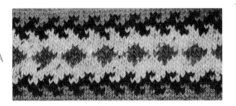

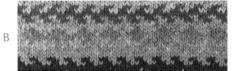

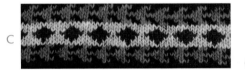

Fairisle Stitch Pattern 30, examples A, B, C. Three very different borders depending how the colours are changed.

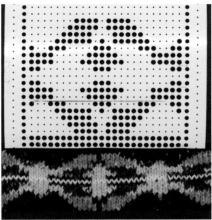
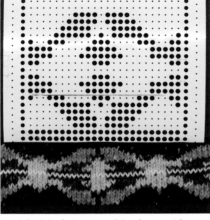

Fairisle Stitch Pattern 31, chart with example A. Worked over 17 rows, 24 sts rep, colours change on rows 4, 4, 1, 4, 4.

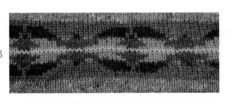

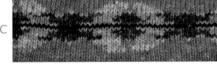

Fairisle Stitch Pattern 31, examples B, C.

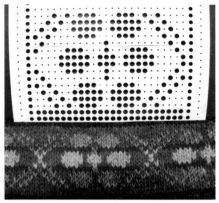

Fairisle Stitch Pattern 32, chart with example A. Worked over 14 rows, 24 sts rep, colours change on rows 4, 1, 4, 1, 4.

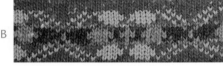

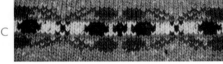

Fairisle Stitch Pattern 32, examples B, C.

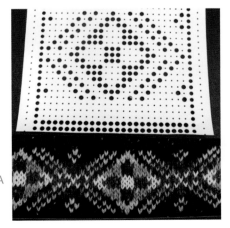

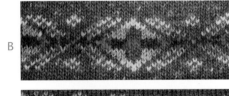

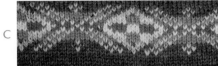

Fairisle Stitch Pattern 33, chart with example A. Worked over 15 rows, 24 sts rep, colours change on rows 3, 3, 3, 3, 3.

Fairisle Stitch Pattern 33, examples B, C.

Sometimes while working and experimenting with colour and stitch patterns the results can be surprising. If your sketch-book knitted strips are all the same length, they can be sewn together to make a colourful blanket.

These are the stitch patterns I find most useful, but there is a legion of others that all have equal merit. I have added three different colourways to show how they can be adapted to change their character.

Numbers 31, 32, 33 stitch patterns have a different character to many of the other patterns as they are larger and have longer floats at the back of the work. They are based on Navajo rug designs.

I find it useful to write in pencil lightly down the side of the card when I change colours – for example when using Stitch Pattern 3, I write 2, 2 and for Border Pattern 19, I write 2, 3, 3, 3, 2, as it helps to prevent counting errors.

All the patterns and charts in this section can be mixed together and worked into a scarf or jacket. There are some that have proved to be more versatile than others. They are all 'works in progress', and can be adapted by moving a stitch to the left or right, adding a few pattern stitches, blocking some out with tape or changing the colour choice. There is no doubt that by experimenting and gaining confidence with colour combinations you will discover more pattern and colour variations as well as their versatility.

FAIRISLE DESIGNS TO KNIT

The basic edge-to-edge knitted jacket absorbs any stitch pattern you wish to use. By mixing borders of Fairisle stitch patterns and all-over patterns, you can create an unstructured garment that can be pinned for closure or have a single button added. Many traditional Fairisle patterns can be adapted and used as all-over patterns, and when the colours are used in a controlled yet random way, the resulting stitch pattern appears and disappears in a dynamic fashion. You will find this technique of colour changing useful when working the sideways jackets.

Basic Pattern

The basic pattern can be altered depending on the collar style chosen and the border size. You can also change the number of stitches to accommodate the stitch pattern to ensure the motif you are using is complete, and not ending half way through a repeat. The sizing is to approximately fit UK sizes 12 to 16, and

you will need roughly 600g of Knoll Soft Donegal yarn.

FRONTS
E wrap cast on 176 sts and work the required rows for the collar, depending on the stitch pattern chosen.

Collar Shaping
Cast off 20 sts RHS.
Work approx. 120 rows completing a stitch patt.

Shape Armhole
Cast off 70 sts, cast on 70 sts.

BACK
Work approx. 280 rows.

Shape Armhole
Cast off 70 sts, cast on 70 sts; work as for front and inc for collar to match. Cast off.

SLEEVES
E wrap braid cast on 70 sts using three ends of yarn. Work a bottom border of choice, RC 000 work the main chart

Turquoise Stripe Jacket.

patt at the same time inc to 130 sts RC approx. 115 rows, cast off.

This basic pattern can be adapted and made longer, shorter, larger or smaller by adding extra stitches or rows, or casting on fewer stitches and knitting fewer rows. The pattern below shows an example of this.

The stitch pattern used was an adaptation of Fairisle Stitch Pattern 25 offset and used as an all-over pattern. Border Stitch Pattern 20 was placed down the front edges and as a cuff for the sleeves.

Stitch Pattern 25 is a versatile Fairisle design, and when re-imagined as an

Materials
Finished weight 570g
Knoll Soft Donegal:

5564 Peacock, 5566 Fuchsia, 5568 Goldilocks, 5550 O'Byrne, 5503 Abbert, 5567 Cardinal, 5565 Deep Blue, 5528 Beltra, 5516 Dingle, 5532 Dariana, 5514 Glyde, 5535 Rea, 5522 Brosna, 5526 Liscannor, 5572 Vichy, 5538 Fitzgerald, 5531 Bantry

Measurements
One size to fit 12–16 (UK size)
Chest round 133cm
Back neck to bottom 60cm
Sleeve length 37.5cm

Tension
31 sts and 40 rows = 10cm
MT 8

Machines
Suitable for all standard gauge punchcard and electronic machines

Turquoise Stripe Fairisle Jacket.

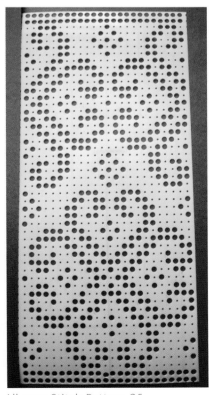

All-over Stitch Pattern 25.

overall design for a jacket it takes on a different character – and with the colour choice becomes a vibrant fabric. The colours used in Feeder 1 are dark maroon, and blues with highlights of peacock and turquoise, while the colours in Feeder 2 are reds, pinks, oranges and bright purple. The fronts consist of five of the motifs offset and twelve across the back, so when the armhole shaping is completed, make sure the stitch pattern is completed to avoid half patterns. Extra stocking stitch rows can be worked between the separate motifs if you require a larger size.

Method

The front collar edging is knitted using garter stitch. Either use a garter bar, or knit by hand and pick up the stitches on to the knitting machine.

Bring 190 sts to WP, cast on using Peacock and k 8 rows garter stitch.
K 4 rows st st Fuchsia and start to follow the colour sequence in Table 5.3 using Stitch Pattern 20.

K 4 rows Fuchsia.

COLLAR SHAPING

Cast off 20 sts RHS RC 000.

Start to knit the Stitch Pattern 25 chart using the colour sequence in Table 5.4.

K 115 rows and shape the armhole as instructed in the Basic Pattern.

K 276 rows across the back and rep the armhole shaping; k the front rows

to correspond, ending with a completed motif.
Shape the collar: cast on 20 sts and rep the front collar border pattern and

garter stitch edging. Cast off loosely.

SLEEVES
Bring 70 sts to WP E wrap braid cast on.

Variation using red, gold and green colours.

Table 5.3: Colour Sequence for Stitch Pattern 20

Rows	Stitch Pattern	Pattern Setting	Feeder 1	Feeder 2
3	20	Fairisle	Fuchsia	Goldilocks
3	20	Fairisle	Abbert	O'Byrne
1	20	Fairisle	Cardinal	Peacock
3	20	Fairisle	Abbert	O'Byrne
3	20	Fairisle	Fuchsia	Goldilocks

Table 5.4: Colour Sequence for Stitch Pattern 25

Rows	Stitch Pattern	Pattern Setting	Feeder 1	Feeder 2
4	25	Fairisle	*Deep Blue	**Fuchsia
4	25	Fairisle	Deep Blue	Forbes
4	25	Fairisle	Peacock	Forbes
4	25	Fairisle	Peacock	Cardinal
4	25	Fairisle	Vichy	Cardinal
4	25	Fairisle	Vichy	Clare
4	25	Fairisle	Beltra	Clare
4	25	Fairisle	Beltra	Brosna
4	25	Fairisle	Deep blue	Brosna
4	25	Fairisle	Deep Blue	Rea
4	25	Fairisle	Glyde	Rea
4	25	Fairisle	Glyde	Liscannor
4	25	Fairisle	Fitzgerald	Liscannor
4	25	Fairisle	Fitzgerald	Fuchsia
4	25	Fairisle	Dariana	Rep **
4	25	Fairisle	Dariana	
4	25	Fairisle	Bantry	
4	25	Fairisle	Bantry	
4	25	Fairisle	Rep *	

Using three ends of any colour, wrap clockwise and return anticlockwise, to make a braid cast on. RC 000 k 4 rows Fuchsia, rep the stitch patt for the front border. K 4 rows Fuchsia and cont as instructed for the front. At the same time inc evenly to 130 sts RC 115 ending with a completed motif. K 2 rows, last row MT+2 and latch off.

MAKING UP

Join the shoulder seams. Join the centre back seam of the collar, and sew the collar along the back neck. Set in the sleeves and sew down the side seams.

The following jacket is a variation of the Turquoise Stripe. The collar is knitted using a double fabric hem, and a section of the motif is adapted and worked. The colourway uses golds and reds with flashes of yellow and green. The whole garment is then placed in the washing machine at 40°C for 60 minutes to felt lightly, making the fabric feel denser and the pattern more compacted. The overall look is less distinct and more intricate. Jamiesons of Shetland Spindrift was used, as Shetland wool felts more firmly than Soft Donegal wool, and a texture and fluffiness was added to the overall fabric. The joy of this yarn is that there are very few flat colours. The Shetland range of wools blends several shades of a similar colour together, all spun into a single thread. This adds to the depth and intricacy of the overall effect.
   The same pattern as the previous Turquoise Stripe was used.

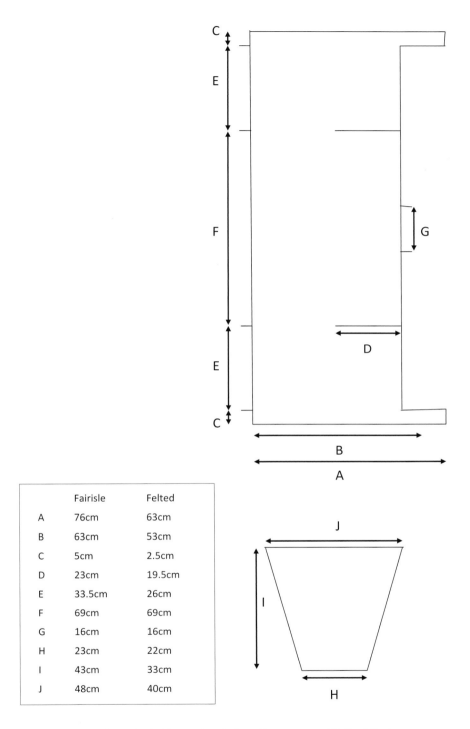

	Fairisle	Felted
A	76cm	63cm
B	63cm	53cm
C	5cm	2.5cm
D	23cm	19.5cm
E	33.5cm	26cm
F	69cm	69cm
G	16cm	16cm
H	23cm	22cm
I	43cm	33cm
J	48cm	40cm

Diagram for Fairisle Turquoise Stripe, Sanquar and Felted Red and Gold Jacket.

RED AND GOLD JACKET

Method

The border stitch pattern was adapted from the main motif.

FRONTS AND BACK

Follow the instructions for the previous jacket but cast on using WY and work the border pattern shown in Table 5.5.

Pick up sts between WY and continue knitting using Stitch Pattern 25 in the colour sequence given in Table 5.6. Follow the instructions for the previous jacket until the final collar piece is reached and reverse the stitch chart border pattern and colour sequence. Cast off loosely. Fold back the collar facing and slip stitch in place.

Red and gold version.

Materials
Jamiesons of Shetland Spindrift using small amounts of 727 Navy, 259 Leprechaun, 231 Bracken, 998 Autumn, 226 Thyme, 261 Paprika, 294 Blueberry, 633 Jupiter, 293 Portwine, 235 Grouse, 237 Thistledown, 1290 Loganberry, 587 Madder, 423 Burnt Ochre, 249 Fern, 1260 Raspberry, 390 Daffodil, 750 Petrol, 242 Ruby, 470 Pumpkin, 198 Peat, 187 Sunrise

Finished weight 550g

Measurements
Around chest 128cm
Length from back neck to hem 56cm
Sleeve length 34.5cm

Tension
After felting: 31 sts and 41 rows = 10cm
MT 8

Machines
Suitable for all standard gauge punchcard and electronic machines.

SLEEVES
Bring 70 sts to WP E wrap braid cast on using three strands of colour, wind clockwise and then anticlockwise.

K 2 rows Madder and k border patt, K 2 rows RC 000, start to work Stitch Pattern 25 until RC 115, ending with a completed motif. Inc evenly to 130 sts. K 4 rows, last row MT+2, latch off.

Table 5.5: Border Pattern Colour Sequence for Red and Gold

Rows	Stitch Pattern	Pattern Setting	Feeder 1	Feeder 2
15		Knit	Madder	
4	Border	Fairisle	Madder	Burnt Ochre
4	Border	Fairisle	Raspberry	Daffodil
5	Border	Fairisle	Loganberry	Pumpkin
2		Knit	Madder	

Fairisle red and gold jacket showing stitch-pattern adaptation to make the border pattern.

SANQUHAR JACKET

The final jacket in this section uses the Sanquhar Fairisle stitch pattern as an all-over colourful interpretation, mainly using various shades of blue with highlights of emerald green and cerise. There is a real sense of movement, with colours swinging back and forth, and the pattern disappearing only to reappear a few rows later.

The diamond shape in the border Stitch Pattern 19 is reflected in the overall Sanquhar pattern, and they mirror each other throughout the design. You could decide to change the all-over pattern and border and

Table 5.6: Fronts, Back and Sleeves Colour Sequence for Stitch Pattern 25

Rows	Stitch Pattern	Pattern Setting	Feeder 1	Feeder 2
4	25	Fairisle	*Blueberry	**Thyme
4	25	Fairisle	Grouse	Thyme
4	25	Fairisle	Grouse	Leprechaun
4	25	Fairisle	Fern	Leprechaun
4	25	Fairisle	Fern	Daffodil
4	25	Fairisle	Peat	Daffodil
4	25	Fairisle	Peat	Bracken
4	25	Fairisle	Portwine	Bracken
4	25	Fairisle	Portwine	Thistledown
4	25	Fairisle	Navy	Thistledown
4	25	Fairisle	Navy	Jupiter
4	25	Fairisle	Sunrise	Jupiter
4	25	Fairisle	Sunrise	Autumn
4	25	Fairisle	Madder	Autumn
4	25	Fairisle	Madder	Petrol
4	25	Fairisle	Ruby	Petrol
4	25	Fairisle	Ruby	Paprika
4	25	Fairisle	Raspberry	Paprika
4	25	Fairisle	Raspberry	Pumpkin
4	25	Fairisle	Loganberry	Pumpkin
4	25	Fairisle	Loganberry	Rep from **
4	25	Fairisle	Blueberry	
			Rep from*	

Sanqhuar Jacket.

Materials
Knoll Soft Donegal 5572 (Turquoise) Vichy, 5514 (Navy) Glyde, 5504 (Light Blue) Annalee, 5565 (Bright Blue) Deep Blue, 5539 (Dark Navy) Sheridan, 5519 (Aqua) Moy, 5532 (Purple) Dariana, 5582 (Mid Purple) Purple Heart, 5527 (Royal Blue) Roe, 5566 (Cerise) Fuchsia, 5535 (Pink) Rea, 5507 (Cream) Swilly, 5506 (Mid Green) Neagh, 5586 (Jade) Jade, 5550 (Lime) O'Byrne, 5536 (Grass) Killala, 5528 (Blue-Green) Beltra, 5564 (Peacock) Peacock

Finished weight 550g

experiment with scale and colour, by making the main motif larger by using the large snow flake Stitch Pattern 26, or by making it smaller using the star Stitch Pattern 15. All experimentation is exciting, and new ways of knitting and thinking will emerge – but be aware that the larger the motif, the more problematic it is to fit in complete motifs when shaping and completing a front, back or sleeve.

Follow the previous pattern depending on the size required. Alter the number of rows to complete the diamond motif within the all-over Sanquhar pattern when shaping the armhole and at the top of the sleeve.

Method
Start the all-over pattern given in Table 5.8.

SLEEVES
Bring 70sts to WP E wrap braid, cast on using three ends of yarn in Fuchsia, Jade and O'Byrne, wind clockwise round the needles and back anticlockwise.

K 2 rows Vichy and start the border patt, omitting the 17 k rows from the chart.

Complete the border and k 2 rows Vichy RC 000; k the Sanquhar stitch patt RC 120.

At the same time inc evenly to 130 sts.

Cast off having completed a patt.

MAKING UP
Make up as the previous jacket.

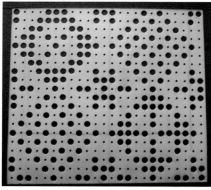

Sanqhuar pattern all-over stitch pattern.

Table 5.7: Border Sequence for Sanquhar Jacket

Rows	Stitch Pattern	Pattern Setting	Feeder 1	Feeder 2
17		Knit	Vichy	
2	19	Fairisle	Vichy	Glyde
3	19	Fairisle	Annalee	Deep Blue
3	19	Fairisle	Swilly	Rea
3	19	Fairisle	Annalee	Deep Blue
2	19	Fairisle	Vichy	Glyde
2		Knit	Vichy	

Table 5.8: The All-Over Pattern Colour Sequence

Rows	Pattern Setting	Feeder 1	Feeder 2
4	Fairisle	*Deep Blue	**Moy
4	Fairisle	Deep blue	Vichy
4	Fairisle	Sheridan	Vichy
4	Fairisle	Sheridan	Peacock
4	Fairisle	Roe	Peacock
4	Fairisle	Roe	Beltra
4	Fairisle	Dariana	Beltra
4	Fairisle	Dariana	Killala
4	Fairisle	Purple Heart	Killala
4	Fairisle	Purple Heart	O'Byrne
4	Fairisle	Fuchsia	O'Byrne
4	Fairisle	Fuchsia	Jade
4	Fairisle	Rep*	Jade
4	Fairisle		Neagh
4	Fairisle		Neagh
			Moy
			Rep**

STRIPES AND FAIRISLE

Fairisle stitch patterns are ideal for making a sideways knitted vertical patterned jacket, and if based on the classic T shape then no shaping takes place to disrupt any of the peerie or border stitch patterns. A variety of the Fairisle patterns can be used, and here is an opportunity for you to make up your own design. Work out which patterns will fit into the number of rows, alternate large and small patterns, and add flashes of bright colour to add rhythm. For the best effect you will need to work three to four stocking stitch rows between each Fairisle band.

Border patterns can be made into larger statement bands by joining two or three borders together. For example, work Stitch Pattern 10, place Stitch Pattern 19 in the middle, and repeat Stitch Pattern 10 using different colours, and immediately the overall effect is of a larger pattern with an altogether bigger visual impact.

Use the basic instructions for the jacket.

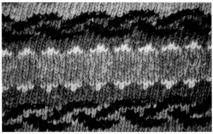
Example of combining two stitch patterns.

Materials
Small amounts of various colours Knoll Soft Donegal and Jamiesons of Shetland Spindrift

Finished weight 580g

Change the colours and use fewer if you don't have many colours in your workroom. I have used the following colours in this design: Bright Blue, Silver, Pale Pink, Pink, Bright Pink, Peacock, Turquoise, Silver, Charcoal, Cream, Dark Pink, Cerise, Purple, Pale Blue, Black, Dark Navy, Green Blue, Mid Blue, Navy, Royal Blue, Aqua, Grey, Mid Purple, Purple

Measurements
Length from shoulder 56cm
Across chest 66cm
Length of sleeve 37cm

Tension
31 sts and 38 rows = 10cm
MT 7••

Machines
Suitable for standard gauge punchcard and electronic machines

Peerie patterns are often used to change the background colour in Feeder 1. When working any peerie stitch pattern change the colour in Feeder 1 in the centre row of a stitch pattern so avoiding a hard line

Fairisle Striped Jacket back view.

Table 5.9: Stitch Pattern and Colour Sequence for Fairisle Striped Jacket

Rows	Stitch Pattern	Pattern Setting	Feeder 1	Feeder 2		Rows	Stitch Pattern	Pattern Setting	Feeder 1	Feeder 2
3		knit	Bright Blue			3	23	Fairisle	Turquoise	Bright blue
2	7	Fairisle	Bright Blue	Silver		3	23	Fairisle	Peacock	Navy
3	7	Fairisle	Pale Pink	Charcoal		4		Knit	Peacock	
2	7	Fairisle	Bright Blue	Silver		1	2	Fairisle	Peacock	Cream
3		Knit	Bright Blue			1	2	Fairisle	Bright Blue	Cream
2	14	Fairisle	Bright Blue	Cream		1	2	Fairisle	Royal Blue	Cream
2	14	Fairisle	Peacock	Light Blue		3		Knit	Royal Blue	
1	14	Fairisle	Purple	Cerise		3	15	Fairisle	Royal Blue	Silver
2	14	Fairisle	Peacock	Light Blue		2	15	Fairisle	Peacock	Cream
2	14	Fairisle	Charcoal	Cream		1	15	Fairisle	Turquoise	Pink
3		Knit	Charcoal			2	15	Fairisle	Peacock	Cream
3	13	Fairisle	Charcoal	Pink		3	15	Fairisle	Mid Blue	Silver
3	13	Fairisle	Cream	Bright Pink		2		Knit	Mid Blue	
3	13	Fairisle	Turquoise	Pink		2	6	Fairisle	Mid Blue	Peacock
3		Knit	Turquoise			2	6	Fairisle	Mid Purple	Turquoise
2	19	Fairisle	Turquoise	Cerise		2	6	Fairisle	Bright Blue	Peacock
3	19	Fairisle	Pale Blue	Purple		3		Knit	Bright Blue	
3	19	Fairisle	Cream	Dark Pink		4	24	Fairisle	Bright Blue	Pale Blue
3	19	Fairisle	Pale Blue	Purple		3	24	Fairisle	Purple	Turquoise
2	19	Fairisle	Turquoise	Cerise		1	24	Fairisle	Cerise	Cream
3		Knit	Turquoise			3	24	Fairisle	Purple	Turquoise
3	17	Fairisle	Turquoise	Dark Navy		4	24	Fairisle	Bright Blue	Pale Blue
2	17	Fairisle	Peacock	Black		3		Knit	Bright Blue	
1	17	Fairisle	Cream	Pink		2	5	Fairisle	Bright Blue	Cerise
2	17	Fairisle	Peacock	Black		2	5	Fairisle	Mid Blue	Bright Pink
3	17	Fairisle	Turquoise	Dark Navy		2	5	Fairisle	Pale Blue	Pink
3		Knit	Turquoise			3		Knit	Pale Blue	
1	2	Fairisle	Turquoise	Black		3	20	Fairisle	Pale Blue	Bright Blue
1	2	Fairisle	Peacock	Black		3	20	Fairisle	Cream	Navy
1	2	Fairisle	Bright Blue	Black		1	20	Fairisle	Purple	Pink
3		Knit	Bright Blue			3	20	Fairisle	Cream	Navy
3	25	Fairisle	Bright Blue	Silver		3	20	Fairisle	Pale Blue	Bright Blue
3	25	Fairisle	Green/Blue	Pale Blue		3		Knit	Pale Blue	
3	25	Fairisle	Peacock	Pale Grey		2	10	Fairisle	Pale Blue	Black
5	25	Fairisle	Turquoise	Cream		4	10	Fairisle	Mid Blue	Black
3	25	Fairisle	Peacock	Pale Grey		2	10	Fairisle	Purple	Black
3	25	Fairisle	Green/Blue	Pale Blue		2		Knit	Purple	
3	25	Fairisle	Bright Blue	Silver		2	19	Fairisle	Purple	Cream
3		Knit	Bright Blue			3	19	Fairisle	Peacock	Pink
1	1	Fairisle	Bright Blue	Grey		3	19	Fairisle	Turquoise	Cerise
1	1	Fairisle	Charcoal	Grey		3	19	Fairisle	Peacock	Pink
1	1	Fairisle	Peacock	Grey		2	19	Fairisle	Purple	Cream
4		Knit	Peacock			2		Knit	Purple	
3	23	Fairisle	Peacock	Navy		2	10	Fairisle	Purple	Black
3	23	Fairisle	Turquoise	Bright Blue		4	10	Fairisle	Turquoise	Black
1	23	Fairisle	Silver	Pink		2	10	Fairisle	Peacock	Black

Table 5.9: *Continued*

Rows	Stitch Pattern	Pattern Setting	Feeder 1	Feeder 2
3		Knit	Peacock	
2	20	Fairisle	Peacock	Silver
2	20	Fairisle	Turquoise	Aqua
2	20	Fairisle	Pale Blue	Pink
1	20	Fairisle	Bright Blue	Bright Pink
2	20	Fairisle	Pale Blue	Pink
2	20	Fairisle	Turquoise	Aqua
2	20	Fairisle	Peacock	Silver
3		Knit	Peacock	
4	26	Fairisle	Peacock	Black
4	26	Fairisle	Turquoise	Charcoal
4	26	Fairisle	Mid Blue	Grey
1	26	Fairisle	Purple	Cream
4	26	Fairisle	Mid Blue	Grey
4	26	Fairisle	Turquoise	Charcoal
4	26	Fairisle	Peacock	Black
3		Knit	Peacock	
2		Knit	Pale Pink	
3	8	Fairisle	Pale Pink	Peacock
1	8	Fairisle	Bright Pink	Turquoise
3	8	Fairisle	Pale Pink	Peacock
2		Knit	Pale Pink	
3		Knit	Mid Blue	
3	22	Fairisle	Mid Blue	Cream
3	22	Fairisle	Royal Blue	Grey
1	22	Fairisle	Purple	Pink
3	22	Fairisle	Royal Blue	Grey
3	22	Fairisle	Mid Blue	Cream
3		Knit	Mid Blue	
2	3	Fairisle	Mid Blue	Grey
2	3	Fairisle	Bright Blue	Pink
3		Knit	Bright Blue	
7	9	Fairisle	Bright Blue	Aqua
3		Knit	Bright Blue	
2	3	Fairisle	Bright Blue	Pale Pink
2	3	Fairisle	Pale Blue	Bright Pink
3		Knit	Pale Blue	
3	21	Fairisle	Pale Blue	Black
3	21	Fairisle	Light Blue	Charcoal
1	21	Fairisle	Cream	Bright Blue
3	21	Fairisle	Light Blue	Charcoal
3	21	Fairisle	Pale Blue	Black
3		Knit	Pale Blue	
2	3	Fairisle	Pale Blue	Mid Purple
2	3	Fairisle	Peacock	Purple
3		Knit	Peacock	
3	17	Fairisle	Peacock	Cream
2	17	Fairisle	Bright Blue	Turquoise
1	17	Fairisle	Black	Pink
2	17	Fairisle	Bright Blue	Turquoise
3	17	Fairisle	Peacock	Cream
3		Knit	Peacock	
1	2	Fairisle	Peacock	Cream
1	2	Fairisle	Black	Cream
1	2	Fairisle	Charcoal	Cream
3		Knit	Charcoal	
3	25	Fairisle	Charcoal	Turquoise
3	25	Fairisle	Pale Blue	Bright Blue
3	25	Fairisle	Silver	Royal Blue
5	25	Fairisle	Cream	Navy
3	25	Fairisle	Silver	Royal Blue
3	25	Fairisle	Pale Blue	Bright Blue
3	25	Fairisle	Charcoal	Turquoise
3		Knit	Charcoal	
1	2	Fairisle	Charcoal	Cream
1	2	Fairisle	Black	Cream
1	2	Fairisle	Bright Blue	Cream
4		Knit	Bright Blue	
2	19	Fairisle	Bright Blue	Bright Pink
3	19	Fairisle	Peacock	Pink
3	19	Fairisle	Turquoise	Pale Pink
3	19	Fairisle	Peacock	Pink
2	19	Fairisle	Bright Blue	Bright Pink
4		Knit	Bright Blue	
2	15	Fairisle	Bright Blue	Turquoise
3	15	Fairisle	Cerise	Peacock
1	15	Fairisle	Black	Cream
3	15	Fairisle	Cerise	Peacock
2	15	Fairisle	Purple	Turquoise
3		Knit	Purple	
2	14	Fairisle	Purple	Cream
2	14	Fairisle	Mid Blue	Light Blue
1	14	Fairisle	Navy	Pale Pink
2	14	Fairisle	Mid Blue	Light Blue
2	14	Fairisle	Royal Blue	Cream
3		Knit	Royal Blue	
3	17	Fairisle	Royal Blue	Pale Pink
2	17	Fairisle	Peacock	Pink
1	17	Fairisle	Purple	Cream
2	17	Fairisle	Peacock	Pink
3	17	Fairisle	Royal Blue	Pale Pink
2		Knit	Royal Blue	

Table 5.9: *Continued*

Rows	Stitch Pattern	Pattern Setting	Feeder 1	Feeder 2
2		Knit	Navy	
3	1	Fairisle	Navy	Pale Blue
2		Knit	Navy	
3		Knit	Charcoal	
3	21	Fairisle	Charcoal	Peacock
3	21	Fairisle	Black	Turquoise
1	21	Fairisle	Purple	Cream
3	21	Fairisle	Black	Turquoise
3	21	Fairisle	Charcoal	Peacock
4		Knit	Charcoal	
2	5	Fairisle	Charcoal	Pale Pink
2	5	Fairisle	Royal Blue	Pink
2	5	Fairisle	Peacock	Bright Pink
4		Knit	Peacock	
3	22	Fairisle	Peacock	Cream
3	22	Fairisle	Bright Blue	Pale Blue
1	22	Fairisle	Navy	Pink
3	22	Fairisle	Bright Blue	Pale Blue
3	22	Fairisle	Peacock	Cream
2		Knit	Peacock	
2		Knit	Turquoise	
3	8	Fairisle	Turquoise	Cream
1	8	Fairisle	Peacock	Charcoal
3	8	Fairisle	Turquoise	Cream
2		Knit	Bright Blue	

Table 5.10: Sleeve Border Stitch Pattern and Colour Sequence

Rows	Stitch Pattern	Pattern Setting	Feeder 1	Feeder 2
2		Knit	Royal Blue	
3	18	Fairisle	Royal Blue	Cream
3	18	Fairisle	Mid Blue	Turquoise
3	18	Fairisle	Pale Blue	Blue/Green
3	18	Fairisle	Light Blue	Peacock
2		Knit	Light Blue	

Table 5.11: Front Edging and Collar Stitch Pattern and Colour Sequence

Rows	Stitch Pattern	Pattern Setting	Feeder 1	Feeder 2
2	2	Fairisle	Bright Blue	Cream
1	2	Fairisle	Turquoise	Cream
1	2	Fairisle	Peacock	Cream
2		Knit	Peacock	
2	20	Fairisle	Peacock	Cream
2	20	Fairisle	Turquoise	Pale Blue
2	20	Fairisle	Mid Blue	Pink
1	20	Fairisle	Bright Blue	Bright Pink
2	20	Fairisle	Mid Blue	Pink
2	20	Fairisle	Turquoise	Pale Blue
2	20	Fairisle	Peacock	Cream
2		Knit	Peacock	
1	2	Fairisle	Peacock	Cream
1	2	Fairisle	Turquoise	Cream
1	2	Fairisle	Bright Blue	Cream
2		Knit	Bright Blue	

Method

The collar is knitted separately and picked up on to the left and right front edge and back neck. This means that you need to start working from the Front instruction by bringing 176 sts to WP cast on using WY and knit a few rows. Change to the main colour and work through the stitch patterns as set, casting off and on for the armholes instructed in the basic pattern.

SLEEVES

Follow the instructions for the basic pattern using Stitch Pattern 18 for the bottom border.

Repeat pattern stitch chart numbers 20, 2, 19, 5, 21, 5, 17, 16, 22, 10, 16, 10, changing the colours if you wish. Cast off.

Join the shoulder seams.

FRONT EDGING AND COLLAR

Bring forward 196 sts to WP and cast on WY, k a few rows, change to Bright Blue k 1 row.

Work through the stitch pattern and colour sequence chart shown in Table 5.11.

K 26 rows Bright Blue.

Pick up sts from WY and k 1 row. Pick up 20 sts from centre of back neck and down front edge, k I row MT, k 1 row MT+2 and latch off.

Rep for second front edge and neck. Join collar at back of neck. Insert sleeves and sew down seam.

Sew in ends.

MOCK FAIRISLE

A mock Fairisle pattern can be worked by using a single colour yarn and a variegated sock yarn for the stitch pattern. This certainly saves a great deal of colour changing. However, you are constrained by the colours of the variegated yarn which are random, and so you have less control on the outcome.

If the colour in Feeder 1 is close to some of the shades within the yarn, the stitch pattern is less distinct and will appear and then disappear, making for a softer, more ethereal design. If the colour in Feeder 1 is a strong contrast, then the stitch pattern becomes clearer and brighter.

Any of the overall Fairisle patterns works well when making this collar design, so experiment by using several shades of variegated yarn in a jacket.

Method

Bring 120 sts to WP, cast on using WY, change to MC, k 1 row. Start to Fairisle patt. Depending on your chosen stitch patt work approx 220 rows. Complete a motif so the join is matched. Remove from machine WY.

Materials
50g variegated yarn
50g single colour yarn

Measurements
Circumference 66cm
Depth 16.5cm when folded over

Tension
37 sts – 36 rows = 10cm
Approx MT 8

Machines
Suitable for standard gauge punchcard and electronic machines

Fairisle jacket.

RS together. Pick up sts from WY and corresponding sts k 1 row MT +1 and cast off. Mattress stitch along the long edge to complete.

Mock Fairisle collars.

CHAPTER 6

PAINTING WITH YARN

The process of painting with yarn takes the path of firstly looking at and experiencing a scene or object with excitement and pleasure. Secondly, of distilling and focusing on aspects of the emotions triggered by the experiences, and allowing the imagination to evolve and create an original design. And finally, to create a piece of work that conveys and communicates a glimpse of what you experienced, and hopefully communicates your feelings and memories to a wider audience. It is, broadly speaking, an attempt to create an original design from your point of view.

Live and design through your eyes – look at the world around you and enjoy the sights and sounds and smells of the city, the countryside and the sea. Discover and dissect what it is that excites you, and try to convey this through your work as a design concept. It can help to sketch, draw, paint, sculpt, or even listen to music, as this can help focus your creativity and design sensibilities as you continue to absorb your surroundings. The more you attempt this, the easier it will become. You then need to translate the design concept into the colours of the yarn that you have on the shelf – and if you don't have a particular shade available then you can mix some ends of yarn to blend the elusive hue. Always have courage. You know you have the technical skill to knit a garment, so

Gold and Chrome Coat.

design and colour choice is merely the vehicle with which to express this.

Designing is an expression of excitement, and conveying this emotion to another person is a perfect outcome. To help this process and analyse what aspects of a scene trigger the excitement, simplify the scene, study shapes, and register different outlines and their relationship to other shapes. For example, in a seascape study a solid dark mass of rocks against the ethereal quality of surf and wispy blown sand, juxtaposed with the pearly

sea and sky. Notice and absorb the textures, identify the differences, look at the rhythms they create, and the constant colour changes that occur with restless movement. The original scene has now changed as you focus on one aspect and then another. The variety of textures, colours and shapes are what excites. Express this excitement with yarn and stitch choice to convey and capture the spirit and wonder of your personal reaction to something seen and experienced.

Focus again on a small section, for

example a wave. Isolate and simplify the main catalysts and extend and experiment with new fluid shapes, textures and colour combinations. Consider how to express the movement of waves or a flight of birds through a knitted fabric. An interplay of curved lines through a stitch pattern and a variety of colour sensations can express whatever feelings were felt. Consider looking at abstract expressionist artists such as Mark Rothko, Jackson Pollock or Helen Frankenthaler, and study how they mix colours and shape.

Consider the work of certain impressionist artists such as Georges Seurat and Paul Signac, who approached colour from a Pointillist point of view and dissected each colour and shade by painting with a small brush full of a pigment on to a canvas, relying on the ability of the eye and mind of the viewer to blend the small points of single colours into a full range of tones. Our eyes view this mix of dots by filling in the gaps and creating a bright and vivid scene, while the point itself retains its pure colour. Trying to re-create this effect and character in my knitting has kept me busy for many years.

Experimenting and playing with a motif, garment shape and colour has led me in many different directions, all mesmerizing and enjoyable, and providing yet another catalyst for a new shape and stitch pattern. This process also teaches you to be selective and to focus on one idea at a time. You can start with the nub of an idea, which is then worked through and experimented with, mixing stitches, shapes and colours to create a vision of the finished piece of work. A spark of an idea can create a huge and intricate body of work, which can be revisited years later with further developments branching out into other directions.

Malvern and the cabinet plate as inspiration.

This is the absolute joy and excitement of designing.

Acknowledge the texture, thickness and colour in a yarn, and allow the painterly aspect of the thread to show through and express its character within a garment. This is paramount when designing a stitch pattern.

Some colour conventions are worth being familiar with. Many base wardrobe colours are navy, grey or brown. These do change with fashion, but they are nevertheless standard variations of the base colour. Be bold, you don't have to stick to these – be more adventurous, and experiment and develop variations on your own colour theme.

There are three basic processes in designing knitwear: first, to have an idea for a particular market and price point; from this, to create a piece of knitted fabric and a garment so the idea is made tangible; and third, to market and sell it.

The reaction of the market will very likely initiate a response either to make

more in a similar way, or to shelve the idea and revisit it at a later stage – maybe reinventing aspects of it. If the market is favourable and production takes off, be aware that this can also be a difficult time, for the following reasons:

* If you are so busy fulfilling orders then there may be no time to develop new ideas and you can easily lose your way.
* If you are not developing new ideas then you are regressing.
* It is vital to be constantly moving forwards and discovering new projects to work on that will keep your work fresh and vibrant.

If the last successful design was floral there is a great temptation to keep recreating florals, but this is only possible for a few years before they become hackneyed and are churned out by low-cost copycat producers using inferior yarns and cheap labour. There is no pleasure in standing still in terms of your designs and being overcome by events, because in that way lies financial disaster. Public taste and fashion change, but there is always a new and just as exciting original idea to create around the corner – it just needs you to focus and to seek out and absorb new design catalysts. There is a real balance to master here, but being realistic and aware of the problem keeps you and your work progressing and thriving. Over the years I have found inspiration from many unexpected sources. For many decades Worcester, my home town, was a centre for the porcelain industry, and this became an inspiration for many of my designs.

There are many and varied stages that design ideas can take. For example, when researching in my local museum the shapes, patterns and colour combinations used by Royal Worcester porcelain since it was founded in 1751, my first reaction was to sit and look for hours and generally study all the patterns, shapes and colours. This was a mass of stimulation. I have inherited a few pieces of Royal Worcester porcelain, so I could look, feel and hold them in my hands – I sketched and studied them, took photographs, and researched books and articles detailing the history of the designs produced by the factory. I absorbed all these views and worked on

ideas for colour, pattern and shape – the contrast and strength of the colours set off by the gold gilding was incredibly ornate, and in some cases it was so thick round the edge of a plate or cup that it formed a crust. Slowly, after about six to nine months in gestation, I was building up an image in my mind, and the motifs chosen were transferred from the porcelain on to a sheet of paper and then on to a punchcard.

The porcelain designs used by Royal Worcester had to be simplified to be suitable for use in a knitted fabric – some trials were too busy and the quality was lost in a chaos of colour and stitch, which became confused and lost the initial clarity and freshness. The way I overcame this confusion was to rely partly on the memory of the excitement and interest that I experienced when I first saw the designs, and to create the essence of several pots in one design. The skill of the Royal Worcester designers became obvious the more I looked at and studied their work, especially in the brave colours they used and their attention to detail.

It is interesting to note that it was the oldest blue and white porcelain designs that caught my attention when I was designing the Mulberry Blossom Sweater. The small motifs from the blue and white porcelain cups and saucers were very similar to Japanese print designs reproduced in the Victoria and Albert Museum. The spatial relationships of the motifs and the textures created by cross hatching, and the freshness and lightness, created a clean and vibrant vase or dish that transposed very well to the knitted fabric. On a practical note, this design was very easy to wear for all ages, and it suited many styles.

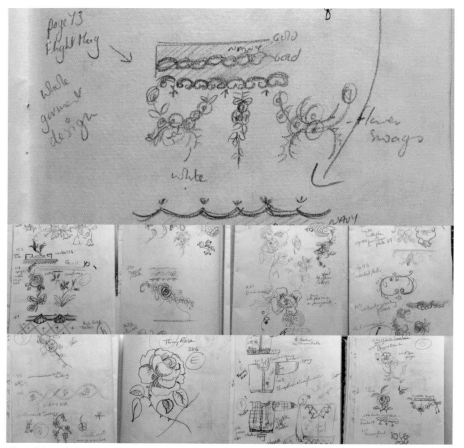

Sketchbook from Worcester Porcelain Museum visits and working drawings for a knitwear collection.

Designs to Knit

MALVERN CARDIGAN

The Fairisle stitch pattern harks back to the 1950s, and reminds me of a cardigan knitted for me as a child with sprigs of brightly coloured flowers. The colours in the Malvern version closely follow the design inspiration; however, replacing the lime with grey or navy blue would work just as well and give a very different character to the cardigan.

Method

BACK

Push 146 Ns to WP and k a few rows WY. Work the pattern and colour sequence as set out. Note that the 6 rows XX00XX00 at the beginning are

Materials
Finished weight 580g
MC Lime, Cream and Gold
Small amounts of Grass Green, Bright Green, Bright Pink, Dull Pink, Maroon, Red, Turquoise, Bright Blue, Terracotta, Lilac, Pale Blue, Mid Blue

Measurements
One size
Around chest 104cm
Length from shoulder 78cm
Length of sleeve 49cm

Tension
30 sts – 40 rows = 10cm
MT 8

Machines
Suitable for all standard gauge punchcard and electronic machines

Pattern Notes
Left top to bottom: Scallop, Leaf, Twigging, Scroll

Right top to bottom: Right Roses 1, turn the card over for Roses 2, Twigging

Malvern Cardigan.

picked up to make a rolled textured edging and this device was used to emulate the gilding around the edge of the Worcester Porcelain plate. Cont to work the hem and pick up the sts between the WY to make the hem. Remove the WY. RC 000.

Work through the pattern sequence to RC 130.

If you require a longer cardigan add extra rows; however, the overall design will be neater if the shoulder ends after a pattern and while working plain rows, so you may need to recalculate the row numbers of the basic pattern.

Back view of Malvern Cardigan.

Table 6.1: Stitch Pattern and Colour Sequence for Malvern

Rows	Stitch Pattern	Pattern Setting	Feeder 1	Feeder 2
10		Knit	Lime	
6	XXOOXXOO	Fairisle	Gold	Ecru
4		Knit	Lime	
5	Twigging	Fairisle	Lime	Gold
2		Knit	Lime	
2	Scallop	Fairisle	Lime	Gold
2	Scallop	Fairisle	Cream	Gold
6		Knit	Cream	
2	Rose 1	Fairisle	Cream	Mid Blue
2	Rose 1	Fairisle	Cream	Pale Blue
1	Rose 1	Fairisle	Cream	Mid Blue
4	Rose 1	Fairisle	Cream	Terracotta
2	Rose 1	Fairisle	Cream	Maroon
3	Rose 1	Fairisle	Cream	Dull Pink
3	Rose 1	Fairisle	Cream	Lilac
4	Rose 1	Fairisle	Cream	Bright Green
4		Knit	Cream	
3	Scroll	Fairisle	Cream	Gold
4	Scroll	Fairisle	Lime	Gold
4		Knit	Lime	
5	Twigging	Fairisle	Lime	Gold
4		Knit	Lime	
2		Knit	Gold	
3	Leaf	Fairisle	Cream	Gold
6		Knit	Cream	
2	Rose 2	Fairisle	Cream	Pale Blue
2	Rose 2	Fairisle	Cream	Mid Blue
1	Rose 2	Fairisle	Cream	Pale Blue
4	Rose 2	Fairisle	Cream	Red
2	Rose 2	Fairisle	Cream	Maroon
3	Rose 2	Fairisle	Cream	Dull Pink
3	Rose 2	Fairisle	Cream	Bright Pink
4	Rose 2	Fairisle	Cream	Grass Green
4		Knit	Cream	
Rep Scroll				

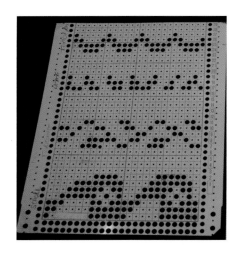

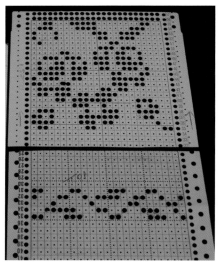

Stitch pattern chart for Malvern Cardigan.

Cont as patt sequence, referring to the images of the *Malvern* Cardigan.

Shape Armholes
Cast off 10 sts at the beg of the next 2 rows. Cont RC 230. Mark either side of centre 50 sts and remove from machine on to WY.

RIGHT FRONT
Work as for half of back to RC 200. Cast off 5 sts on neck edge, and 2 sts on the foll alt rows twice and cont to dec 1 st ff on every alt row until 25 sts have been dec in total.

Cont to RC 230, remove from the machine using WY.

LEFT FRONT
Work as for right front, reversing the shaping.

With right sides together join the shoulder seams from the fronts to the back.

SLEEVES

Push 65 Ns to WP. Using WY k a few rows and work the bottom hem as set out. RC 000.

Follow the patt sequence inc 1 st at each end of every 6th until 140 sts, cont to follow the stitch patt RC 168 approx.

End with the 6 row roll edging and cast off.

BUTTON BANDS

Left Band

Push 130 Ns to WP and work the bottom hem starting with the twigging sequence, work the roll edging, k 10 rows st st using Lime. Pick up the band and k 1 row. Pick up the front of the cardigan k 1 row and cast off.

Right Band

As for the left, but work 6 buttonholes evenly spaced. The top button is placed into the neckband.

NECKBAND

Approx 138 sts, work as for button bands placing a buttonhole for the top button. Pick up right and left front and back of neck. K 1 row and cast off loosely.

Sew sleeves into armholes, sew side and sleeve seams. Sew in ends. Sew on buttons. Wash and press lightly.

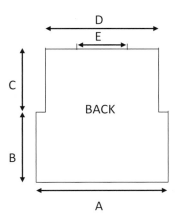

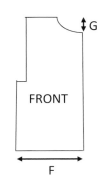

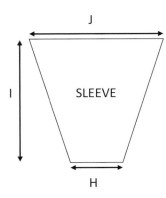

A	52cm	F	26cm
B	31cm	G	14cm
C	25.5cm	H	24cm
D	47cm	I	48.5cm
E	21.5cm	J	52cm

Diagram for Malvern Cardigan.

BLUE SCALE SWEATER

Another design adapted from the Worcester Porcelain Museum collection was based on the rich, exotic Blue Scale pattern, so called because the two shades of blue looked like fish scales when painted. The stitch pattern is reminiscent of the Spider/Louse Scandinavian Fairisle patterns. It is the contrast between the Blue Scale and Floral white deep border pattern that makes this an eye-catching design. The background of the Floral border changes from cream to white to add depth and texture. Further study found examples of the Scale pattern using shades of green, pink and orange, and exotic fantasy birds that produced a vibrant juxtaposition.

The Blue Scale stitch pattern can be used as a variation to the Malvern Cardigan shape, using stripes of the Floral pattern and stripes of the Blue Scale. Alternatively, the Floral design can be used as a deep bottom border to a sweater with the main part knitted

Blue Scale Sweater.

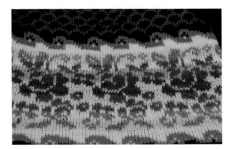

Detail showing Floral border.

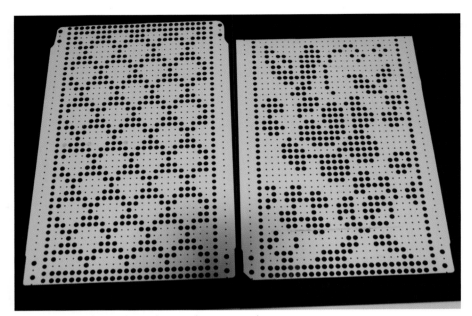

Blue Scale and Floral border stitch pattern chart.

Floral Border

Although there is a lot of colour changing with the background colours in Feeder 1 it is of course possible to knit using only one colour; however, using several shades and textures of yarn creates depth and interest, so the completed result is worth the effort.

The Blue Scale stitch pattern is worked in two shades of Blue, Navy and Denim.

A scarf was knitted using this design, and this can be found in the Accessories section of this book.

The basic instructions for this are E wrap cast on 100 sts and work the Floral patt, enclosed top and bottom with the Malvern Scrolls, work 400 rows approx. Using the Scale patt, rep the Scroll/ Floral/Scroll stitch patt and cast off.

When working a scarf, reverse the stitch patterns at the end of the scarf and reverse the colour chart sequence so it will appear the right way up when worn.

in Scale pattern, the sleeves having the Floral border at the bottom and top. From the image you will see that there is a small circular stitch pattern border: this was to emulate little porcelain pearls placed around the decorative edges of some the plates. The inspiration provided by this study gave me many ideas that I have yet to fully develop and create.

The Scroll pattern from the Malvern design has been added to the top and bottom to enclose the Floral border.

Table 6.2: Stitch Pattern and Colour Sequence for Floral Border

Rows	Stitch Pattern	Pattern Setting	Feeder 1	Feeder 2
4	Floral	Fairisle	Cream	Lime
4	Floral	Fairisle	White	Pink
2	Floral	Fairisle	White	Dark Pink
2	Floral	Fairisle	Off white	Dark Pink
4	Floral	Fairisle	Off White	Terracotta
2	Floral	Fairisle	Off White	Cerise
2	Floral	Fairisle	Cream	Red
2	Floral	Fairisle	Cream	Cerise
2	Floral	Fairisle	Ecru	Red
3	Floral	Fairisle	Ecru	Raspberry
2	Floral	Fairisle	Ecru	Mid Green
3	Floral	Fairisle	White	Mid Green
5	Floral	Fairisle	Cream	Lime

FANTASY BIRD

The inspiration for the Fantasy Bird design was a medallion in a Blue Scale Worcester Porcelain tea-set. It is a purely stylized bird and I tried to keep to the same colours. This panel is really using the idea of painting with yarn, trying to create a picture – embroidery stitches are added to highlight certain areas of the scene, which further makes a picture. The Scale colours chosen were brave and risky as I wanted to avoid sugar pink, so went for a dark pink and dull pink and the result was an echo of the colours used in the bird.

A scarf was worked using this as a border pattern, enclosed by the Scallop stitch pattern from the Malvern Cardigan, and inverted at the top. The instructions are the same as set out in the Blue Scale Floral pattern scarf.

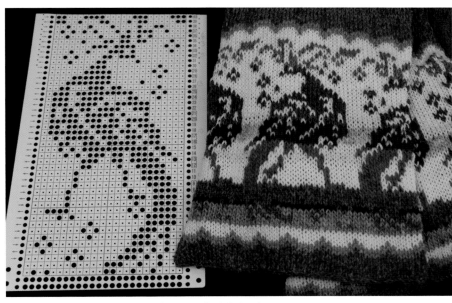

Fantasy Bird stitch pattern chart and Pink Scale.

Fantasy Bird design inspiration with Blue Scale.

Table 6.3: Stitch Pattern and Colour Sequence for Fantasy Bird

Rows	Stitch Pattern	Pattern Setting	Feeder 1	Feeder 2
4	Fantasy Bird	Fairisle	Lime Green	Redmix
1	Fantasy Bird	Fairisle	Juniper	Redmix
2	Fantasy Bird	Fairisle	Grass Green	Terracotta
2	Fantasy Bird	Fairisle	Ochre	Terracotta
2	Fantasy Bird	Fairisle	White	Terracotta
4	Fantasy Bird	Fairisle	White	Orange
2	Fantasy Bird	Fairisle	Cream	Orange
2	Fantasy Bird	Fairisle	White	Orange
1	Fantasy Bird	Fairisle	White	Rust
4	Fantasy Bird	Fairisle	Off white	Rust
2	Fantasy Bird	Fairisle	Cream	Denim
2	Fantasy Bird	Fairisle	White	Denim
5	Fantasy Bird	Fairisle	White	Mauve
5	Fantasy Bird	Fairisle	White	Cerise
3	Fantasy Bird	Fairisle	White	Dark Pink
4	Fantasy Bird	Fairisle	White	Lavender

RICH QUEENS CARDIGAN

Rich Queens is a further idea to use the Floral pattern from the Blue Scale design, which can be worked in a twenty-four-stitch repeat and knitted as a strip, alternating with a strip of Twigging using Navy and Gold chenille. For each Floral reverse the stitch pattern over. The strips are then sewn together. A large coat with minimal shaping can be made, or even furnishings such as cushions.

The Twigging pattern can also be knitted using different colours to emulate seaweed, and mixed in with other motifs, for example shells.

STRIP COAT

This Strip Coat is an interesting exercise in mixing patterns and colours together. It can be used to make a patchwork of squares, or in long strips sewn together using a contrast of colours, as seen here. The back consists of ten strips, twenty-two stitches wide, and approximately 240 rows depending on the required length.

The fronts have minimal shaping. On the relevant front strip, on row 140 decrease on the neck edge on every third alternate row until all the stitches have been decreased. The strip to the side of this will require shaping from

row 196. Decrease on the neck edge every third row three times. Continue to work to row 240, cast off.

The sleeves are made up of eight strips. For each single strip, E wrap cast on ten stitches and increase evenly to twenty stitches while working in your chosen stitch pattern to row 160. Cast off. Make seven more.

Sew all the strips together.

Make a simple double hem and pick up the main body or sleeves on to the machine, knit one row MT+1 and latch off.

This pattern can be adapted to make a larger coat by adding more stitches to the strips and shortening the sleeve row count.

The pattern can easily be adapted to use another stitch pattern and create an original garment with a completely different character, such as the Country Herringbone Cardigan shown below. The neck shaping starts lower as it is a V neck.

Rich Queens Pattern Worcester Porcelain.

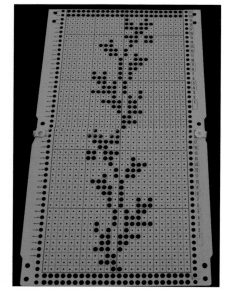

Twigging vertical stitch pattern.

Strip Jacket variation herringbone.

MULBERRY BLOSSOM SWEATER

The Mulberry Blossom design was inspired by a small book entitled Japanese Stencils published by Webb and Bower for the Victoria and Albert Museum in London. A tiny, seemingly simple motif floating on a background of bamboo and interspersed with cloud-like organic shapes was hugely appealing as the effect was almost ethereal and the unfocused edges gave a sense of movement to the stencilled fabric.

The elements of a knitted design were drawn out on a sheet of paper and transferred to a twenty-four-stitch punchcard. To keep to the spirit of the blue and white stencil image I honoured this colour palette – although I added other shades of blue and navy to sharpen up the branches of the mulberry blossom tree and add contrast.

The design kept the blossom indistinct by mixing shades of pale blue and using the yarn as if I were painting a picture. The stitch pattern was reversed for any repeat, which kept the design motif travelling up the garment to create a sense of movement. I also wanted to add some small borders to break up the overall intensity of the design, and I found, in the same Japanese stencil book, some small edging motifs that I adapted to work on a punchcard knitting machine.

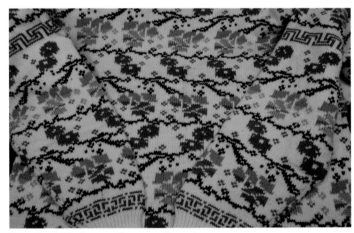

Detail of Mulberry Blossom Sweater.

Mulberry Blossom inspiration showing Blossom and small border stitch patterns.

Table 6.4: Stitch Pattern and Colour Sequence for Mulberry Blossom Sweater

Rows	Stitch Pattern	Pattern Setting	Feeder 1	Feeder 2
6	Mulberry Blossom 1	Fairisle	White	Navy
6	Mulberry Blossom 1	Fairisle	White	Cornflower
2	Mulberry Blossom 1	Fairisle	White	Grey
3	Mulberry Blossom 1	Fairisle	White	Cornflower
6	Mulberry Blossom 1	Fairisle	White	Pale Blue
13	Mulberry Blossom 1	Fairisle	White	Navy
8	Mulberry Blossom 1	Fairisle	White	Mid Blue
9	Mulberry Blossom 1	Fairisle	White	Cornflower
*6	Mulberry Blossom 2	Fairisle	White	Navy
4	Mulberry Blossom 2	Fairisle	White	Pale Blue
2	Mulberry Blossom 2	Fairisle	White	Grey
5	Mulberry Blossom 2	Fairisle	White	Pale Blue
6	Mulberry Blossom 2	Fairisle	White	Mid Blue
13	Mulberry Blossom 2	Fairisle	White	Navy
8	Mulberry Blossom 2	Fairisle	White	Cornflower
9	Mulberry Blossom 2	Fairisle	White	Mid Blue

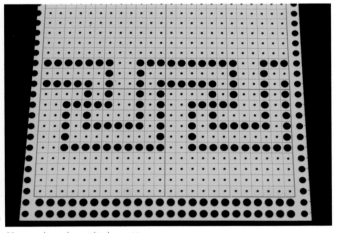

Sleeve border stitch pattern.

The pattern sequence in Table 6.4 indicates the colour changes of the Blossom stitch pattern. The reversed side of the stitch pattern occurs at *.

Repeat from the beginning reversing the stitch pattern.

The sweater was knitted using the Basic Sweater pattern below, with the main background yarn being white. The two one-row stripes after the cast-on circular rib rows are Mid Blue and Pale Blue, and the ribs completed using white. The small border nine-row pattern was placed after the rib, before commencing the Mulberry Blossom for the main body of the garment.

The sleeves end with the small nine-row border but also accommodated a larger Greek Key border stitch pattern just above half way between two sets of Blossom repeats. This breaks up the overall pattern and adds a further interest by a change of texture.

The neckband was knitted in white and folded over with the two contrast stripes worked half way through.

Within every garment there are several elements that all work together and create a unique garment.

BASIC SWEATER PATTERN

The Mulberry Blossom, Florette and Orchard Blossom sweaters all use this basic pattern with only minor alterations to rows to accommodate a border or complete a stitch pattern.

The ribs are always enhanced when after knitting the circular cast-on rows using MY, the next two rows are knitted using a contrasting colour to reflect the colours used in the design. Return to the MY and continue to work the rest of the rib. This is a small detail that makes a big difference aesthetically.

Method
BACK
Bring forward 160 sts to WP for a 1 x 1 rib and work 40 rows. Transfer sts to back bed RC 000, work in patt to RC 134.

Shape Armhole
Cast off 8 sts at the beg of the next 2 rows.

RC 234 shape shoulder.

Place into HP Ns at beg of the next rows 12 sts twice, 10 sts 6 times.

Mark the centre 60 sts for the back of neck. Remove work from machine WY.

FRONT
As for back to RC 207.

Shape Neck
Knit centre 20 sts on to WY.

Cont to work each side separately casting off at the neck edge 4 sts once, 2 sts twice, and cont to dec 1 st ff until 42 rem.

Pick up back shoulder sts on to the front shoulder sts. K 1 row M+ 1 and cast off.

Leave one shoulder unattached until neckband is completed.

Materials
Finished weight 580g

Measurements
Around chest 112cm
Length to shoulder 70cm
Length of sleeve 54cm

Tension
36 sts – 40 rows = 10cm over
Fairisle stitch pattern
Approx MT 7

Machines
Suitable for a standard gauge punchcard and electronic machines with ribber

SLEEVES (MAKE 2)
Bring forward 70 Ns to WP and work 40 rows 1 x 1 rib transfer to back bed. Work in patt inc 1 st at each end of every 3rd row until 160 sts. Cont to work until measures 54cm, approx 190 rows, and cast off loosely.

NECK RIB
Bring forward 160 sts to WP for a 1 x 1 rib, work 16 rows, transfer sts to back bed and pick up 60sts from back neck, 40 sts down side neck, and 20 sts centre neck and a final 40 sts and k 1 row MT+2 and cast off loosely.

The neckband is folded over and sl st into place.

Join the final shoulder seam.

Sew sleeve into armhole, and side of sleeve into armhole shaping. Sew together sleeve side seams and front and back side seams. Sew in ends.

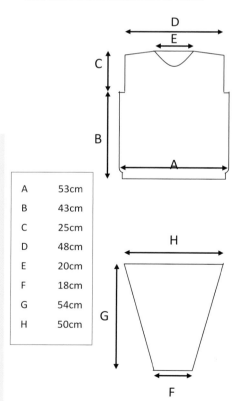

A	53cm
B	43cm
C	25cm
D	48cm
E	20cm
F	18cm
G	54cm
H	50cm

Diagram for Basic Sweater pattern.

Wash and press lightly.

To make a slightly larger version cast on 168 sts for the back and front ribs and work to row 138 before shaping the armholes. Neck shaping starts on row 210 and shoulder shaping on row 238; the extra stitches are incorporated into the shoulder.

colour palette of Terracotta and Gold on a Navy background. The neckband is not ribbed, but the small border Rose pattern hem is used.

All the different elements in this

pattern could be taken and used in a variety of ways. For example, the Rose border could be worked in with traditional Fairisle stitch patterns to add a contrast band.

FLORETTE

This stitch pattern was inspired by a Laura Ashley wallpaper and fabric design, but I wanted the cottage garden appeal without the 'twee' appearance. The design incorporates a large Cabbage Rose border with swags of roses gently zigzagging down the front and back; the main Florette stitch pattern is knitted and then reversed to create this effect. Each florette is joined by a small sprig.

The top of the sleeve and collar has a Small Rose design to echo the roses on the Florette design. The sweater image also shows a variation using a different

Table 6.5: Stitch Pattern and Colour Sequence for Cabbage Rose

Rows	Stitch Pattern	Pattern Setting	Feeder 1	Feeder 2
4	Cabbage Rose	Fairisle	Navy	Grass Green
2	Cabbage Rose	Fairisle	Navy	Mid Green
4	Cabbage Rose	Fairisle	Green	Dark Red
2	Cabbage Rose	Fairisle	Mid Green	Bright Red
4	Cabbage Rose	Fairisle	Green	Pink
2	Cabbage Rose	Fairisle	Grass Green	Cranberry
4	Cabbage Rose	Fairisle	Grass Green	Red
2	Cabbage Rose	Fairisle	Green	Red
2	Cabbage Rose	Fairisle	Navy	Green
2	Cabbage Rose	Fairisle	Navy	Mid Green
3	Cabbage Rose	Fairisle	Navy	Grass Green

Navy colourway; this also looks attractive using a cream background.

Cabbage Rose lower border, top of sleeve and collar Small Rose border stitch pattern chart.

Florette and Sprig stitch patterns

Table 6.6: Florette and Sprig Stitch Pattern and Colour Sequence

Rows	Stitch Pattern	Pattern Setting	Feeder 1	Feeder 2
2	Florette	Fairisle	Navy	Bright Blue
1	Florette	Fairisle	Navy	Pale Blue
4	Florette	Fairisle	Navy	Bright Blue
7	Florette	Fairisle	Navy	Grass Green
4	Florette	Fairisle	Navy	Bright Red
2	Florette	Fairisle	Navy	Bright Pink
2	Florette	Fairisle	Navy	Pink
4	Florette	Fairisle	Navy	Cranberry
4	Florette	Fairisle	Navy	Dark Red
7	Florette	Fairisle	Navy	Bright Blue
2		Knit	Navy	
3	Sprig	Fairisle	Navy	Bright Green
5	Sprig	Fairisle	Navy	Gold
3	Sprig	Fairisle	Navy	Lime Green
2		Knit	Navy	

Any repeat of the florette stitch pattern is reversed and a few of the colours changed to create depth and interest.

Table 6.7: Rose Border Stitch Pattern and Colour Sequence

Rows	Stitch Pattern	Pattern Setting	Feeder 1	Feeder 2
2		Knit	Navy	
4	Rose Border	Fairisle	Navy	Bright Red
2	Rose Border	Fairisle	Navy	Bright Pink
2	Rose Border	Fairisle	Navy	Pink
2	Rose Border	Fairisle	Navy	Cranberry
2		Knit	Navy	

This occurs at the top of the sleeve and on the neckband.

QUEEN'S STRIPE CARDIGAN

A variation of the Florette stitch pattern was to knit the design in twenty-four-stitch wide strips, the cream strip working the Florette pattern in all the colours and the dark red strip using two colours only – Red and Gold Chenille. The strips are sewn together to make a large jacket. Luck sometimes favours the knitwear designer, and the meandering of the floral swags creates an (unintentionally) attractive circular shape across the jacket. The colour choice was harking back to the study of Worcester Porcelain and a large dinner

Queen's Stripe Cardigan.

service painted with maroon and cream stripes overlaid with hand-painted roses and gilding.

ORCHARD BLOSSOM SWEATER

I am lucky enough to live in the fruit bowl of England, surrounded by orchards of apples, pears, damsons, plums and cherries, to say nothing of the soft fruits such as strawberries, raspberries and blackcurrants. Market gardens are everywhere, and the smell of spring onions percolating the air in the early summer can be quite overwhelming!

The blossom season in early spring is so welcome and lifts the spirits after a long winter, and the aim with this design was to try and capture some of this pleasure. Sketches were produced, photographs of blossom and fruit taken, and the colours of each duly noted and transcribed back to the colours of yarn in the workroom. The overall shape of the fruit was simplified to a motif, and textured yarns added to give shape and form.

It is always useful to sketch ideas, and to use a variety of media to carry out rough sketches, such as ink, charcoal, pastel, crayon or gouache. This is a useful aide-memoire to have when choosing yarn colours for each motif, and it will also help to inform the shape of the motif. It is better to keep to a simple, bold, definite shape as this will absorb the yarn and colours.

Gather together all the yarns in the colours of your choice. For example, the plums consist of four varying shades of purple and violet and three shades of green for the leaves. Build up and layer the colours to create a round plum with textural interest. The colours used are in the Spindrift range by Jamiesons of Shetland with Purple, Lavender, Iris and Lupin for the plum, and Eucalyptus, Mermaid and Woodgreen for the leaves.

The knitted Fairisle row sequence is as follows: in Feeder 1, Navy

Sweater taken from the front of the knitwear catalogue.

throughout, with the colours in Feeder 2 changing as follows – three rows Purple, two rows Lavender, two rows Purple, one row Violet, two rows Lupin, one row Violet, three rows Purple, eight rows Eucalyptus, four rows Mermaid, four rows Eucalyptus, four rows Woodgreen.

Placed in between each fruit is a branch and blossom, although I do realize that it is not possible in real life to have blossom and fruit on the tree at the same time. The blossom was knitted in a textured white or chenille yarn with two rows of a pale contrasting colour for the centre. So, in Feeder 2 – three rows White, two rows Lavender, three rows White, and the branch being four rows Shaela.

The Leaf stitch pattern is also repeated after each branch: this consists of twelve rows, just before the apple motif – five rows Bottle and seven rows Moorgrass.

The apple is made up of fifteen rows and four shades of red – Madder, Crimson, Scarlet and Poppy. So work Fairisle – two rows Madder, eight rows Crimson, two rows Scarlet, and three rows Poppy. The apple leaf consists of five rows Verdigris and ten rows Moorgrass.

The blossom and branch are repeated in varying pale pink and white tones, and Shaela branch.

For the repeated Leaf stitch pattern work twelve rows Woodgreen.

The pear consists of twenty rows and four shades – Burnt Ochre, Camel, Oatmeal and Burnt Umber. Work four rows Burnt Ochre, two rows Camel, two rows Burnt Ochre, four rows Oatmeal, four rows Camel and four rows Burnt Umber, and for the pear leaf, fourteen rows of Woodgreen.

The blossom and branch are repeated, and the repeated leaf consists of six rows Spruce and six rows Mermaid.

The cherry requires two shades, Poppy and Crimson, and Woodgreen for the stalk, and two shades of green for the leaf, Forest and Verdigris. Work six rows Poppy, two rows dark Crimson, two rows Poppy, seven rows Woodgreen, three rows Verdigris, and seven rows Bottle.

The Blossom and Branch patterns are repeated, as is the Leaf stitch pattern.

Depending how long you require your knitted piece, start to repeat the Plum pattern again.

It will make the piece more interesting to knit and view if the colours are changed each time a fruit, blossom, branch or leaf is repeated. Alter the rows of the colours to create a different colour emphasis. Add chenille or angora to create a fluffy blossom. This is a great way to use up small amounts of varying textured yarn.

The stitch pattern for the Orchard Blossom was punched in its entirety on to a card and with all the repeats of the blossom and branches. It became very long, but saved time when knitting many sweaters. The sweater pattern for this is the Basic Pattern outlined previously. Follow the stitch pattern and colour sequence set out in the scarf pattern.

Inspiration: fruit and drawings, stitch pattern and knitted sample.

ORCHARD BLOSSOM SCARF

The Orchard Blossom design can also be adapted to make a scarf.

Method

Cast on 120sts using MY and k 1 row, follow stitch patt and colour sequence chart. Note that the punchcard will need to be turned upside down half way through the scarf so the design is the correct way up when worn. Do this after a leaf or fruit so the design moves from one to the other seamlessly.

Rep from beg for required length approx 600 rows. K 1 row Navy MT + 2 and latch off.

Sew in ends. Wash and press.

Materials

Finished weight 330g
Jamiesons of Shetland Spindrift in oil
MY Navy 730
Leaf shades – Eucalyptus 794, Mermaid 688, Woodgreen 318, Bottle 820, Moorgrass 286, Spruce 805, and Verdigris 772
Blossom and Branch shades – Natural White 104, Blossom 555, Shaela 118, Lemon 350, Sunglow 185
Plum, Purple 610, Lavender 617, Violet 600, Lupin 629
Apple and Cherry – Madder 587, Crimson 525, Scarlet 500, Poppy 524
Pear – Burnt Ochre 423, Camel 141, Oatmeal 337, Burnt Umber 1190

Measurements

Width 38cm
Length 170cm

Tension

MT 8
35 rows and 32 sts = 10cm

Machines

Suitable for all standard gauge punchcard and electronic machines

EVESHAM SCARF

This design can be altered and made more formal and stylized by separating the fruit motifs and placing them within a band – this changes the emphasis and anchors them so they become a definite motif rather than part of a natural picture.

With each change of fruit, the background colour changes, for example from blackberry, to dark green, to dark brown. Six stocking stitch rows have been knitted between each fruit motif, two rows of a contrasting colour and another two rows of main yarn before the Butterfly stitch pattern is worked. Each Fairisle band changes colour to add interest and each repeat.

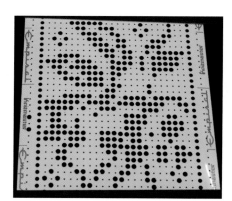

Blossom and Branch stitch pattern.

Orchard Blossom Scarf.

Evesham knitted piece shown as a scarf.

Table 6.8 Orange Blossom Scarf Stitch Pattern and Colour Sequence

Rows	Stitch Pattern	Pattern Setting	Feeder 1	Feeder 2
3	Plum	Fairisle	Navy	Purple
2	Plum	Fairisle	Navy	Lavender
2	Plum	Fairisle	Navy	Purple
1	Plum	Fairisle	Navy	Violet
2	Plum	Fairisle	Navy	Lupin
1	Plum	Fairisle	Navy	Violet
3	Plum	Fairisle	Navy	Purple
8	Leaf	Fairisle	Navy	Eucalyptus
4	Leaf	Fairisle	Navy	Mermaid
4	Leaf	Fairisle	Navy	Eucalyptus
4	Leaf	Fairisle	Navy	Woodgreen
3	Blossom	Fairisle	Navy	White
2	Blossom	Fairisle	Navy	Lavender
3	Blossom	Fairisle	Navy	White
4	Branch	Fairisle	Navy	Shaela
5	Leaf	Fairisle	Navy	Bottle
7	Leaf	Fairisle	Navy	Moorgrass
2	Apple	Fairisle	Navy	Madder
8	Apple	Fairisle	Navy	Crimson
2	Apple	Fairisle	Navy	Scarlet
3	Apple	Fairisle	Navy	Poppy
5	Leaf	Fairisle	Navy	Verdigris
10	Leaf	Fairisle	Navy	Moorgrass
3	Blossom	Fairisle	Navy	White
2	Blossom	Fairisle	Navy	Blossom
3	Blossom	Fairisle	Navy	White
4	Branch	Fairisle	Navy	Shaela
12	Leaf	Fairisle	Navy	Woodgreen
4	Pear	Fairisle	Navy	Burnt Ochre
2	Pear	Fairisle	Navy	Camel
2	Pear	Fairisle	Navy	Burnt Ochre
4	Pear	Fairisle	Navy	Oatmeal
4	Pear	Fairisle	Navy	Camel
4	Pear	Fairisle	Navy	Burnt Ochre
14	Leaf	Fairisle	Navy	Woodgreen
3	Blossom	Fairisle	Navy	White
2	Blossom	Fairisle	Navy	Lemon
3	Blossom	Fairisle	Navy	White
4	Branch	Fairisle	Navy	Shaela
6	Leaf	Fairisle	Navy	Spruce
6	Leaf	Fairisle	Navy	Mermaid
6	Cherry	Fairisle	Navy	Poppy
2	Cherry	Fairisle	Navy	Crimson
2	Cherry	Fairisle	Navy	Poppy
7	Stalk	Fairisle	Navy	Woodgreen
3	Leaf	Fairisle	Navy	Verdigris
7	Leaf	Fairisle	Navy	Bottle
3	Blossom	Fairisle	Navy	White
2	Blossom	Fairisle	Navy	Sunglow
3	Blossom	Fairisle	Navy	White
4	Branch	Fairisle	Navy	Sheala
12	Leaf	Fairisle	Navy	Moorgrass

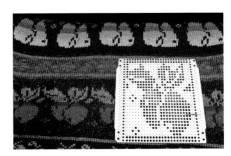

Apple stitch chart.

Pears and Butterfly stitch pattern chart.

Plums and Cherries stitch pattern chart.

ALMOND BLOSSOM

The blossom design has been used by Chinese and Japanese artists for centuries. The overall shape is circular, which as an appealingly shaped motif lends itself to a reimagination of the scale to make a smaller, more delicate design, an example of which is Almond Blossom.

This scale of the Almond Blossom stitch pattern is smaller than that used for the Orchard Blossom, yet when placed on a black background becomes dramatic. Note that the stitch pattern is reversed for the second repeat (Blossom 2), and this has the effect of movement with the branches zigzagging up the worked swatch. The floats on the back are long, so if this is not practical more blossom can be added, or a diamond shape of four stitches randomly spaced throughout the design. This not a problem if the design is worked as a cushion or scarf folded over.

The introduction of the Butterfly motif creates space, interest and variety within the overall design.

Almond Blossom with Butterfly.

Table 6.9: Almond Blossom Stitch Pattern and Colour Sequence

Rows	Stitch Pattern	Pattern Setting	Feeder 1	Feeder 2
2	Blossom 1	Fairisle	Black	Green
2	Blossom 1	Fairisle	Black	Cream
2	Blossom 1	Fairisle	Black	Pale Pink
1	Blossom 1	Fairisle	Black	Cream
4	Blossom 1	Fairisle	Black	Brown
6	Blossom 1	Fairisle	Black	Green
8	Blossom 1	Fairisle	Black	Cream
2	Blossom 2	Fairisle	Black	Grass Green
5	Blossom 2	Fairisle	Black	Cream
4	Blossom 2	Fairisle	Black	Brown
6	Blossom 2	Fairisle	Black	Mid Green
2	Blossom 2	Fairisle	Black	Pale Pink
1	Blossom 2	Fairisle	Black	Cream
5	Blossom 2	Fairisle	Black	Pale Pink
2		Knit	Black	
3	Butterfly	Fairisle	Black	Terracotta
2	Butterfly	Fairisle	Black	Rust
4	Butterfly	Fairisle	Black	Mustard

BUTTERFLY SWEATER

The Butterfly Sweater was knitted using cotton to create a light, summery design. Many years after I designed it for a designer knitwear catalogue I was amazed and pleased to see this design in a book of paintings by Lucien Freud. I was also interested to read the comments of one journalist, which stated that this is a typical sweater worn by old ladies with pink nail polish!

Knitted using a soft cotton yarn, the design incorporates five separate smaller stitch patterns which are placed together. The Arch bottom border has been used in several designs as it is versatile and always looks attractive when placed at the bottom of the sleeve. The Wolf's Paw deep border has also been worked countless times as a border and also as an overall design. The main Leaf and Butterfly designs are a statement motif. This is followed by the Butterfly silhouette and Dragonfly motif. For the repeat the stitch pattern is offset and the colours changed. The top of the sleeve has a stylized border of a butterfly, which is enclosed within a subtle stripe.

The design lends itself to a complete change and dramatic contrast by replacing the cream background with a black background.

Naturalistic elements can be mixed in with seemingly unrelated borders and motifs, but a balance is always required in any design – all the patterns need to be in unison, with no single one overwhelming the others. The only way in which you can see if this is happening is to knit a good-sized swatch. Try out other colour combinations and be critical. Take an image on a camera or phone and view it after a few days. Is the design in harmony? Always make a note of any changes as it is easy to forget after the event.

Butterfly Sweater painted by Lucien Freud, black colourway and stitch pattern chart.

Stitch pattern charts: Arch bottom border, Butterfly/Leaf and Butterfly/Dragonfly.

Basic Cream Colourway

Table 6.9: Stitch Pattern and Colour Sequence for Butterfly Sweater in Basic Cream Colourway

Rows	Stitch Pattern	Pattern Setting	Feeder 1	Feeder 2
1		Knit	Pale Blue	
1	Arch border	Fairisle	Pale Blue	Cream
1	Arch border	Fairisle	Beige	Cream
1	Arch border	Knit	Beige	
4	Arch border	Fairisle	Cream	Apricot
4	Arch border	Fairisle	Cream	Lilac
5	Arch border	Fairisle	Cream	Silver Grey
8		Knit	Cream	
1	Wolf's Paw	Fairisle	Cream	Pale Green
2	Wolf's Paw	Fairisle	Cream	Sand
1	Wolf's Paw	Fairisle	Cream	Pale Green
1	Wolf's Paw	Knit	Cream	
4	Wolf's Paw	Fairisle	Cream	Lilac
4	Wolf's Paw	Fairisle	Cream	Sand
4	Wolf's Paw	Fairisle	Cream	Beige
4	Wolf's Paw	Fairisle	Cream	Pale Green
4	Wolf's Paw	Fairisle	Cream	Pale Blue
4	Wolf's Paw	Fairisle	Cream	Silver Grey
4	Wolf's Paw	Fairisle	Cream	Pale Blue
7	Wolf's Paw	Fairisle	Cream	Grey
8		Knit	Cream	
1		Knit	Pale Green	
1		Knit	Pale Grey	
2		Knit	Cream	
10	Butterfly 1	Fairisle	Cream	Beige
10	Butterfly 1	Fairisle	Cream	Mid Green
7	Butterfly 1	Fairisle	Cream	Lilac
7	Butterfly 1	Fairisle	Cream	Apricot
6	Butterfly 1	Knit	Cream	
17	Butterfly 1	Fairisle	Cream	Silver
6		Knit	Cream	

Reverse the stitch pattern for Butterfly 2 and change the colours.

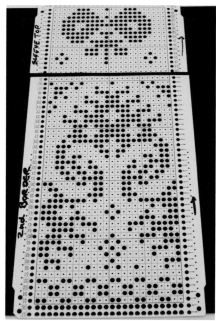

Wolf's Paw and top of the sleeve Butterfly border.

Table 6.10: Stitch Pattern and Colour Sequence for Top of Sleeve Border Only

Rows	Stitch Pattern	Pattern Setting	Feeder 1	Feeder 2
2		Knit	Apricot	
2		Knit	Lilac	
1		Knit	Silver	
4		Knit	Cream	
6	Top border	Fairisle	Cream	Apricot
8	Top border	Fairisle	Cream	Silver
4		Knit	Cream	
1		Knit	Pale Green	
2		Knit	Cream	

To knit the sweater follow the instructions for the Basic Sweater, altering the rows to fit the stitch pattern.

EMBROIDERY EMBELLISHMENT

To enhance a variety of designs and motifs Swiss Darning or duplicate stitch can be added to define highlights, and give form to a motif.

The Daisy motif is an ideal example to show this technique – there are many varieties of daisy but the most familiar are the white and yellow flower heads that appear in lawns and verges. The smaller lawn flowers trigger memories of the rhyme 'he/she loves me, he/she loves me not' and making fiddly daisy chains for children. The following Daisy variations show how this embellishment technique can transform a very basic motif.

The first Daisy pattern has an Art Nouveau feel with the scrolling leaf. In Feeder 2 the first thirteen rows are knitted with green, and the final twelve rows knitted using white, and the centre of the daisy can then be Swiss Darned with a contrasting colour. The colour in Feeder 1 could also have been changed for the first six rows to anchor the daisy, which can give it the appearance of being more naturally placed in a landscape.

The second Daisy variation is based on a William Morris tapestry design, and relies on the embellishment of Swiss darning to give the small flowers shape. The first six rows, in Feeder 2, are worked using green, the next six rows worked using an off white, and the final six rows worked using cream. The centre and top of some of the Daisy motifs are Swiss Darned. If used as a repeat it would create a more balanced feel to offset the stitch pattern.

The third Daisy pattern is also derivative of a William Morris tapestry. The centres of the daisy flowers are embellished with Swiss Darning. I originally used this daisy with a Wall/Path Check pattern. This was to anchor the daisy within a band of colour to create a more formal design. The Check border is worked over sixteen rows changing the colour in Feeder 2 every fourth row, while the daisy was worked in shades of gold and the Swiss Darning sewn with cream.

The fourth Daisy pattern has a neat and compact shape and creates a stylized motif. This small stitch pattern can be easily incorporated into a border, or mixed in with other more traditional Fairisle patterns. For an all-over pattern offset the pattern repeat.

Second Daisy pattern.

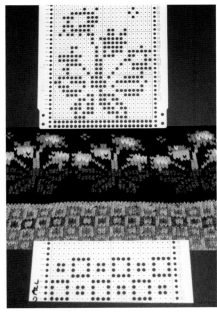

First Daisy pattern.

Wall and third Daisy pattern.

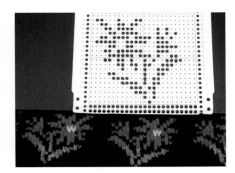

Fourth Daisy pattern.

Table 6.11: Daisy 3 Stitch Pattern and Colour Sequence

Rows	Stitch Pattern	Pattern Setting	Feeder 1	Feeder 2
10	Daisy 3	Fairisle	Black	Green
4	Daisy 3	Fairisle	Black	Gold
4	Daisy 3	Fairisle	Black	Yellow
8	Daisy 3	Fairisle	Black	Ochre

Table 6.12: Daisy 4 Stitch Pattern and Colour Sequence

Rows	Stitch Pattern	Pattern Setting	Feeder 1	Feeder 2
7	Daisy 4	Fairisle	Black	Green
5	Daisy 4	Fairisle	Black	Red
2	Daisy 4	Fairisle	Black	Pink
5	Daisy 4	Fairisle	Black	Red

DESIGN, EMBROIDERY AND ADAPTATIONS

Charity or second-hand bookshops are a rich source of old embroidery books and leaflets. These treasures are full of border patterns, all-over designs, and some naturalistic motifs. Hours can be spent rummaging amongst them and picking out any designs, however small, that you may be able to incorporate within a knitted design.

When you spot a whole design motif, or part of one that interests you, make a sketch and colour it in to see if it works for you – it will give you an outline design which is there for you to adapt or use as is. You may have to extend or shorten the design to fit within the restrictions of your knitting machine, but it is all a matter of careful editing and deciding which part or shape is the important one for your design.

Cornflowers

These flowers are also known as 'bachelors' buttons'. The colours of the golden wheat ears and the bright blue of the cornflower react perfectly together and will trigger memories of hot summer days, so try to capture the spirit of this feeling within the design. The shape of the cornflower and the ears of wheat is quite distinct, and this was easily adapted to a knitted stitch pattern. A tapestry cross-stitch pattern was adapted for use with a knitting machine, and the shapes of the cornflowers that had the most impact were then coloured in to use as a guide for the final knitted design. The leaves and ears of corn were incorporated to conjure up long summer days, and the ears of corn then highlighted with Swiss Darning.

The pattern repeat is long, as this is what was required to gain the idea of a field of cornflowers and wheat. It can be repeated as many times as is wanted to make, for example, a scarf.

Draw out the design on squared paper or directly on to the twenty-four stitch punchcard or mylar sheet. Firstly, knit in two colours to ascertain if any other shapes and stitches need to be added, and check that the proportions are what you intended.

Only when you are satisfied that the motif is correct, start to work out the colours and quantities of different

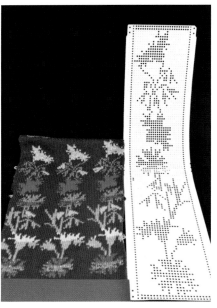

Cornflower stitch pattern chart and sample.

shades. Try out a few variations – these can be added to your sketchbook for reference. This is great fun, and you can try out both a naturalistic version and a wacky version, with lots of colours and changes of background.

Embroidery books as sources.

Cornflower and Wheat embroidery inspiration.

Table 6.13: Cornflower Stitch Pattern and Colour Sequence

Rows	Stitch Pattern	Pattern Setting	Feeder 1	Feeder 2
4	Cornflower	Fairisle	Navy	Bright Blue
4	Cornflower	Fairisle	Navy	Blue
5	Cornflower	Fairisle	Navy	Bright Blue
8	Cornflower	Fairisle	Navy	Grass Green
5	Cornflower	Fairisle	Navy	Lavender
6	Cornflower	Fairisle	Navy	Pale Lavender
22	Cornflower	Fairisle	Navy	Grass Green
4	Cornflower	Fairisle	Navy	Denim
4	Cornflower	Fairisle	Navy	Purple
7	Cornflower	Fairisle	Navy	Denim
15	Cornflower	Fairisle	Navy	Klein Blue
21	Cornflower	Fairisle	Navy	Green
15	Cornflower	Fairisle	Navy	Pale Turquoise

FERNS

For this design I started off with a fern cross-stitch pattern and adapted it into a stitch pattern that I used in a design for a cushion. The front of the cushion uses shades of green in Feeder 2 and darker shades in Feeder 1, and these are reversed seamlessly for the reverse of the cushion cover.

Fern inspiration.

Fern stitch pattern and cushion.

Fern cushion cover front view.

ABSTRACT LANDSCAPE COATS

I have tried over the years to establish a relationship between my work and the landscape by repeatedly observing and absorbing the colours and textures into my work. One way that I have done this is to study the sea and observe how the seagulls fly, dip and play with the air currents – they wheel around rocks and dance over the waves, squeezing the space between the two. My aim was to express this form and atmosphere through colour, texture and tension in various pieces of work.

Physical memories play a part when designing, and in my designs I look to express the warmth of the sun and the surf against my legs, and the dragging of the sand under my feet as the waves recede. All these feelings and emotions are remembered and expressed in my work through choice of colour and stitch pattern, even at an unconscious level. The raw material, which is the yarn, becomes a tangible image portraying a myriad of thoughts, ideas and feelings.

To design well you need to understand both the limitations and the advantages of the techniques that you are looking to use in your design, so that you are able to design something that can be brought to fruition successfully – the design idea and technique are therefore inseparable. It is always worth having in mind that your work is a visual memory, and this can in turn be a visual explanation to others as to why you have chosen to put certain colours and patterns together within a particular shape. If you have succeeded in this process then they become actively engaged in the knitted piece, enjoying your process and thoughts, and actually become part of the process by trying it on and wearing it – you are essentially creating a psychological contract with your customer through the integrity of your design. It is always a delight to see a customer several years later wearing a design and seeing how they have customized and accessorized it – the garment has moved away from being my design to being their design, and has taken on a new lease of life.

Vertical shapes and stripes are easily adapted to the sideways knitted jackets and coats. For example, a scene of mountains, lakes and a forest of trees can inspire a design of vertical and horizontal stripes of varying widths, with the emphasis on a small but rich colour range such as yellow, ochre, and shades of blue such as slate blue, green blue and grey blue; and to sharpen up all the shades and make them brighter, add black and white in small amounts.

Decisions need to be made as to the spacing between the colours and shapes:

* Too crowded, and the design will not have room to breathe.
* Experiment with textures of yarns and blending your own yarns to obtain subtle colour variations.
* Look at an object or scene in your surroundings and create a visual subjective response.
* Try to capture the elemental character in your observations.

This way you are creating a work of art, just like a painted picture, which will relate your passion and enthusiasm to others, and they will be able to share your ideas and experience your observations. Use the yarn and pattern to express your thoughts and feelings, and knit into your design visual memories and experiences.

ST IVES YELLOW AND CHROME COAT

It is interesting to note that scientists say that it is easier to look horizontally along the horizon rather than to look up or down, and also that there is something non-threatening and calming about the circular shape (which represents wholeness and a natural sense of completion). Both of these observations I have used endlessly as they are great catalysts and a wonderful starting point for a new design or colourway.

The intention with the *St Ives Yellow and Chrome Coat* was to knit some hard-edged stripes and to create a contrast by knitting other stripes with a softer edge by blending several ends of fine yarn and similar colours together. The juxtaposition of hard and soft edges creates depth and adds to the sense of colour and space.

While it is possible to plan each row to a certain extent, the result is only really known when a sample is knitted, so keep an open mind and be prepared to change a colour or stripe width or blend of yarn to achieve the result you are looking for.

There is a creative excitement in designing and knitting in this way, and always be prepared to leave a piece of work pinned up on a board for a few days and view it from a distance (in both senses of the word).

Give yourself time and space to consider, contemplate and reflect on the best way forwards for your design – very often simple ideas are the most complex to achieve. Reconsider the techniques used, the forms and motifs, and the colours required, and treat this exercise as a meditation for design refinement by softening or hardening the line and the repeat shapes and colours.

St Ives Yellow and Chrome Coat.

Materials
Finished weight 750g

A variety of colours were used to include six shades of Yellow and Chrome, three shades of Pale Blue, one of Beige, one Chocolate Brown, four shades of Cream, three shades of Grey, one Black, one Pale Green, and one Pale Pink

The yarns used consisted of Cashmere, Raw Silk, Silk Marl, Tussah Silk, Mulberry Silk weaving yarn, Donegal Soft Wool, Shetland Wool, and Alpaca

No yarn was used singly – two and three ends were blended to make up the colour and the weight required

Working directly from a sketch, change the blend of the yarns and the texture as you work along the rows, and then repeat. Keep working directly from the sketch as you will see the repeat differently with fresh eyes and the colours will change slightly as the way you blend the yarns varies.
This is truly painting with yarn!

Measurements
The sizing is flexible
Around chest 146cm
Length to shoulder 71cm
Sleeve length 34cm

Tension
28 sts and 35 rows = 10cm
Approx MT 8

Machines
Suitable for all standard gauge punchcard and electronic machines.

St Ives Yellow and Chrome Coat and sketch.

Method
E Wrap cast on 190 sts. K 100 rows, changing colours and yarns as required.

COLLAR SHAPING
Cast off 25 sts RHS.

FRONT
K 120 rows.

Armhole Shaping
RHS cast off 60 sts, cast on 60 sts.

BACK
K 320 rows.

Armhole Shaping
RHS cast off 60 sts, cast on 60 sts.

FRONT
K 120 rows.

COLLAR SHAPING
RHS cast on 25 sts, k 100 rows and cast off loosely.

SLEEVES (MAKE 2)
E wrap braid cast on 70sts using three ends of contrasting yarn, wind clockwise and back anticlockwise. Change to MY and inc evenly to 130 sts over 140 rows and cast off loosely.

MAKING UP
Join shoulders and collar to back. Join centre back of collar. Set sleeves in armholes, join sleeve seams.

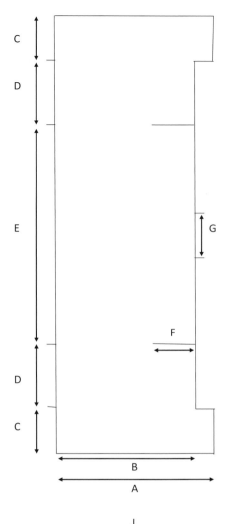

A	83cm
B	64cm
C	22cm
D	33cm
E	81cm
F	21.5cm
G	18cm
H	24cm
I	36m
J	42cm

Diagram for St Ives Yellow and Chrome.

ATLANTIC ROCKS COAT

Dark and subtle shades were used so any sense of scale can be lost, and the scene becomes an abstract expression of the rocks. The focus was on the depth of colour and a loose, draped shape was required to enhance this.

Method
MAIN BODY
E wrap cast on 190 sts using a thin and thicker yarn. Change the thick or thin yarn alternately every 8, 12, 16 rows to create a colour mix.
K 120 rows.

Collar Shaping
Cast off 20 sts at RHS. K 110 rows.

Shape Armhole
Cast off 60 sts at RHS, cast on 60 sts.
Back k 270 rows, rep from *–*.

Materials
Finished weight 650g

Choose a thicker and finer yarn to mix together. A variety of shades were used to include Black, Dark Brown, Mid Brown, Chestnut, Mid Blue, Dark Green, Forest Green, Navy, Mustard, Slate Grey, Dark Red, Maroon

Measurements
The sizing is flexible. The sample garment is:
Around the chest 122cm
Length to shoulder 85cm
Sleeve length 41cm

Tension
22 sts and 48 rows = 10cm after washing
MT 8

Machines
Suitable for all standard gauge punchcard and electronic machines

Atlantic Rocks Coat.

Diagram for Atlantic Rocks Coat.

A	94cm
B	78cm
C	22cm
D	26cm
E	30cm
F	15cm
G	28cm
H	43cm
I	42cm

FRONT
Knit 110 rows.

Shape Collar
Cast on 20 sts RHS. K 120 rows. Cast off loosely.

SLEEVES (MAKE 2)
E wrap cast on 60 sts. RC 000 cont to change colours as required and inc

each end of every 4th row until 130 sts. Cont to k until RC 170 cast off loosely.

MAKING UP
Join shoulders and collar to back. Join centre back of collar. Set sleeves in armholes, join sleeve seams.

FELTING
A completely different finish can be obtained by felting in a washing machine at 40° and 800 spin speed for 60 minutes. Some yarns will felt firmly, while others are looser and less dense. You will need to experiment and decide if this is a feature you require. The pattern will need to be altered to accommodate the felting and yarn shrinkage, but this is not a daunting task if using a loose, unstructured pattern such as the ones above.

It is worth noting that the colours become less distinct and the edges softer, which can be an ideal characteristic when knitting an abstract landscape coat.

It is vital to know your yarn and its characteristics, so experiment with tension and yarn combinations. This knowledge will help in other projects when you require a certain finish.

Before and after felting.

Kimonos

The sideways knitted pattern creates a classic T shape which is ideal for a loose, unstructured edge-to-edge kimono with rectangular body and square sleeves. Using a silk marl yarn for drape, a relaxed fabric was knitted. The stitch pattern required was one that would shimmer and create movement but have no definition or recognizable motif.

The stitch pattern was inspired by Monet's Water Lily paintings. The colours and shapes are fluid and the background disappears into the foreground and re-emerges. The colour choice for Reflected Blossom was taken from several of Monet's paintings of blossom reflected on to the water of the famous lily ponds at Giverny, France; while Dark Reflections, in red, reflects the leaves and vegetation under a tree floating on the water.

Both designs were a complete joy to knit as I had no firm idea as to the overall outcome of the stitch pattern and colour, just the desire to create impressionistic designs within an evocative colour palette. Creating both designs proved to be a dynamic process, as the colour choice changed throughout the knitting process as certain shades proved more suitable than the original ones chosen.

The colour sequence is rotated and the colours in Feeders 1 and 2 alternate by changing every twelve rows, starting with six rows in Feeder 1.

Both kimonos are knitted using the sideways pattern variation with an edge-to-edge front opening. The Reflected Blossom version has a back neck measurement, whilst the Dark Reflections does not. The two fronts join at the centre of the back neck so the drape at the front reflects this.

Blossom and Dark Reflections Kimono.

REFLECTED BLOSSOM KIMONO

Reflected Blossom Kimono.

Materials
Finished weight 370g

1 ply 2/28s silk marl in various colours:
Dark Green, Marine Blue, Purple, Aqua,
Mint Green, Grass Green, Turquoise,
Brown, Mustard, Pale Lemon, Bright
Green, Grey, Lemon

Measurements
The silk marl yarn lengthens
considerably when washed

One size:
Around the chest 102cm
Shoulder to hem 72cm
Sleeve length 38cm

Tension
24 sts – 40 rows
MT 7•
Measured after washing

Machines
Suitable for all standard gauge
punchcard and electronic machines

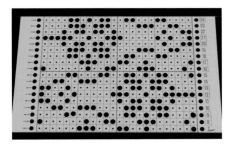

Reflected Blossom stitch pattern
chart.

Method

MY Dark Green.

Feeder 1 colour sequence as follows:
*Marine Blue, Purple, Aqua, Mint
Green, Grass Green, Turquoise, Dark
Green and Brown. Rep from *.

Feeder 2 colour sequence as follows:
**Mustard, Pale Lemon, Bright Green,
Grey, Lemon; rep from **.

FRONTS AND BACK

Left Front
Bring forward 180 Ns to WP and cast
on using WY. K a few rows and change
to MY MT-1; k 30 rows. MT start the
Reflected Blossom stitch patt and work
30 rows. Pick up the first knitted MY
row and work I row. Cast off 20 sts RHS.
RC 000 work 120 rows.

Shape armhole RHS. Cast off 75 sts,
cast on 75 sts.

Back
Cont to work the stitch patt for a
further 260 rows. RC 380.

Shape armhole: cast off 75 sts, cast
on 75 sts.

Right Front
Cont to work a further 120 rows, RC
500.

Shape Collar
Cast on 20 sts at RHS and work 30
rows, stop patt and k 30 rows st st
using MY. K 1 row MT+ 1 and cast off
loosely.

Join shoulder seams and sl st the right
facing back to the inside of the right
front. Attach the collar to the back
neck. Join collar.

SLEEVES (MAKE 2)
Bring 130 sts to WP and complete hem
as for left front. Cont in patt, inc 1 st at
each end of the next 10 rows until 140
sts. Cont to RC 130 from start of
Reflected Blossom stitch pattern. Cast
off loosely.

Insert sleeves and sew in ends.

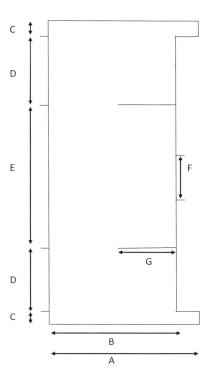

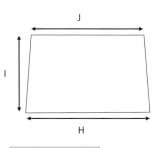

A	78cm
B	68.5cm
C	6cm
D	32cm
E	66cm
F	19.5cm
G	26cm
H	56cm
I	36cm
J	50cm

Diagram for Reflected Blossom
Kimono.

DARK REFLECTIONS KIMONO

With a few small alterations the previous kimono-style jacket can be changed to create more drape at the front edge. This style is easy to wear as it drops from the shoulders and skims the body. The drape at the front requires a fine yarn so as not to appear bulky. The sleeves are shorter than the previous version.

Method

Feeder 1 colour sequence: *Chocolate Brown, Cerise, Maroon, Rust Red, Chili Orange, Dark Red, Brown, Grape; rep from *.

Feeder 2 colour sequence: **Gold, Orange, Sand, Pale Green, Grass Green, Beige, Yellow Ochre; rep from **.
The colour sequence is rotated and the colours in Feeders 1 and 2 change

Detail of Dark Reflections Kimono.

Materials
Finished weight 380g
1 Ply 2/28s silk marl in various colours
MY Chocolate Brown

Small amounts of Cerise, Maroon, Rust Red, Chili Orange, Dark Red, Brown, Grape, Gold, Orange, Sand, Pale Green, Grass Green, Beige, Yellow Ochre

Measurements
The silk marl yarn lengthens considerably when washed
One size:
Around chest 102cm
Shoulder to hem 77cm
Sleeve length 29cm

Tension
24 sts – 40 rows
MT 7•
Measured after washing

Machines
Suitable for all standard gauge punchcard and electronic machines

every twelve rows starting with six rows in Feeder 1.

LEFT FRONT
Bring forward 180 Ns, cast on using WY and k a few rows. Change to MY MT -1 and k 30 rows, MT RC 000 start the Fairisle stitch patt RC 30; pick up sts from first row to make hem, cont RC 130.

Shape Armhole
RHS cast off 75 sts, cast on 75 sts.

BACK
Cont RC 390.

Shape Armhole
Cast off 75 sts, cast on 75 sts.

RIGHT FRONT
Cont to patt to RC 520 MT-1 MY k 29 rows st st, MT+1 k 1 row and latch off loosely.

SLEEVES (MAKE 2)
Follow patt as for previous version. Note the sleeves are shorter and work to RC 110.

Turn back the right front facing and sl st into place. Join the right and left collar together and place at the centre back. Sew shoulder seams together. Inset sleeves and sew side seam. Sew in ends.

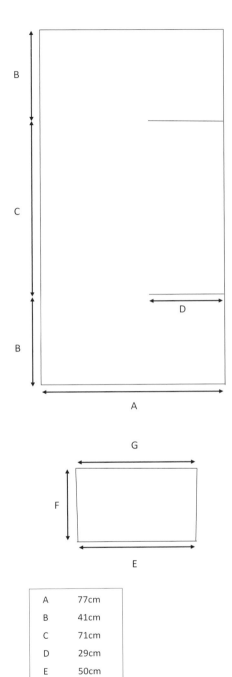

A	77cm
B	41cm
C	71cm
D	29cm
E	50cm
F	29.5cm
G	51cm

SHORT FAIRISLE KIMONO JACKET

The same pattern can be used to make a shorter version of the kimono jacket, knitting with silk and using traditional Fairisle stitch patterns. The final shorter jacket is based on the first version. The stitch pattern uses traditional Fairisle stitch patterns so a certain amount of planning has to take place to make sure that the Fairisle peerie and border patterns will fit within the row count.

When knitting with wool it is possible to sew in the ends from the lower edge and they will weave into the fabric when washed and become secure. When using a fine slippery yarn, the ends although sewn in well, tend to slip out and create an untidy bottom edge. With this in mind a double hem was added; this also gives weight to the base of the garment, and the result is that it becomes less diaphanous and firmer. Knitting with a textured silk yarn

Short Fairisle Kimono Jacket.

the Fairisle pattern fabric has a very different feel to the jackets knitted with Donegal Soft Wool. This in itself is an interesting exercise, observing as a usually firm, woolly, slightly hairy Fairisle fabric is transformed into a light, distorted, stitch-pattern motif.

The traditional Fairisle stitch patterns I used for the left front were stitch patterns 25, 24, 3, 20, 5, 19, 4 and 18. For the back I used stitch patterns 18, 3, 23, 1, 9, 2, 21, 8, 25, 5, 15, 7, 13, 11 and 21, and for the right front, stitch patterns 18, 3, 21, 22, 11 and 25. K approx 3 st st rows between each Fairisle band. The stitch patterns I used for the sleeves were 27, 3, 21, 5 and 22.

Method
FRONTS AND BACK

Left Front
Bring forward 100 Ns to WP and using WY cast on and work a few rows. Change to MY MT-1 k 30 rows st st. Start the Fairisle stitch patts of your choice and work 30 rows. Pick up the first knitted row and work I row. Shape collar, cast off 20 sts RHS. RC 000 MT work 100 rows.

Materials
Finished weight 250g
Colours in various small amounts

Measurements
Around chest 114cm
Length from shoulder to hem 57cm
Sleeve length 16cm

Tension
24 sts – 40 rows
MT 7•
Measured after washing

Machines
Suitable for all standard gauge punchcard and electronic machines

Shape armhole RHS. Cast off 70 sts and cast on 70 sts again.

Back
Cont to work the Fairisle pattern for a further 240 rows RC 340.

Shape armhole. Cast off 70 sts, cast on 70 sts.

Right Front
Cont to work a further 100 rows RC 440.

Shape Collar
Cast on 20 sts at RHS and MT-1 work 30 rows in patt, stop patt and k 30 rows st st using MY. K 1 row MT+ 1 and cast off loosely.

SLEEVES (MAKE 2)
Bring forward 130 Ns, complete hem as for left front. Cont in patt and work a further 50 rows. Cast off loosely.

BOTTOM BORDERS

Right Front Bottom Border
Bring forward 85 Ns to WP and cast on, k a few rows WY, change to MY and work a Fairisle border of your choice, work the corresponding amount of st st rows and pick up the hem. K 1 row. With wrong side facing pick up the bottom edge sts of the right front. K 1 row, K 1 row MT+1 and latch off.

Rep for left front.

Back Border
Bring forward 140 Ns and cast on using WY and work the bottom border as before. With wrong side facing pick up the back bottom edge. K 1row, k 1 row MT+1 and latch off.

Sl st the right facing to the inside of the right front, join shoulder seams. Attach the collar to the back neck. Join right and left collar. Insert sleeves and sew in ends.

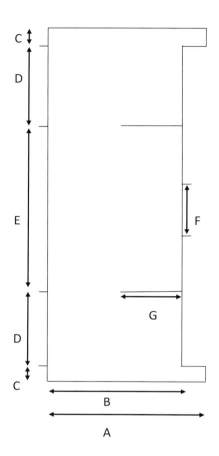

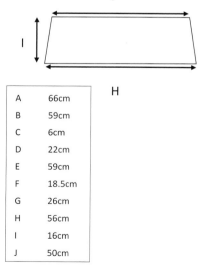

A	66cm
B	59cm
C	6cm
D	22cm
E	59cm
F	18.5cm
G	26cm
H	56cm
I	16cm
J	50cm

Diagram for Short Fairisle Kimono Jacket.

CHAPTER 7

DESIGNING WITH PANELS AND BORDERS

The overall impression of a finished garment should be pleasing, and it will then draw in the viewer to discover details such as the stitch pattern and subtle colour changes. The design should appeal on numerous levels.

Contrasting colour and stitch pattern creates an immediate effect and this in turn creates variations. I always try to envisage what a completed piece will look like, as this helps enormously when working and developing an idea from conception to realization. It may well be that during the design process an element or further idea will be triggered – which may be immediately useful, in which case I will look to incorporate it in my design, or decide not to use it at this time and make a note to explore this precious nugget at a later date.

Creative imagination has endless possibilities, and ideas can spring up out of the blue, so be receptive as your creative ideas may well feed into lots of your other projects. Try not to be too rigid in your ideas, and keep an open mind – observation is the key to creating an original design, and you are surrounded by things that are a catalyst to inspire your creative imagination. Small everyday objects or scenes around the home or garden can inspire, so it is not necessary to look very far afield for ideas to act as a catalyst for your designs.

Try observing the inside of a flower or

Detail of Rose Border Cardigan.

the layers of petals, the shapes, the colours, the shadows, and use your creative imagination to transfer your experience into yarn, pattern, colour and stitch. The petal shape can be envisaged into a slip-stitch circle, add three or more colours to the circle, surround it with smaller or larger circles and experiment with ideas. If something unforeseen happens when you are putting your ideas into practice, question if it reveals another avenue to explore. Many original design ideas can be realized from one small accidental discovery.

Give yourself time and space to focus and go rummaging about with an idea, and consider what you are looking to achieve, and work it through from a variety of angles. For example, you could change your design from using a slip stitch to a tuck stitch or even Fairisle. Try variations of colours, change the yarn, change the scale, and keep adding to your design knowledge – and above all, be reflective and critical, and ask yourself which ideas trigger your creative imagination, and which ideas are likely to create a successful design.

Beware of having too many design choices under consideration at any one time, as this can be mesmerizing and stupefying when deciding upon the patterns, colours, yarns, textures and shapes to use in your end design. Choice and discrimination between choices is part of the design process, and when no decisions are made the design generally fails. A narrower choice of ideas can give greater focus and freedom to complete an original project. All design choices require a certain amount of selection, and it is quite possible that at the beginning of the process there is a difficulty in deciding what is wanted – but it is much easier to know what is not wanted.

When picking up a stitch pattern,

colour, yarn or shape you work through a process of elimination, and knowing what to reject will progress your design forwards. For example, if you place together a variety of clashing colours you can experience an immediate jarring sensation; however, if colours of similar hue are placed together, then these will create a calmer sensation of unity and coherence. It can be easier to work with materials that are similar and have a quiet order, rather than with those that are dissimilar. However, this is not to say that selecting a clashing range of colours that 'ping' should not be considered if that is the effect that you are after.

When working through ideas don't disregard traditional methods, techniques or shapes, as you can use them to create something new. As the twelfth-century French philosopher Bernard of Chartres is quoted as saying, 'We are all standing on the shoulders of giants', and this is true of the design process, because we are inspired by the designers who have gone before us in order to make progress and underpin our designs. We do this by observing and studying a well-honed technique, which can be developed further to create something new.

For example, everyone knows the standard shape of a cardigan – however, any basic garment shape can be broken down into sections. Front panels can be knitted and edgings added vertically. Side panels can be knitted using a contrasting stitch pattern. This is a fun exercise, and once you have worked out the basic pattern, a variety of stitch patterns can be used to create countless garments, each with a completely different character. Deeper border patterns can be worked, and traditional Fairisle juxtaposed with florals or geometric stitch patterns, which will create a different character and style.

ROSE BORDER CARDIGAN

The Rose Border Cardigan illustrates how a rose and rose-bud motif can be edged with a traditional Fairisle stitch pattern border. It is interesting to note that the Fairisle border reverses the colours and stitch pattern over the final five rows.

The Bluebell swatch laid over the Rose Cardigan shows how variations can be tried out. A large bluebell motif is offset by a smaller one, and the colours changed with each repeat. The basic cardigan shape remains the same.

Rose Border Cardigan.

BLUEBELL BORDER CARDIGAN

Method

BACK
Cast on 164, 170, 176 sts for a 2 x 1 rib using contrasting yarn, k 2 rows, MY knit 28 rows.

Transfer sts to single bed machine. RC 000.

K 1 row.

K Fairisle border stitch pattern, k 2 rows MY.

Follow Bluebell stitch pattern sequence until RC 238, 246, 254. Remove from machine on WY.

RIGHT FRONT
Cast on 52 sts to R of centre and 35, 38, 41 sts to left.

Cont as back for rib.

Materials
Finished weight 600g
Various shades using Jamiesons of Shetland Spindrift, wool in oil
MY 500g Navy
50g each of colours chosen for the bluebells or chosen motif
8 buttons

Measurements
Around chest 104cm, 110cm, 116cm
Length to shoulder 62cm, 66cm, 70cm
Sleeve length to inc cuff 51cm, 63cm, 63cm

Tension
34 sts – 43 rows = 10cm
MT 7•

Machine
Standard gauge punchcard and electronic with ribber attachment

The Rose and Rose Bud stitch patterns can be found in my book *Machine Knitting: Designing with Colour*

Rose and Bluebell swatch.

	Small	Med.	Large
A	51cm	54cm	57cm
B	35cm	42cm	90cm
C	22cm	24cm	26cm
D	52cm	55cm	58cm
E	11cm	12cm	12cm
F	5cm	5cm	5cm
G	48cm	49cm	49cm
H	46cm	48cm	48cm
I	16cm	16cm	16cm

K the Fairisle border pattern, dec 15 sts evenly on the LHS. Cont as patt set to RC 217, 225, 233.

Neck Shaping
On neck edge cast off 5 sts on the next two rows, 2 sts on the next two rows, and cont to dec 1 st on the neck edge until 52, 55, 58 sts rem RC 238, 246, 254. Pick up corresponding shoulder sts from back and k 1 row MT+2, and latch off.

Right Front Fairisle Border
With wrong side facing, pick up approx 131, 134, 138 sts down the right front. K the Fairisle border reversing the punchcard and colour sequence. Inc 15 sts evenly on the LHS and dec 3 sts evenly on the RHS for neck shaping. K off on to WY.

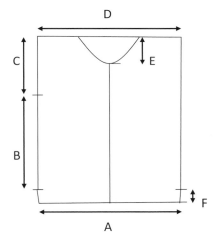

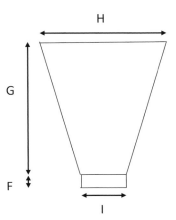

Diagram for Rose and Bluebell Border Cardigan.

LEFT FRONT BORDER

As for right front, reversing all shaping.

SLEEVES

Cast on using WY 78, 83, 90 sts and complete the Fairisle border and knit the Bluebell patt as required, completing the second small bluebell; at the same time inc 1 st at each end of every 4th row until 160, 168, 170 sts. Approx 180 rows.

CUFF

Cast on 70, 75, 80 sts for a 2 x 1 rib. K 40 rows. Transfer sts to back bed. Attach sleeve by picking up sts between WY and placing two sts on Ns evenly to gather the sleeve on to the cuff. K 2 rows and cast off.

BUTTONHOLE BAND

Cast on 146, 156, 166 sts and work a 2 x 1 rib for 12 rows at the same time. Dec 3 sts on the neck edge to mitre band. Place 7 buttonholes evenly down the front, transfer sts to back bed and k 1 row, pick up sts along front edge, k 1 row and cast off.

Rep without buttonholes for left front, reversing shaping.

For neckband cast on 142, 148, 152 sts and work a 2 x 1 rib for 12 rows. Dec 3 sts evenly to mitre with front bands. Transfer sts to the back bed. K 1 row. Pick up front and back neck sts. K 1 row, MT+2 and latch off.

MAKING UP

Join the mitres leaving an opening for the 8th buttonhole. Set in sleeves. Join side seams.

Sew on buttons.

BLUEBELL AND BORDER PATTERN

There is nothing like a bluebell carpet glowing in the wood: it is a truly beautiful spectacle and heralds spring. The bluebell flower has an iconic shape and is unmistakable with its delicate heads bowing gently.

The stitch patterns here are used in place of the roses in the cardigan pattern. The colours in the Fairisle border reflect the colours of a bluebell woodland and the floral motif.

Bluebell Fairisle Border Cardigan and stitch patterns.

Table 7.1 Stitch Pattern and Colour Sequence for Bluebell Border

Rows	Stitch Pattern	Pattern Setting	Feeder 1	Feeder 2
2		Knit	Black	
3	Border	Fairisle	Black	Pale Blue
1	Border	Fairisle	Green	Turquoise
1	Border	Knit	Green	
1	Border	Fairisle	Green Blue	Purple
2	Border	Fairisle	Green	Purple
1	Border	Fairisle	Turquoise	Purple
2	Border	Fairisle	Green	Purple
1	Border	Fairisle	Green blue	Purple
1	Border	Knit	Green	
1	Border	Fairisle	Green	Turquoise
3	Border	Fairisle	Black	Pale Blue
2		Knit	Black	

Table 7.2 Stitch Pattern and Colour Sequence for Bluebell 1 and Bluebell 2

Rows	Stitch Pattern	Pattern Setting	Feeder 1	Feeder 2
22	Bluebell 1	Fairisle	Black	Grass Green
4	Bluebell 1	Fairisle	Black	Turquoise
4	Bluebell 1	Fairisle	Black	Pale Turquoise
13	Bluebell 1	Fairisle	Black	Bright Blue
6	Bluebell 1	Fairisle	Black	Denim
10		Knit	Black	
12	Bluebell 2	Fairisle	Black	Bright Green
10	Bluebell 2	Fairisle	Black	Pale Blue
10		Knit	Black	

The stitch pattern can be reversed for a pattern repeat and the colours changed.

WOOD VIOLET CARDIGAN

Cardigans and sweaters can be further broken down into blocks and smaller panels knitted and fitted back together, rather like a jigsaw. Borders can be added by picking up at right angles to a front panel. An example of this is the Wood Violet Cardigan design.

The inspiration for the Violet plant motif was seen in an embroidery cross-stitch pattern book, and I then simplified the basic shape of the plant and flower for a knitted design. Look for a strong, bold, characteristic shape, and transfer this to a knitted design. The Leaf pattern was more stylised than natural to fit neatly into a border.

The Wood Violet Cardigan images show two variations:

* In the first variation a central panel can be knitted using the violet flowers only, with the Leaf border being picked up and knitted at right angles.

Side panels are then knitted using the Violet plant motif and offset for any repeat. The plant design is reflected in the sleeves and knitted after the Leaf border to tie the design together.

* The second version uses the flowers almost like a yoke enclosed by the Leaf border. A further variation and example of this is the Star and Tassel Cardigan, which uses the same basic pattern but creates a very different style through the change of stitch pattern.

Both basic patterns can be used for an infinite variety of stitch patterns and themes.

Method

BACK PANEL
Push 100 Ns at centre to WP, cast on WY, change to MY Bantry and k 1 row RC 000.

Materials
Finished weight 560g
A combination of Knoll Soft Donegal and Jamiesons of Shetland Spindrift in oil

250g each in MC Knoll Soft Donegal 5517 Mourne (Dark Green), 5531 Bantry (Blackberry), 5539 Sheridan (Navy)

100g Dariana (Purple), 5582 Purple Heart (Mid Purple), 5566 Fuchsia (Cerise), 5526 Liscannor (Dark Pink), 5572 Vichy (Turquoise)

100g each Jamiesons of Shetland Spindrift in oil Shades of Green, Thyme 226, Moorgrass 286, Leprechaun 259, Woodgreen 318, Verdigris, Marjoram 789, Shades of Purple Jupiter 633, Anemone 616, Lavender 617, Paprika (Red) 261, Autumn (Brown) 998

Or small amounts from your stash

7 buttons

Measurements
To fit 92–102cm
Length to shoulder 56cm
Sleeve length 50cm

Tension
32 sts – 39 rows = 10cm
MT approx 8

Machines
Suitable for standard gauge punchcard and electronic machines

Wood Violet Cardigan.

Embroidery chart and punchcards.

Start to work the Violet Flower Head stitch pattern as set out in Table 7.3. Shape side by inc 1 st at each end of the next and every foll 10th row until 120 sts. Cont to work patt until RC 202. Place a marker at each side of centre 40 sts for neck. Using WY release from machine.

Note: Flower Head 2 is the reversed stitch pattern.

RIGHT FRONT PANEL
Push 50 Ns at the right of centre 0 to WP, cast on WY, change to MY Bantry and k 1 row. RC 000.

Start to work the Violet Flower Head stitch pattern as set in Table 7.3. Shape

side by inc 1 st at right edge of next and every foll 10th row until there are 60 sts. K 75 rows. RC 175.

Shape Neck
Cast off 5 sts at neck edge and foll alt row, K 1 row. Cast off 2 sts on the neck edge and foll alt row, K 1 row. Dec 1 st at neck edge on the next row and every foll alt row until 40 sts rem. K 8 rows RC 202. Pick up back corresponding shoulder sts. K 1 row. MT + 1 cast off.

LEFT FRONT PANEL
Work as for right panel reversing cast on and shaping.

RIGHT BACK BORDER LEAF

BORDER
Push 150 Ns at centre of machine to WP. With wrong side of back facing, pick up 150 sts along right edge up to shoulder and place on to Ns. Work Leaf border stitch pattern. K 1 row MT + 2 and latch off.

LEFT BACK BORDER
Work as for right back border, reading left for right.

Table 7.3: Stitch Pattern and Colour Sequence for Violet Flower Heads 1 and 2

Rows	Stitch Pattern	Pattern Setting	Feeder 1	Feeder 2
6		Knit	Bantry	
2	Flower Head 1	Fairisle	Bantry	Jupiter
4	Flower Head 1	Fairisle	Bantry	Purple Heart
2	Flower Head 1	Fairisle	Bantry	Jupiter
3	Flower Head 1	Fairisle	Bantry	Lavender
5	Flower Head 1	Fairisle	Bantry	Anemone
6		Knit	Bantry	
2	Flower Head 2	Fairisle	Bantry	Fuchsia
4	Flower Head 2	Fairisle	Bantry	Liscannor
2	Flower Head 2	Fairisle	Bantry	Fuchsia
4	Flower Head 2	Fairisle	Bantry	Anemone
4	Flower Head 2	Fairisle	Bantry	Liscannor
Rep from beg.				

Table 7.4: Leaf Border Stitch Pattern and Colour Sequence

Rows	Stitch Pattern	Pattern Setting	Feeder 1	Feeder 2
1		Knit	Paprika	
2		Knit	Autumn	
2		Knit	Mourne	
3	Leaf	Fairisle	Mourne	Leprechaun
3	Leaf	Fairisle	Mourne	Woodgreen
2		Knit	Mourne	
2		Knit	Vichy	
1		Knit	Autumn	

Table 7.5: Violet 1 and Violet 2 Stitch Pattern and Colour Sequence

Rows	Stitch Pattern	Pattern Setting	Feeder 1	Feeder 2
4		Knit	Navy	
8	Violet 1	Fairisle	Navy	Moorgrass
6	Violet 1	Fairisle	Navy	Verdigris
4	Violet 1	Fairisle	Navy	Jupiter
2	Violet1	Fairisle	Navy	Anemone
2	Violet 1	Fairisle	Navy	Lavender
2	Violet 1	Fairisle	Navy	Anemone
4	Violet 1	Fairisle	Navy	Dariana
4		Knit	Navy	
8	Violet 2	Fairisle	Navy	Thyme
6	Violet 2	Fairisle	Navy	Marjoram
4	Violet 2	Fairisle	Navy	Dariana
2	Violet 2	Fairisle	Navy	Anemone
2	Violet 2	Fairisle	Navy	Lavender
2	Violet 2	Fairisle	Navy	Jupiter
Rep from beg.				

A	62cm
B	30cm
C	25cm
D	46cm
E	18cm
F	32cm
G	12cm
H	14cm
I	27cm
J	25.5cm
K	15cm
L	25cm
M	47cm
N	48cm

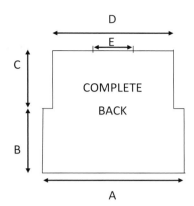

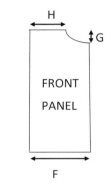

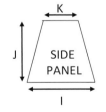

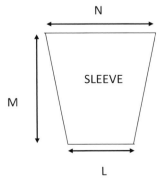

Diagram for Wood Violet Cardigan.

RIGHT FRONT BORDER
Work as for the right back border, reading front for back.

LEFT FRONT BORDER
Work as for the right back border, reading left for right and front for back.

SIDE PANELS (MAKE 2)
Push 90 Ns at centre to WP, Cast on WY, change to MY Navy and start to work the Violet 1 and 2 stitch pattern. Shape sides by dec 1 st at each end of the next and every 4th row until 50 sts rem cont to RC 100 knit 1 row MT + 2 and latch off.

SLEEVES
Push 80 Ns at centre of machine to WP. Using MT and WY, k a few rows; using nylon cord k 1 row. Change to MY and work Leaf border, k 6 rows, work Violet 1 and Violet 2 stitch pattern with 6 rows between each plant as set, complete four Violet plants and finally work a Flower Head. At the same time shape the sleeve by inc 1 st at each end of the next 3rd row and every foll 3rd row until 140 sts. Cont without shaping to approx RC 170.
K 1 row MT + 2, latch off.

CUFF
Push 60 Ns at cent and k a few rows WY.* Change to MY Mourne, k 12 rows, k 1 row Lavender, k 2 rows Anemone, k 1 row Lavender, k 12 rows Mourne, pick up hem k 1 row Dariana.* Pick up sts from sleeve and dec evenly across, k 1 row MC k 1 row MT + 2, and latch off.

LOWER BACK BORDER
Push 160 Ns at cent to WP. Work as for cuffs from *-*. With purl side facing, pick up back panel, leaf borders and half side panels evenly spaced on to the border. K 1 row MC, k 1 row MT + 2, and latch off.

LOWER RIGHT BORDER
Push 80 Ns to WP at RHS of machine.

Work as for cuffs *to* and pick up right front and remaining half of side panel and complete as lower back border.

LOWER LEFT BORDER
Complete as lower right border reversing shaping.

FRONT BUTTON BAND
Push 120 Ns to WP and k a few rows WY. Change to MY Dariana, k 10 rows, placing 6 buttonholes evenly spaced on the fifth row at the same time. Inc 4 sts evenly on the RHS to make the top mitred buttonhole. K 2 rows Fuchsia. Change to MY Dariana k 10 rows, dec 4 sts at the RHS to complete the mitre, pick up the hem and k 1 row Jupiter. Pick up the right front k 1 row and I row MT + 2 and latch off.

Front band rep as button band reversing shaping and omitting buttonholes.

NECKBAND
Push 120 Ns and complete the neckband as before, mitre both ends. Pick up right and left front and back neck, and complete as previous bands.

MAKING UP
Neaten ends of neckband and sew mitres together leaving a gap on the RHS for the final button hole. Join the border seams at the shoulders and lower border seams at sides. Sew cast-off edges at sleeve top to borders, sew rows at top of sleeve to side panels. Join sleeve seams. Finish buttonholes, sew on seven buttons.

KLIMT PANEL CARDIGAN

The following cardigan is a variation of the Wood Violet Cardigan, and has a brighter, more edgy character. Various design elements inspired by the paintings of Gustave Klimt are used within this design. The golden spirals twirl and swirl over the front panel sections, with ochre and chestnut making up the background.

The circular anemone striped design with embroidery in the centre is used in the side panel, with the colours changing with each stripe. Muted subtle colours are used with a blue line to enhance the stripe. The highlights of bright green are Swiss Darned into the flower centre.

The sleeves incorporate large, small, squat and extended triangles, with bright and dark colours to add a rhythmic dynamism to the stitch pattern. Some of the patterns are repeated and the colours reversed, keeping a consistency yet adding interest and pattern conformation. It is interesting to use many unrelated patterns, but by using colour and repetition they all meld together. The flashes of black and white check pattern mirror the checker pattern on the cuffs and bands.

Klimt Cardigan.

Back view.

The side borders to the front and back panels consist of the large triangle motif repeated from the sleeve. However, any of the stitch patterns from the sleeve would have worked just as well.

The cuffs and front edgings are a checkerboard pattern, with the gold

Materials
Finished weight 580g
Various small amounts of colours in 4 ply
7 buttons

Measurements
One size
Around chest 114cm
Length shoulder to hem 58cm
Sleeve length 49cm

Tension
32 sts – 39 rows = 10cm
MT approx 8

Machines
Suitable for standard gauge punchcard and electronic machines

colour alternating in the check stripe.

Any of the stitch patterns could be used as the main pattern for a jumper or cardigan, and they can be used in a different order. Look at your Fairisle 'sketchbook' for inspiration, and work out other stitch-pattern combinations. This is adding to your archive of patterns and helps you to become familiar with mixing patterns and colourways.

Method

Use the basic Violet Cardigan pattern and decide which patterns you are going to use in which sequence and position. Try changing them around and make up your own version – tweak the basic pattern so you can incorporate all the stitch patterns and the correct rows. Avoid incomplete motifs.

The completed cardigan is embellished with Swiss Darning and running stitches, using a DK weight yarn. The side panel circles are Swiss Darned in the centre. The front panels are highlighted with a bright contrasting yarn to outline some of the swirls. A running stitch is sewn up and down, in front of and behind the swirls, in a random way. This decoration adds a richness and depth to the panel.

Using this basic pattern each panel could be a different geometric pattern, or a series of stripes in a varying colour palate – the variations are endless.

Back panel stitch pattern and knitted piece before Swiss Darned embellishment.

Punchcard sleeve stitch pattern and detail of knitted piece.

Sleeve punchcard stitch pattern and detail of knitted sleeve.   Detail showing Swiss embroidery and running stitches.

STAR AND TASSEL CARDIGAN

Yet another development of the panel cardigans can be seen in the Star and Tassel design. The variation moves the mitred border up to the armhole, creating a yoked look. The Rope border is also knitted at the top of the sleeve and mitred to enclose the Star stitch pattern.

Materials
Finished weight 650g of a variety of colours in 4-ply yarn
7 buttons

Measurements
One size only:

Around chest 110cm
Length hem to shoulder 66cm
Sleeve length 50cm

Tension
32 sts – 39 rows = 10cm
MT approx 8

Machines
Suitable for standard gauge punchcard and electronic machines

Detail of bottom borders and Star stitch pattern.

Method

BACK
Push 170 Ns to WP, cast on using WY and work 24 row hem of your choice or 1 x 1 rib for 30 rows.

RC 000. Work the Fairisle bottom border, k 4 st st rows changing colour each row, work one star changing the colour in Feeder 1 on the fourth row. K 2 rows st st changing colour each row. Work the 7 row bottom border using contrasting colours. MY k 6 rows st st. Work the Tassel pattern reversing the stitch pattern for each rep. After each tassel k 2 rows st st. Complete 5 tassels. RC 123.

Stitch patterns for the Rope border, bottom border, Star and Tassel.

A	59cm
B	37cm
C	25cm
D	56cm
E	21.5cm
F	31.5cm
G	9cm
H	18.5cm
I	24cm
J	51cm
K	46cm

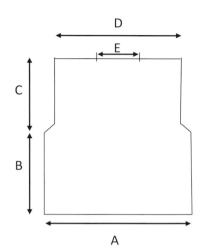

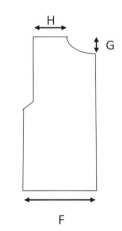

Shape the Armhole

Work the Rope patt and the final 7 rows of the bottom border stitch patt turned upside down, at the same time dec 1 st at each end of every row 11 times (22 sts dec in total). Cont to work the Star patt with 6 st st rows between each star. Complete six stars and the final 6 st st rows RC 230. Mark the centre 54 sts and run work off the machine on to WY.

RIGHT FRONT

Work as for half of the back until RC 123.

Shape the Armhole

Work the Rope patt and the 7 rows of bottom border, at the same time dec 1 st at each end every row until 22 sts have been dec. Work the Star stitch patt RC 210.
Shape the neck. Cast off 5 sts on the neck edge and foll alt row, dec 1 st on the neck edge until 47 sts remain for the shoulder. RC 230. Pick up the corresponding shoulder sts from the back, k 1 row MT + 1 and latch off.

FRONT BORDER

Pick up approx 56 sts along the front edge of the Star patt. Reverse the bottom border and Rope stitch patt and complete. At the same time dec 3 sts evenly on the neck edge, inc 11 sts evenly on the lower edge to shape the mitre for the yoke. Cast off.

LEFT FRONT

Work as for the right front reversing all shaping.

SLEEVES (MAKE 2)

Bring 90 Ns to WP using WY. K a few rows, change to col and work the stitch patts as set out for the back completing 7 tassels. At the same time inc evenly at each end until 140sts. Complete the Rope and bottom border rows, dec 1 st at each end of every row until 11 sts have been dec each side. Cast off loosely.

CUFF

Bring 70 Ns to WP and work the chosen rib or hem, pick up the sts from the sleeve between the WY evenly. K 1 row, MT + 1 k 1 row and latch off.

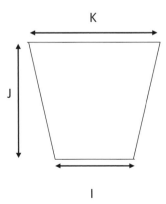

Diagram for Star and Tassel Cardigan.

Sleeve detail.

BUTTON BAND

Either cont working a 1 x 1 rib or use a border Fairisle stitch pattern or part of the border and work a double hem. Bring forward approx 160Ns to WP and work the band placing 7 buttonholes evenly as required.

Pick up the front of the cardigan and k 1 row, k 1 row MT+1 and latch off loosely.

Rep for the second band omitting buttonholes.

NECKBAND

Bring forward approx 150 Ns and work the neckband of choice. Pick up the front of the neck and back neck and k 1 row, k 1 row MT+1 and latch off loosely.

MAKING UP

Join all the mitres neatly matching the stitch patt. Sew in the top of the sleeve to the armhole. Sew side seams. Sew on buttons. Wash and press.

Various all-over patterns and borders can be used to create variations of this shape. Small adjustments may be required to accommodate any stitch pattern.

POPPY AND DAISY CARDIGAN

Big bold daisies were designed and knitted with egg-yolk yellow Swiss Darned centres. This stitch pattern was designed to be used in a vertical panel twenty-six stitches wide and ninety-nine rows before a repeat, therefore the floats across the back were not a problem. The bright daisy would also work well as a furnishing fabric.

The basic shape of the Poppy and Daisy pattern is very simple. To add interest to the rib, work the first circular rows using a contrasting colour, followed by a single row of another contrasting colour and the remaining rib knitted with the main colour.

Method

The back consists of a 28-row, 2 x 1 rib with stitches transferred to the single bed and the first daisy knitted followed by the 7-row bottom border from the previous Star and Tassel design; also 6 repeated poppies with 10 st st rows between each repeat, and the bottom

border repeated once again for the top of the back piece.

The fronts are half the width of the back, so cast on half the stitches. Cast on 13 sts to the right or left of the centre so the Daisy stitch pattern is centred, and complete the rib. Work the first single daisy, continue to knit through the Daisy stitch pattern on the 26 centre stitches having knitted the remaining part of the front on to waste yarn. Work until approx 230 rows.

Shape the neck by casting off 6 sts on the neck edge on the following and alternate row, and 4 sts on the following and alternate row; continue dec 1 st on alt rows until all sts are dec. Pick up the rem sts between the WY and work the poppy patt and bottom border RC approx 245; dec 1 st on the neck edge until 55 sts remain for the shoulder. Cont until RC matches the same as the back.

For the sleeves, cast on 70 sts and work 40 rows 2 x 1 rib and transfer the stitches to the single bed machine. RC 000 evenly inc to 160 sts over approx RC 180 rows. Work the first single daisy,

Poppy and Daisy Cardigan.

Large Daisy heads.

Poppy stitch-pattern chart.

Table 7.6: Poppy Stitch Pattern Colour Chart

Rows	Stitch Pattern	Pattern Setting	Feeder 1	Feeder 2
5	Poppy	Fairisle	Navy	Mid Green
11	Poppy	Fairisle	Navy	Grass Green
4	Poppy	Fairisle	Navy	Maroon
4	Poppy	Fairisle	Navy	Dark Red
2	Poppy	Fairisle	Navy	Red
4	Poppy	Fairisle	Navy	Cardinal Red

Any repeat should be offset, and the colours used should be changed.

followed by the bottom border, then a poppy, followed by the bottom border again and another offset poppy followed by another deep border pattern of your choice.

For the button band cast on approx 160 sts, 12 rows 2 x 1 rib at the same time; dec 4 sts evenly on the neck end to create a mitre. Transfer the sts to the back bed and pick up the front edge of the cardigan, k 1 row, k 1 row MT+1 and cast off.

Work the buttonhole band placing seven buttonholes on the sixth row. The final eighth buttonhole is left as a gap in the mitre when sewn up.

For the shawl collar, cast on approx 142 sts and work 2x1 rib RC 11; cast off 2 sts at the beg of every row until 72 sts remain, approx RC 46. Run off on to WY. Sew the collar to the right and left front and back neck.

To make up, sew sleeves to armholes, sew side seams. Sew on buttons.

Try experimenting with a variety of stitch patterns that can be used together. For example, rather than using a single flower motif, use an all-over pattern with a geometric motif. The patterns don't need to be connected by a theme – they can be diverse, as this will add to the surprise and unique quality of the design.

Revisit the Fairisle sketchbook for ideas, and place patterns together to see how they work with changing colours and emphasis. Question constantly and make notes – combine motifs from other worked designs for example, look at the bottom border stitch pattern features in both the previous designs. Some motifs will be used over and over as they are truly versatile and can easily change their appearance through colour and yarn texture choice.

CORNISH SUN CARDIGAN

The inspiration for these cardigans was the sun and moon reflected on the water and in the sky at various times of day, and after studying the magical effect of the colour changes present in the landscape and seascape. The following two designs are my interpretation, and my attempt to capture the spirit of the experience.

The Cornish Sun Cardigan uses bright oranges, reds and yellows, and the Cornish Moon soft ethereal shades. The moons change shape constantly, by using varying tuck-stitch patterns, with some off set and others placed directly above each other. Notice that the base of the circle is flattened when this happens, with the result that the moon is reflected in the water, which was the effect that I wanted to create.

Materials
The finished weight was 400g

Various colours and weights of yarn. Three ends of a fine I ply were used for the collar, and a 2 ply–3 ply yarn used for the main patterned body part. The sleeves are a combination of the two

Measurements
The measurements are approximate, as it does depend which yarns felt densely and which have a looser feel

One size only:
Around chest 110cm
Length from shoulder to base 53.5cm

Tension
You will need to check the felted piece carefully
26 sts and 54 rows = 10cm
MT 8 after felting

Machines
Suitable for standard gauge punchcard and electronic machines

Front view of Cornish Sun Cardigan.

Cornish Sun Cardigan: back view.

On completion, both garments were felted in the washing machine for 60 minutes at 40 degrees, 800 spin speed.

Method

Divide the pieces of the garment into separate sections – the sleeves, the body and the collar – and use unrelated patterns, stocking-stitch stripes and tuck-stitch circles to create a unique garment. For the right-side collar three ends of yarn in different colours were blended together, and three subtle yet contrasting colours used for the left side of the collar and each sleeve block.

The tuck-stitch pattern OXXXXXXXO was placed in the middle of a stripe. The suns (circles) created with the tuck stitch changed colour in the middle row of the stitch sequence. For example: col 1 k 6 rows st st, col 2 k 4 rows tuck st, col 3 k 4 rows tuck st, col 1 k 6 rows st st. This sequence is repeated throughout, only the colours change.

Bring forward 155 Ns to WP and E wrap, cast on using three ends of fine yarn to create a marled effect, and k st st for 60 rows.

SHAPE COLLAR

Cast off 20 sts at the right edge.
K 120 rows in the tuck-stitch Sun patt.

SHAPE ARMHOLE

Cast off 70 sts at the right.
Cast on again over the 70 sts needles.

BACK

Knit 270 rows.

Shape Armhole

Cast off 70 sts at the right edge.
Cast on again 70 sts.
K 120 rows.

SHAPE COLLAR

Cast on 20 sts at right edge. 155 sts. K 60 rows and cast off.

SLEEVES

Push 70 Ns to WP, and using three strands of fine-weight contrasting yarn, E wrap braid cast on wrapping yarn around the Ns from left to right and right to left.

K several rows st st, work two of the tuck-stitch Sun borders at random intervals as you k up the sleeve. At the same time inc evenly to 140 sts over 160 rows. Cast off.

Note that the colour combination of the three ends of yarn changes between each Sun band placed on the sleeve. The spacing of the Sun border should be different on each sleeve, to create interest.

MAKING UP

Join shoulder seams. Join centre back seam of collar and sew collar into position. Set in sleeves and join side seam.

Machine wash for 60 minutes at 40 degrees, 800 spin speed. Pull firmly into shape after the garment is removed from the machine and still damp and malleable. When dry, give a firm steam press.

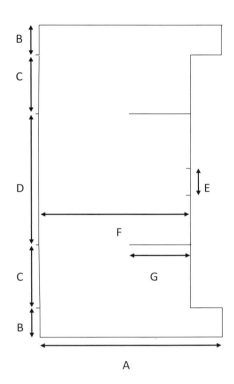

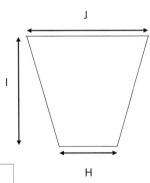

A	69.5cm
B	13cm
C	23.5cm
D	52.5cm
E	11.5cm
F	54cm
G	24cm
H	26cm
I	37.5cm
J	21.5cm

Diagram for Cornish Sun Cardigan.

CORNISH MOON CARDIGAN

Small and large moons were created by using varying tuck-stitch patterns: eight rows tuck OXXXXXO, eight rows tuck OXXXXXXXO, and ten rows tuck OXXXXXXXXXXXO. Some of the moons change colours midway. The stripes between the moons vary in width and texture by using yarns of various weights and blending colours and yarn ends together.

The large collar is worked throughout in stocking stitch, knitted separately, and sewn on afterwards. The sleeves and collar use three ends of fine yarn

Materials
Finished weight 700g

Use a variety of colours to suit the theme you are inspired by

Measurements
To fit various sizes:
Width around chest 142cm
Shoulder to lower edge 75cm
Sleeve length 40cm

Tension
29sts – 42 rows = 10cm
MT 8

Machines
Standard gauge punchcard or electronic machines

together to create a blended, marled look. One colour was changed every sixth row and replaced with another fine yarn in another similar shade to create movement and texture.

Throughout this design colours were blended while others of a thicker weight were used singly. The design used a palette of greys, blues and very pale pink with a small amount of beige. Cashmere, raw silk and lamb's wool yarns were all combined together.

Method
FRONTS AND BACK
Bring forward 180 Ns to WP E wrap cast on C1 RC 000, work the striped and tuck-stitch Moon pattern RC 150.

Armhole Shaping
Cast off 70 sts, cast on 70 sts on RHS.

BACK
Work in patt 320 rows.

Cornish Moon Cardigan.

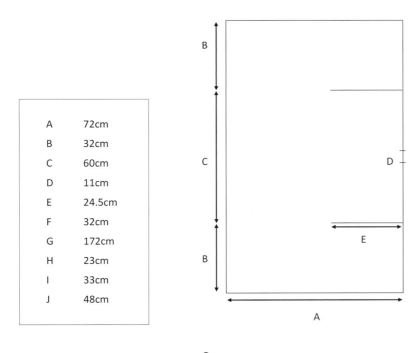

A	72cm
B	32cm
C	60cm
D	11cm
E	24.5cm
F	32cm
G	172cm
H	23cm
I	33cm
J	48cm

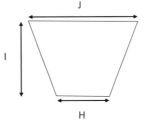

Diagram for Cornish Moon Cardigan.

BLOCK SWEATER

This basic sweater design can be customized to make several variations by adding Fairisle to the sleeves, or an overall pattern using a thick and finer silk marl yarn.

Below are two different colourways of the same garment, one using bright pinks and reds and the other soft greys and blues, showing two very different characters. The yarn chosen is a fine silk marl that will drape well. When a thicker yarn is chosen the basic design is firmer and therefore smaller in size, so adjustments will need to be made to the basic pattern.

Method

Punchcard stitch pattern locked: 0X0X0X0X0.

SLEEVE STRIPED PATTERN

Using G, k 6 rows in sl st. Using D, k 10 rows in st st. Using E, k 6 rows in sl st. Using G, k 10 rows in st st. Using MC, k 6 rows sl st. Using E, k 10 rows st st.

Materials
Finished weight 240g.
MC A, B, C, D for the four blocks of colour right and left front and back. Smaller amounts of yarn for the sleeve stripes D, E, F, G, H, I

Measurements
One size:
Actual size 150.5cm
Length to shoulder 64cm
Sleeve seam 34cm

Tension
22 sts and 40 rows = 4cm over st st
MT 7•

Note: On the completed sweater the knit side of the fabric is the right side

Machines
Suitable for standard gauge punchcard and electronic machines

Armhole Shaping
Cast off 70 sts, cast on 70 sts on RHS. Work in patt 150 rows and cast off.

SLEEVES
Worked throughout in st st.

Bring forward 70 Ns to WP E wrap, cast on using three ends varying colours of fine weight yarn throughout but changing one of the colours every sixth row, at the same time inc evenly to 140 sts RC 140.

COLLAR
Bring forward 100 Ns to WP E wrap, cast on using three ends of yarn as for sleeves, work in st st throughout RC 660 rows.

Cast off.

MAKING UP
Join the shoulders, sew the collar up the fronts and across the back neck. Set in the sleeves and sew side seams. Wash to lightly felt at 40 degrees 800 spin speed for 60min and press.

Harvest Fairisle Block Sweater.

Firebird Block Sweater.

Using H, k 6 rows sl st. Using MC, k 10 rows st st. Using F, k 6 rows sl st. Using H, k 10 rows st st. Using A, k 6 rows sl st. Using F, k 10 rows st st. Using C, k 6 rows sl st. Using A, k 10 rows st st. Using I, k 6 rows sl st. Using C, k 10 rows st st. Using B, k 6 rows sl st. Using I, k 10 rows st st. Using D, k 6 rows slip stitch. Using B, k 10 rows in st st. These 160 rows create the sleeve pattern.

RIGHT BACK
Push 80 Ns to WP. E wrap cast on by hand using MC and MT k 6 rows. Using D, k 6 rows in sl st. Using MC, k 4 rows st st. Using E, k 6 rows in sl st. Using MC, k 2 rows in st st. Using F, k 6 rows sl st. Cont in st st.
    RC 000 using MC, k 19 rows. Inc 1 st

on the right-side edge and every foll 20th row until 85 sts. K 50 rows. RC 150.

Shape Armhole
Dec 1 st ff at the right edge of the next row and every foll alt row until 80 sts remain. * K 81 rows.
    RC 240.

Shape Shoulder
Set to hold, push 10 Ns at right to HP on the next and foll 3 alt rows. K 1 row.

Using WY release from machine.

LEFT BACK
Work as for right back, reversing all shaping and using A instead of MC.

LEFT FRONT
Work as for right back to * using B instead of MC.
    K 44 rows. RC 203.

Shape Neck

Set to hold. Push 5 Ns at left, neck edge, to HP on next and foll alt row. K 1 row. Push 1 N at left to HP on next and every foll alt row until 55 sts rem. K 4 rows. RC 240.

Shape Shoulder

Push 10 Ns at right to HP on next row and foll 3 alt rows. K 1 row. Push Ns at right from HP to UWP. K 1 row. Using WY release from machine. Push remaining Ns to WP using WY release from machine.

RIGHT FRONT

Work as for right back to * reversing all shaping and using C. K 44 rows. RC 203.

Shape Neck

Set to hold. Push 5 Ns to HP on the next row and foll alt row. K 1 row. Push 1 N at right to HP on the next row and every foll alt row until 55 sts rem. K 4 rows. RC 240.

Shape Shoulder

Push 10 Ns at left to HP on next row and foll 3 alt rows. K 1 row. Push Ns at left from HP to UWP. K 1 row. Using WY, release from machine. Push rem 25 Ns from HP to UWP and using WY release from machine.

Join the left and right front centre seam. Join the left and right back centre seam.

Join the left shoulder.

Push 55 Ns to WP. With p side of left front facing, pick up the shoulder sts. With k side of left back shoulder facing, replace sts on to corresponding Ns using appropriate colour MT+2. K 1 row. Cast off using latch tool.

NECK BORDER

Push 118 Ns to WP with p side facing. Pick up the sts around the neck front and back.

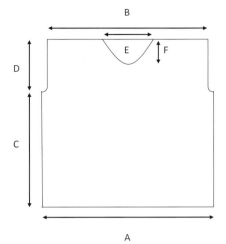

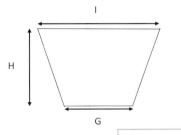

Diagram for Firebird Block Sweater.

A	76cm
B	71cm
C	41cm
D	22cm
E	21cm
F	12cm
G	29cm
H	35cm
I	54cm

Using A, k 2 rows st st. Using D, k 6 rows sl st. Using A, k 2 rows st st. Using E, k 6 rows in sl st. Using A, k 2 rows in st st. Using F, k 6 rows sl st. Using A, k 2 rows st st. Using MT+2, k 1 row. Cast off using latch tool.

Join right shoulder seam.

Rep as for left shoulder seam.

SLEEVES

Push 130 Ns to WP. With p side facing, pick up armhole sts making sure the shoulder seam is at the centre.

RC 000 using MT cont in sleeve stripe patt as set at the same time dec 1 st at each end of the next and every foll 5th row until 70 sts rem. Cont RC 160. Using E, k 6 rows in sl st and 2 rows st st. Using F, k 6 rows sl st and 2 rows st st. Using MT+2, k 1 row and latch off.

MAKING UP

Join side and sleeve seams. Sew in ends.

OXFORD BLUE SWEATER

The coloured front and back blocks of the Oxford Blue version below remain the same as the previous version but the sleeves have been worked using traditional Fairisle patterns. For this, consult the Fairisle Sketchbook for variations of stitch patterns. Unlike the previous sweaters the right side of the garment is the purl side.

Colour variation: Aqua Block Sweater.

The front and back four pieces are knitted using a small Fairisle Peak stitch pattern border; continue to work through the instructions of the *Basic Sweater* as set.

The sleeves are knitted from the armhole down using Fairisle stitch patterns. Choose which ones will fit best and follow the instructions as set in the *Basic Sweater*, ending with the small Peak pattern to match the bottom border of the front and back. The stitch patterns used for the Oxford Blue example are, from top to bottom 20, 3, 19, 5, Rams Horn stitch pattern, see below, 3, 29, 27, 29. You will need to add a few extra stitches as Fairisle stitch patterns are not as stretchy as stocking stitch, so bear this in mind when making pattern adjustments. Alter the row count to the length of sleeve

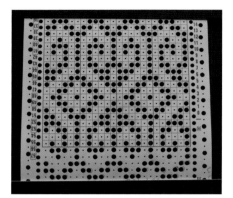

Rams Horn stitch pattern.

required, approximately 138 rows.

The neckband uses Stitch Pattern 3 and is folded over to make a hem.

ORIENTAL SWEATER

The Oriental stitch pattern is based on a vintage fragment of fabric from an antique kimono and represents a stylized pomegranate. An overall stitch pattern is used, and the front and back worked in two pieces, not four as in the previous sweaters. The purl side is the right side.

Method

Using the *Basic Sweater* patt E wrap cast on 160sts; all shaping remains the same. A fine silk yarn was placed in Feeder 2 and a thicker yarn in Feeder 1. The first rows after the E wrap cast on were worked in a XOXOXOXOXOXO sl st patt for 2 rows using a contrasting yarn. The yarn used was soft and dropped considerably in length when knitted and washed, so I had to be mindful of this when knitting the garment. The stitch pattern works equally as well using a variety of 4-ply weight yarn.

The background colours in Feeder 1 consisted of a variety of dark colours and shades of blue such as navy, marine blue, peacock blue, dark green, grape, maroon, purple and black. The colours used in Feeder 2 are brighter, such as bright red, bright pink, violet, bright green, lime green, gold, turquoise and lavender. The colour sequence changes every four rows, so the colour in Feeder 1 changes on the fourth row and the colour in Feeder 2 changes on the eighth row, and this is repeated throughout.

The neckband is worked by picking up the stitches around the neck and knitting the slip stitch pattern worked after the E wrap cast on rows for the front and back pieces. Cast off having worked 1 row MT + 2.

Oxford Blue Sweater with Fairisle sleeve variation.

Oriental Sweater stitch pattern.

SLEEVES

Push 150 Ns to WP. With knit side facing, pick up armhole stitches making sure the shoulder seam is at the centre. Note that the stitch pattern must be worked in reverse to appear the correct way up, and started and finished on the appropriate row to avoid ending mid-pattern. Decrease evenly to 70 sts until RC 136 complete with the sl st patt from the lower edge of the front and back pieces.

Oriental Sweater variation.

COUNTRY SWEATER

This design was made using the same Basic Sweater pattern and working with a variegated yarn that requires no fancy stitch pattern. This version is a classic shaped Country Sweater with a classic simple T shape, worked using a gorgeous luxury cashmere yarn.

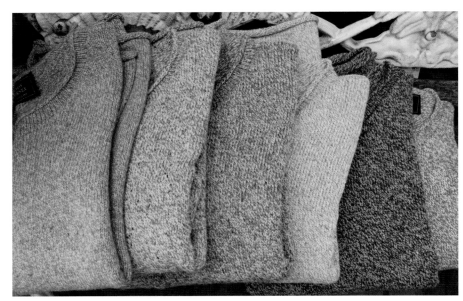

Block Sweater variations.

HARVEST FAIRISLE BLOCK SWEATER

A further development is to knit the Basic Sweater pattern using wool with a variety of Fairisle peerie and border stitch patterns. Refer back to the Fairisle Sketchbook and choose the Fairisle stitch patterns and colourways that best complement your design.

Harvest Fairisle Sweater.

CHAPTER 8

SHAWL COLLAR CARDIGANS

Shawl collar cardigans and jackets are the epitome of winter knitwear as the warm and cosy collar wraps around and creates a comforting garment suitable for indoor and outdoor wear.

BOBBING BOATS FAIRISLE SHAWL COLLAR CARDIGAN

This basic pattern can be altered with very little tweaking to produce an elaborate Fairisle cardigan – decide which Fairisle patterns you want to use, and work out how they will be best spaced. This is a fairly ample garment

Bobbing Boats Jacket in bright colours.

Materials
Finished weight 700g

A variety of colours in keeping with your colour palette, Knoll Soft Donegal, and Jamiesons of Shetland Spindrift in oil

For the bobbing boats I used Cerise, Yellow, Green, Red, Navy, Purple, Dark Pink, Orange, Emerald, Dark Red, Lime, White, Pale Blue, Pink, Grass Green, Turquoise, Blue

5 buttons

Measurements
Around chest 112cm
Length to shoulder 68cm
Sleeve length 46.5cm

Tension
32 sts – 39 rows = 10cm
MT 8

so larger Fairisle motif patterns can be used.

Make sure you calculate the number of rows so that you will not be ending three-quarters of the way through a pattern at the join at the back of the collar. I used between two and four rows of stocking stitch between each Fairisle pattern. The colour palette I used contained bright contemporary colours reminiscent of a myriad of brightly coloured boats bobbing and

weaving about in the harbour on a day with a strong off-shore breeze.

Method
BACK
Push 166 sts to WP and cast on using WY. K a few rows and change to MY, MT -1, k 22 rows MT + 2, k 1 row. RC 000 Follow Fairisle stitch pattern instructions as set out, MT. When RC 22 pick up sts from between WY, continue

to RC 86. Inc 1 st at each end of the next and foll 10th row until 182 sts. K to RC 174.

Shape Armholes
Cast off 14 sts at beg of next two rows. Cont to RC 254.
   Knit on to WY.

POCKET LININGS (MAKE 2)
Push 40 sts to WP and cast on using WY, knit a few rows and change to MY, k 70 rows and k on to WY.

LEFT FRONT
Push 75 sts (Ns 83 R to 9 at L) to WP using WY. K a few rows and change to MY, MT-1 k 22 rows, E wrap cast on 32 sts on the right, 107 sts RC 000, k 1 row MT+2, MT. Start to patt RC 22 pickup sts for hem from WY, Cont RC 74.

Autumn Fairisle Cardigan.

Place Pocket
With right side of pocket lining facing, pick up sts in MY and place on corresponding Ns 63-24 on L. K 1 row and cast off. Place the other end of the lining on to the empty Ns RC 74 and cont to k RC 86 inc 1 st on left on the next row and every foll 10th row until 114 sts RC 147.
   Inc 1 st on the next right row and every foll 10th row until 119 sts RC 156.
   Inc 1 st on left of the next row.
   Inc 1 st on the right on the next and every foll alt row until 129 sts.
   K 1 row RC 175.

Shape Armhole
Cast off 14 sts at beg of next row, inc 1 st at end of the next row.
Inc 1 st at R on next and every foll alt row until 154 sts.
   K 1 row RC 257.

Shoulder
Pick up the corresponding 54 shoulder sts from the back piece. K 1 row MT +2 and latch off.
   Cont to work in patt on rem 100 sts RC 290 cast off.

RIGHT FRONT
Work as for left front, reversing, shaping and working buttonholes on rows 7, 41, 75, 109, 143 on Ns 7, 8 and 2, 1 at centre.

SLEEVES
Push 80 sts to WP using WY k a few rows. Change to MY and MT-1. K 22 rows.
   MT + 2 k 1 row MT RC 000. Start to follow patt sequence, picking up the hem sts RC 22.
   K 6 rows. Inc on the next and every foll 6th row until 150 sts.
Cont to RC 162 and cast off.

POCKET TOPS
Using a suitable stitch patt, make a pocket top and pick up the sts from the cast-off edge from the front piece. K 1 row MT+1 and latch off.
   The Basic Pattern can be adjusted to add or shorten the length by knitting a few more st st rows between the Fairisle patterns, or removing an entire border pattern.
   An autumnal variation using browns, greens, gold, chestnut and ochres creates a more traditional Fairisle style. The stitch patterns used were different from the previous Bright Bobbing Boats version. Returning to the traditional Fairisle Sketchbook will help enormously when designing another version. The yarn used was mainly Knoll Soft Donegal and Jamiesons of Shetland Spindrift. Obviously any variety of yarn that knits up to a similar tension is suitable.
   The Fairisle stitch patterns used in this version were from the lower edge to

Table 8.1: Row Sequence Chart

Rows	Stitch Pattern	Pattern Setting	Feeder 1	Feeder 2
2		Knit	Cerise	
3	2	Fairisle	Cerise	Yellow
2		Knit	Cerise	
2	10	Fairisle	Cerise	Green
4	10	Fairisle	Red	Green
2	10	Fairisle	Cerise	Green
2		Knit	Cerise	
3	2	Fairisle	Cerise	Yellow
2		Knit	Cerise	
2		Knit	Navy	
2		Knit	Purple	
3	23	Fairisle	Purple	Red
3	23	Fairisle	Dark Pink	Green
1	23	Fairisle	Orange	Yellow
3	23	Fairisle	Dark Pink	Green
3	23	Fairisle	Purple	Red
2		Knit	Purple	
2		Knit	Navy	
2		Knit	Emerald	
3	8	Fairisle	Emerald	Yellow
1	8	Fairisle	Lime	Orange
3	8	Fairisle	Emerald	Yellow
2		Knit	Emerald	
4		Knit	Red	
3	22	Fairisle	Red	Lime
3	22	Fairisle	Dark Red	Emerald
1	22	Fairisle	White	Cerise
3	22	Fairisle	Dark Red	Emerald
3	22	Fairisle	Red	Lime
4		Knit	Red	
3	29	Fairisle	Yellow	Red
3	29	Fairisle	Yellow	Lime
3	29	Fairisle	Orange	Lime
3	29	Fairisle	Orange	Purple
1		Knit	Purple	
3	27	Fairisle	Purple	Emerald
2	27	Fairisle	Cerise	Pale Blue
1	27	Fairisle	Red	White
2	27	Fairisle	Cerise	Pale Blue
3	27	Fairisle	Purple	Emerald
1		Knit	Purple	
3	29	Fairisle	Orange	Purple
3	29	Fairisle	Orange	Lime
3	29	Fairisle	Yellow	Lime
3	29	Fairisle	Yellow	Red
2		Knit	Red	
4		Knit	Green	
3	22	Fairisle	Green	Dark Red
3	22	Fairisle	Lime	Red
1	22	Fairisle	Yellow	Cerise
3	22	Fairisle	Lime	Red
3	22	Fairisle	Green	Dark Red
4		Knit	Green	
4		Knit	Cerise	
2	19	Fairisle	Cerise	Emerald
3	19	Fairisle	Pink	Grass
3	19	Fairisle	Dark Pink	White
3	19	Fairisle	Pink	Grass
2	19	Fairisle	Cerise	Emerald
4		Knit	Cerise	
4		Knit	Red	
7	9	Fairisle	Red	Emerald
4		Knit	Red	
3		knit	Cerise	
3	20	Fairisle	Cerise	Yellow
3	20	Fairisle	Dark Red	Lime
1	20	Fairisle	Red	Emerald
3	20	Fairisle	Dark Red	Lime
3	20	Fairisle	Cerise	Yellow
3		Knit	Cerise	
3		Knit	Purple	
3	17	Fairisle	Purple	Emerald
2	17	Fairisle	Dark Red	Grass
1	17	Fairisle	Red	Yellow
2	17	Fairisle	Dark Red	Grass
3	17	Fairisle	Purple	Emerald
4		Knit	Purple	
7	9	Fairisle	Purple	Yellow
4		Knit	Purple	
3		Knit	Yellow	
3	8	Fairisle	Yellow	Turquoise
1	8	Fairisle	Yellow	Red
3	8	Fairisle	Yellow	Turquoise
3		Knit	Yellow	
2		Knit	Navy	
3		Knit	Purple	
3	25	Fairisle	Purple	Orange
3	25	Fairisle	Cerise	Yellow
3	25	Fairisle	Dark Pink	Grass
5	25	Fairisle	Blue	Emerald
3	25	Fairisle	Dark Pink	Grass
3	25	Fairisle	Cerise	Yellow
3	25	Fairisle	Purple	Orange
3		Knit	Purple	
3	2	Fairisle	Purple	Red
2		Knit	Purple	

The sleeve uses the same colours and patterns up to the end of Chart 19, then the smaller Wave Pattern 28 is used for the top of the sleeve. (*See* Table 8.2.)

shoulder 25, 13, 2, 21, 9, 21, 25, 22, 8, 21, 9, 21, 17, 25, and 2. The sleeve sequence is completed after Fairisle Stitch Pattern 8. Many of the same stitch patterns are repeated, but with each repeat the colours are reworked to create interest and variety.

Table 8.2: Stitch and Pattern Settings for the Top of the Sleeve

Rows	Stitch Pattern	Pattern Setting	Feeder 1	Feeder 2
4		Knit	Cerise	
2	28	Fairisle	Grass	Cerise
1	28	Knit	Grass	
2	28	Fairisle	Turquoise	Grass
1	28	Knit	Turquoise	
2	28	Fairisle	Purple	Turquoise
1		Knit	Purple	
3	27	Fairisle	Purple	Orange
2	27	Fairisle	Cerise	Yellow
1	27	Fairisle	Emerald	Red
2	27	Fairisle	Cerise	Yellow
3	27	Fairisle	Purple	Orange
1		Knit	Purple	
2	28	Fairisle	Turquoise	Purple
1	28	Knit	Turquoise	
2	28	Fairisle	Grass	Turquoise
1	28	Knit	Grass	
2	28	Fairisle	Blue	Grass
2		Knit	Blue	

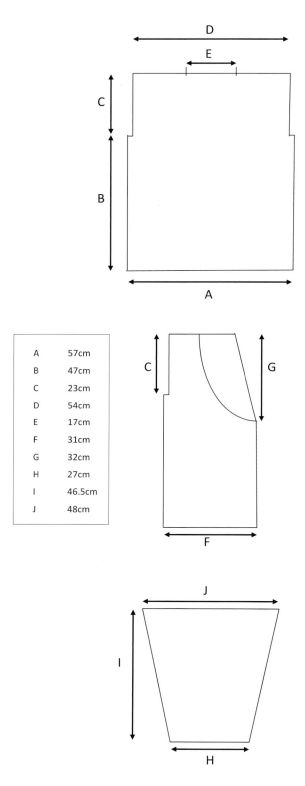

A	57cm
B	47cm
C	23cm
D	54cm
E	17cm
F	31cm
G	32cm
H	27cm
I	46.5cm
J	48cm

Diagram for Shawl Collar Jacket.

CHAPTER 9

DIAGONAL KNITTING

Diagonal knitting has the appearance of being more complicated than it is, as the effect of the rows coming together in a gentle point at the front and back of a garment looks impressive and attractive, but it is merely another shaping tool in our box of techniques. Stitches are increased or decreased to add shaping. You can choose to add pattern to each diagonal band, or keep it plain using stocking stitch and coloured stripes to enhance the diagonal. Below are a few examples detailing how this effect is created – be bold and confident.

SNOWFLAKE TRELLIS CARDIGAN

The stitch patterns used for the diagonal yoke are 3, 4, 5, 6, 7, 11, 12, 13, 14 and 15.

The back and front panels use the traditional Fairisle Stitch Pattern 19 for the hem with a change of colours for the front button bands and the all-over Snowflake Trellis pattern for the main body. The neckband is worked with Stitch Pattern 3. The sleeve consists of Stitch Pattern 19 for the hem, the all-over Snowflake Trellis stitch pattern and finally Stitch Pattern 20 for the border at the top of the sleeve.

Snowflake Trellis Cardigan.

Materials

Finished weight 650g of Knoll Soft Donegal

Main colours Peacock 5564, Silver Mist 5580, various small amounts in the chosen yoke and border shades

Measurements

Around chest 90cm
Length to shoulder 71cm
Sleeve length 57cm

Tension

32 sts and 34 rows = 10cm
MT 8

Machines

Suitable for standard gauge punchcard and electronic machines

Method

It is easy to use other small Fairisle patterns for the yoke – just try and keep to small repeat patterns as they are neater to match up at the centre back and front. Use another all-over pattern for the hem and front panels, and a motif can be used with plain rows in between. The sleeves can be striped with all-over Fairisle patterns for a very intricate look, but keep to a colour palette to avoid the overall look becoming too busy and chaotic. Embroidery can be added later to the trellis pattern to create a rich brocade feel.

LEFT BACK YOKE

Having decided on your chosen Fairisle stitch pattern, using the first appropriate yarn colour, work as follows:
E wrap cast on 78 sts (60 sts at the left and 18 at the right of the centre bed). K 2 rows.

Inc 1 st on right and dec 1 st on left every row until 71 sts remain.

Cont to dec 1 st on left edge every row and dec 1 st on right edge every

Diagonal Snowflake Trellis Cardigan.

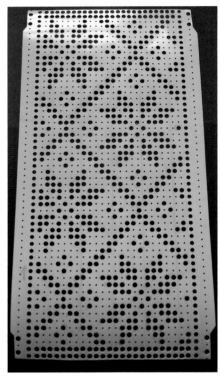

Snowflake Trellis stitch pattern.

4th row until 32 sts remain. RC 106.

Dec 1 st on left edge every row and dec 1 st on right edge every alt row until 2sts remain. Cast off.

RIGHT BACK YOKE

Work as for left back yoke reversing all shaping, right for left and left for right.

LEFT FRONT YOKE

Work as for left back yoke until RC 103, 36 sts and cast off.

RIGHT FRONT YOKE

Work as for right back yoke until RC 103, 36 sts and cast off.

BACK PANEL

Push 150 Ns to WP and k a few rows WY. MY k 17 rows st st, MT+1 k 1 row, MT work the Fairisle Stitch Pattern 19.

Pick up the sts on the first row to

make a hem sts and k 1 row RC 000. Start the Snowflake Trellis patt. K 62 rows.

Place half the needles in HP. Make a note of the pattern row *dec 1 st at the centre every row, work 1 row without shaping*. Rep from *to*until 15 sts remain, cast off. RC 132.

Pick up the sts on the other side and repeat shaping.

RIGHT FRONT PANEL

Push 75 sts to WP. Work the hem as the back panel, cont to work as right half of back.

LEFT FRONT

Rep as right front reversing shaping.

SLEEVES

MT 7.
Push forward 70 Ns to WP and k a

few rows WY. Work Stitch Pattern 19 for the cuff.

MT8. RC 000. Work the Snowflake Trellis pattern, inc 1 st each end of every 3rd row until 170 sts. Cont to row 158. Change to Stitch Pattern 20 and work a further 17 rows. Cast off.

FRONT BAND

T 7. Bring forward 170 Ns, cast on using WY, change to MY and work Stitch Pattern 19 using contrasting colours. K 17 rows st st, pick up hem sts and k 1 row. Pick up along left front right sides facing together, k 1 row MT, k 1 row T10 and cast off.

BUTTONHOLE BAND

Rep as for previous band but place 7 buttonholes evenly down the centre of the band. Bear in mind that the top buttonhole is placed on the neckband so the buttons will start approx 22 sts from the top. Try and place them in the centre of the diamond shape created by the Snowflake Trellis as this will look neater when completed.

NECKBAND

Bring forward 120 Ns and cast on using WY, change to MY, make the neckband using the appropriate Fairisle Stitch Pattern 3. Place a buttonhole on the appropriate side of the band. When completed pick up 35sts from right side of the cardigan, 50 sts across the back neck and 35sts down the left front side. Rep as for other bands, cast off.

MAKING UP

Attach sleeves to armhole, sew top of side seam to cast off panel top. Sew side seams and sleeve seams together. Join all hems using mattress stitch.

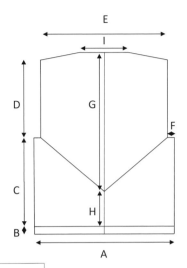

A	55cm
B	3.5cm
C	38cm
D	31cm
E	38cm
F	4cm
G	52cm
H	14.5cm
I	20cm
J	27cm
K	9cm
L	3cm
M	24cm
N	53.5cm
O	62cm

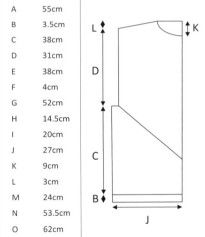

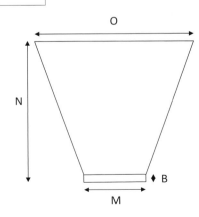

Diagram for Diagonal Yoked Cardigan.

FAIRISLE TWEED CARDIGAN

Another version of a diagonal front-panelled cardigan is the Fairisle Tweed Cardigan. This pattern has a wide V neck, and the tweedy front and back panels contrast with the intricate bottom borders and traditional Fairisle peerie pattern sleeves.

The front and back panels are knitted on the cross using the diagonal technique. The stitch pattern used adapts the Louse/Spider motif from the sketchbook to make an all-over stitch pattern. It was a revelation when knitted in a large piece as visually the stripe pulled the pattern one way while the circular plain colour Spider seems to point in the other direction: this created a more dynamic overall effect than I had anticipated when studying the original small swatch. It is always inspiring to see how some patterns change visually when knitted in a larger piece, or scaled down.

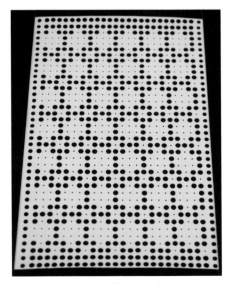

All-over Louse/Spider stitch pattern.

Fairisle Tweed Cardigan.

Table 9.1: Stitch and Pattern Settings for Fairisle Tweed

Rows	Stitch Pattern	Pattern Setting	Feeder 1	Feeder 2
*1	Spider	Fairisle	Lime	Purple
4	Spider	Fairisle	Tweed Col 1	Navy

A combination of Knoll Soft Donegal and Jamiesons of Shetland Spindrift was used. The Tweed colours used for the front and back diagonal panels are 1 Olive Green, 2 Brown, 3 Vichy (Turquoise), 4 Blue Green, 5 Autumn Brown, 6 Ochre.

The stitch pattern repeats again from the first row using the same colours. The four-row pattern changes the Tweed colour in Feeder 1 but keeps the navy in Feeder 2 for every repeat.

Repeat from *changing col to Tweed 2 for the four-row pattern. Continue working through the Tweed colours as required.

Lower Border

The gold and blue lower border highlights some of the colours used in the front and back panels. The back panels are sewn together down the centre back seam and picked up right side facing on to the machine.

Start by working a single repeat of the Spider all-over pattern knitted with navy and cerise to add contrast. This is followed by the deep Rams Horn border pattern, which appears intricate but is easy to knit. Finally, a further Spider single repeat is worked, along with the plain stocking-stitch turn-back hem rows. Pick up stitches from the first

row knitted to make a hem. Knit 1 row MT+1 and cast off.

Sleeves

The sleeves are a combination of Peerie Fairisle patterns, many of which were adapted from the designs found on Norwegian Selbu mittens. The Rams Horn border pattern is worked with a change of colour for the middle rows from gold and blue to ochre and red. Also note that the colours are reversed in the second half of the pattern for a few rows. While the overall pattern remains the same, the effect is to add interest and keep the eye moving over the fabric.

Small design details such as this add to the unique originality of the garment, and it is also great fun to experiment and play with swapping colours within a design, and reversing others from Feeder 1 to Feeder 2. Always consider attention to detail, as small changes can make a huge difference and create a truly dynamic and individual design.

The main part of the sleeve consists of various peerie patterns and a repeat of the Spider pattern half way up the

Materials
Various colours of Knoll Soft Donegal and Jamiesons of Shetland Spindrift
Finished weight 500g
6 buttons

Measurements
Width around chest 106cm
Length to shoulder 53cm
Length of sleeve 45cm

Tension
30st – 38 = 10cm
MT 7•

Machines
Suitable for standard gauge punchcard and electronic machines

sleeve to reflect the front and back panels. The image [below] shows the Rams Horn stitch pattern used with other colour changes.

The button bands are a singular repeat of the Spider pattern using cerise and navy.

Method

RIGHT FRONT

Using MY, cast on 3 sts, k 3 rows. RC 000 start stitch patt, inc 1 st on RHS and every foll alt row, at the same time inc 1 st LHS every row until 104 sts.

Shape Armhole

RC 72, dec 1 st at LHS, cast off 6 sts at RHS.

Cont to dec 1 st on LHS every foll alt row until 84 sts. RC 100

Cont to dec on LHS as set, inc 1 st every row on RHS until 100 sts, RC 130.

Shoulder and Neck Shaping

Cast off 5 sts every alt row on LHS, RHS dec 1 st every foll alt row until 2 sts rem, cast off.

LEFT FRONT

Repeat as for right front, reversing all shaping.

RIGHT BACK

Follow instructions for right front to RC 130.

Dec 1 st LHS every alt row, RHS dec 1 st every alt row to RC 162.

Shoulder and Neck Shaping

RHS cast off 5 sts every alt row, dec 1 st every row LHS until 2 sts rem. Cast off.

LEFT BACK

Rep as set for right back, reversing all shaping.

Join the shoulders and centre back panels.

BACK LOWER BORDER

There are two ways of completing this: either cast on 142 sts WY, work the lower border as detailed. Pick up the hem and k 1 row. Pick up the lower edge of the back diagonal panels, k 1 row and cast off.

Or pick 142 sts across the back panels and work the Spider patt, the Rams

Horn border patt and rep the Spider patt for the hem. K st st for the underside of the hem, cast off loosely and sl st into place.

FRONT LOWER BORDERS

Rep as for back, casting on or picking up 72 sts.

SLEEVE

Using WY, cast on 70 sts and knit a few rows. Change to MY and work the cuff hem of your choice.

RC 000. Start to patt at the same time, inc evenly to 150 sts. RC 140.

Shape Top of Sleeve

Cast off 6 sts at the beg of the next 10 rows. Cast off.

BUTTONHOLE BAND

Using WY, cast on 174 sts and work the button band placing 6 buttonholes evenly up to the V neck shaping, work the chosen patt, pick up the hem and k 1 row. Pick up 36 sts from the centre of the back, 66sts down the front V neck shaping, and 72 sts front edge. K 2 rows MT+2, cast off.

Rep for final band omitting the buttonholes.

MAKING UP

Sew sleeves into armholes. Sew together side seams and sleeve seams. Sew in ends. Sew on buttons. Wash and press firmly.

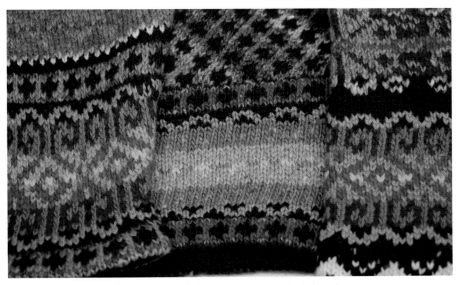

Various changes to the colours of the Rams Horn stitch border pattern.

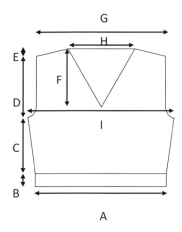

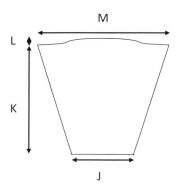

A	49cm	H	25cm
B	9.5cm	I	55cm
C	20.5cm	J	24cm
D	24cm	K	42cm
E	3cm	L	3cm
F	24cm	M	50cm
G	50cm		

Diagram for the Fairisle Tweed Cardigan.

HEBRIDEAN SEAS CARDIGAN

The subtle grading of greys and blues in the front panel gives a different character to this diagonal panel cardigan. The colours change every eight rows starting with navy, green, peacock blue, turquoise, aqua, pale blue and finally mid blue. The aim was to capture the spirit of the Hebrides and emulate the turquoise clear sea and crashing waves. The pinks pick up the heathery shades of the hills and glens. There is always a breeze, if not a gale blowing across the islands, yet the freshness of the air and clear bright skies create a magical spirit and induce meditative reflection, which is so often triggered by the sea and the rhythm of the waves.

An all-over Paisley pattern worked

Materials
Finished weight 570g

Variety of colours of your choice Knoll Soft Donegal and Jamiesons of Shetland Spindrift
8 buttons

Measurements
One size only:
Around chest 114cm
Length from shoulder including hem 57.5cm
Length of sleeve 51cm

Tension
32 sts and 36 rows = 10cm over Fairisle stitch pattern
MT 8

Machines
Suitable for standard gauge punchcard and electronic machines

Hebridean Seas Cardigan.

into the sleeves and side panels compliments the traditional Fairisle border patterns. The all-over Paisley pattern changes colours every six rows and rotates between Feeder 2 and Feeder 1. The sequence of the colours in Feeder 1 is navy, green, peacock blue, mid blue, dark grey and purple. The colours in Feeder 2 rotate through pale grey, off white, aqua, pale blue and pink.

The side panel border is knitted at right angles to the centre panels and uses the traditional Fairisle Stitch Pattern 19. The hem Fairisle Stitch Pattern 14 uses similar colours. The front button bands and neckband use Fairisle Stitch Pattern 3.

As always, any of these patterns are interchangeable. A deeper hem or button band can create a very different style, however minor adjustments will need to be made regarding the length and width of the finished garment.

Method

LEFT BACK PANEL
Change colour every 8 rows.
The chart shows the Ns in WP and the row count as the increases and decreases take place.

*E wrap cast on over 3 Ns on RHS of the machine bed 38, 39, 40th Ns (if the centre of the bed is number 1, count to N 38, 39 and 40).

RC 000. Work 3 rows st st start to inc each end evenly so the correct number of sts is achieved as suggested by the chart.

RC 48 start to dec on the RHS evenly while cont to inc on the LHS. Follow the chart to RC 160 shoulder and neck shaping.

Dec 1 st on LHS every row, at the same time dec 1 st on RHS every 4th *row until 2 sts remain. Cast off. RC 216.

LEFT FRONT PANEL
Work from * to * as back panel until 32 sts remain. Cast off rem sts.

Work the right back and front panel as the left panel reversing all shaping. Join the centre back and shoulders.

SIDE FAIRISLE BORDER
Pick up 140 sts down the outside edge of the left back panel. K 2 rows MY. Work the Fairisle border patt no 19, k 2 rows MY. Cast off.

Rep for all outside edge panels.

LOWER SIDE PANELS (MAKE 2)
E wrap cast on 90 sts and work the all-over Paisley stitch patt. RC 000

Dec evenly until 50 sts remain. Cont to RC 110, cast off.

SLEEVES
Bring forward 80 NS to WP and k a few rows using WY. RC 000. Change to MY and work the all-over Paisley pattern. Inc evenly to 150 sts, RC 96. Cast off.

Table 9.2: Row Count as the Increases and Decreases Take Place

Rows	Left	Right
8	32	47
16	25	52
24	20	58
32	15	65
40	10	70
48	5	75
56	0	70
64	5	65
72	10	60
80	15	55
88	20	50
96	25	45
104	30	40
112	35	35
120	40	30
128	45	25
136	50	20
144	55	15
152	60	10
160	65	5

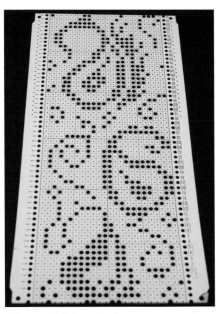

All-over Paisley stitch pattern chart.

CUFF
Bring forward 70 Ns to WP and k a few rows WY. MT 7.

Change to MY and k 2 rows. Work the Fairisle border Stitch Pattern 14, k 2 rows, MT + 1 k 1 row contrast colour, MT – 1, MY k 12 rows st st and pick up the hem. K 1 row in contrast colour. Pick up the sts between the WY on the sleeve and evenly gather excess sts. K 1 row MT + 2 and cast off.

Rep for cuff on second sleeve.

Making Up
Join the top of the sleeve to the side panel border front and back. Join the side seams of the lower panels to the side border and the top edge to the side sleeve seam.

Join the remaining side sleeve seams.

BACK HEM
Bring forward 144 Ns and work from *to* as cuff. Pick up 32 sts from the bottom edge of half the right-side lower panel, 7 sts from the side border, 33 sts from the right back panel, 33 sts

from the left back panel, 7 sts from the side border and 32 sts from the left side lower panel.

K 1 row, k 1 row MT+2 and cast off.

FRONT HEM
Bring forward 72 Ns and rep as for half of back hem.

BUTTONHOLE BAND
Bring forward 130 Ns to WP and k a few rows WY. Change to MY MT–1 k 2 rows, inc 3 sts evenly on the neck edge. Place 7 buttonholes evenly spaced noting that the top buttonhole is the mitred shaping at the top of the band. K Fairisle Stitch Pattern 3, k 2 rows. K 1 row contrasting yarn MT +1, MY MT-1 k 8 rows st st, dec 3 sts evenly on the neck edge. Pick up as cuff hem.

Pick up front edge of cardigan. K 1 row and cast off.

Make further band omitting buttonholes.

NECKBAND
Bring forward 130 Ns to WP and cast on WY. Rep as for button bands, mitre both ends.

Pick up around neck and cast off. Mitre neckband and front bands leaving a hole for the button.

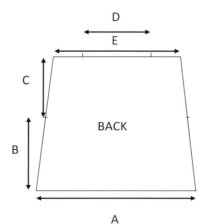

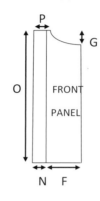

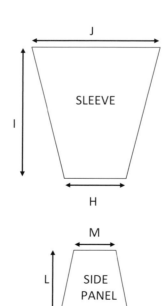

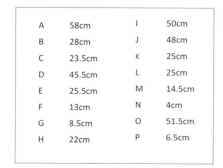

A	58cm	I	50cm
B	28cm	J	48cm
C	23.5cm	K	25cm
D	45.5cm	L	25cm
E	25.5cm	M	14.5cm
F	13cm	N	4cm
G	8.5cm	O	51.5cm
H	22cm	P	6.5cm

Diagram for Hebridean Seas Cardigan.

PORTHMEOR GARDEN DIAGONAL WAISTCOAT

This design is a neat waistcoat that is rich in colour and peerie patterns. The colours chosen were those of a jewel-coloured summer flower border, with intricate traditional Fairisle patterns layered one on top of another.

The peerie stitch patterns used when knitting this sample are as follows: 3, 4, 6, 7, 11, 12, 13, 14, 15, 16, three with four stocking stitch rows in between each Fairisle pattern band. Fairisle Stitch Pattern 3 was used for the lower hem, arm and button bands.

Porthmeor Garden Waistcoat front view.

Materials

Finished weight 250g
A small amount of various colours ranging from Knoll Soft Donegal and Jamiesons of Shetland Spindrift Finished
5 Buttons

Measurements

Around underarm 96cm
Armhole depth 20cm
Length to shoulder 50cm

Tension

32 sts and 34 rows = 10cm
MT 8

Machines

Suitable for standard gauge punchcard and electronic machines

Method

RIGHT BACK

Cast on 3 sts and knit 4 rows.

Inc 1 st each end of every row, until 117 sts RC 61.

Side seam is on the right, centre back seam is on the left.

Dec 1 st on the back seam every row while shaping the armholes.

Dec 1 st on the side seam edge every row 6 times*. K 1 row.

Dec 1 st on next row * rep from * to *.

Continue to dec on back edge only until 83sts remain RC 84.

Inc 1 st on armhole edge every row and cont to dec on back seam until armhole measures 29cm. RC 118.

Shape Top

Dec 1 st on armhole edge every row and back seam until 2 sts remain. Cast off.

LEFT BACK

As for right back but reverse all shaping.

LEFT FRONT

Work as for left back until row 106. Continue armhole shaping as set.

On the front edge transfer 2 sts on to the next two Ns. Next row dec 1 st on the front edge. Rep the last 2 rows shaping the front until RC 118.

Shape Top

Dec 1 st on armhole and front edge every row until 2 sts remain; latch off.

RIGHT FRONT

Work as for left front, reversing shapings.

Join shoulder seams, and centre back seam.

ARMBANDS

MT T7. Cast on 130 sts and k the border patt of your choice. Pick up and k 1 row.

Pick up sts from the front and back pieces around armhole and k 1 row T8 and 1 row T10; latch off.

LEFT FRONT BAND

Rep. the border stitch patt as for

Garden Waistcoat back view.

armband but cast on 126 sts for front edge and 20 sts to centre back neck.

BUTTONBAND

Rep as for left band, but place 5 buttonholes from V shaping to lower edge of waistcoat.

MAKING UP

Join side seams. Sew in ends and sew on buttons.

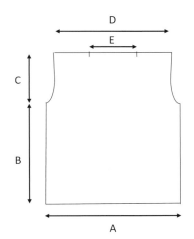

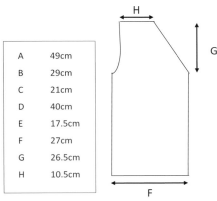

A	49cm
B	29cm
C	21cm
D	40cm
E	17.5cm
F	27cm
G	26.5cm
H	10.5cm

Diagram for Diagonal Waistcoat.

CHAPTER 10

WAISTCOATS

Waistcoats (or 'vests' in the USA) are sleeveless upper body garments. The waistcoat was first worn in Persia and brought back to England by the explorer Sir Robert Shirley who had seen Shah Abbas the Great wearing one at court. It was later adopted by King Charles II of England as part of correct dress for men to wear at court. The French word for a waistcoat is gilet, and this has now come into common use in the English-speaking world – the word 'gilet' being derived from the Turkish word yelek, which means a waistcoat or sleeveless jacket.

After the Great Fire of London in 1666 it was thought that to wear more sober dress would fit in with the country's mood. The early waistcoats were knee length and tightly fitting to wear under a coat, but by the 1700s waistcoats had become shorter, and the skirts cut away at the front for sporting purposes. They were now lavishly embroidered, and pockets were introduced with small flaps.

By the 1800s they became a fashionable feature in a gentleman's wardrobe and were no longer to be hidden under a coat but required to be ostentatious and flamboyant. No holds were barred – single or double breasted, waist length, stand-up collar, lapels, round cut, square cut and flaps of various shapes were all available. Dandies took to wearing two at a time, one buttoned and the other undone –

Diamond Slipover.

Queen Victoria's husband Albert favoured a tight-fitting short waistcoat. However, this fashion passed, and by the mid-nineteenth century they were worn as part of a suit and lost their status as being only for rich and wealthy owners.

During the nineteenth century they became such a staple garment that not wearing one indicated that you were too poor to buy one. However, by the early twentieth century suits became more unstructured, and waistcoats were no longer needed as men started to wear wrist watches, and the waistcoat was no longer needed to carry a pocket watch. Nevertheless they were a useful garment, so never went totally out of fashion.

In the 1960s the waistcoat was adopted and customized by their owners, and 'Teddyboys' wore them as a fashion accessory. At the other end of the scale they still held their place as conservative attire worn with a three-piece suit.

Other names for the waistcoat-shaped garment without buttons are slipover, which is designed to be slipped over the head; sleeveless pullover; or tank top.

During the 1912 Stockholm Olympic Games, twenty-seven female swimmers were deemed immodest by the press and some spectators for wearing one-piece sleeveless bathing costumes. Swimming pools were then known as 'tanks', and the costumes were called 'tank suits', and they were the only practical swimming garment available at the time that gave free movement of the swimmer's arms. The costumes they wore were very similar to modern-day tank tops, but with an added piece that resembled shorts to cover the top half of the thighs. The 'tank top' is named after these 'tank suits', and are buttonless, collarless and pocketless.

During the 1930s and 1940s, tank tops were often seen worn by men (usually villains) in American movies; in the early 1950s Marlon Brando wore a tank top when starring as Stanley Kowalski in A Streetcar Named Desire. In the 1970s both men and women wore brightly coloured hippy tank tops teamed up with bell-bottom trousers. The 1990s saw the rise of the simple fashion trend that has continued into the present day – a tank top and a pair of jeans. Today they have developed into strappy tops, cropped to show the midriff, and are now very much a sportswear staple.

Tank tops, sleeveless pullovers, slipovers and waistcoats are practical garments to wear because they fit under coats and jackets, adding an extra layer of warmth whilst not restricting body and arm movement. The shape is versatile – it can be long, short, buttoned or unbuttoned. They can complement a dull outfit, can be tailored for a tight fit, or made loose and baggy.

A sweater pattern can easily be altered to make a waistcoat, a sleeveless pullover or a tank top by removing the sleeves. The overall shape required is narrow on the shoulders, so the armhole needs to be larger than for a sweater or cardigan – at least 5cm deeper and more stitches cast off or decreased when shaping the armhole.

An alternative way is to design wide shoulders where the armhole is still deeper but the shaping decease is less – see the Sunset Sky Boxy Slipover as an example of this. The shoulder sits between 3cm and 4cm over the shoulder and down the top of the arm.

V-NECK DIAMOND SLEEVELESS PULLOVER

The image shows the smaller size V-neck sleeveless pullover knitted using the Diamond stitch pattern and Knoll Soft Donegal and Jamiesons of Shetland Spindrift wool and cashmere in a 4-ply weight. There are no stocking-stitch rows as this is an all-over pattern, and as such the overall feel of the garment is firm and not stretchy.

The ribs edgings are knitted using the E wrap braid cast on. Using three ends of contrasting yarn E wrap left to right

Diamond stitch pattern knitted examples.

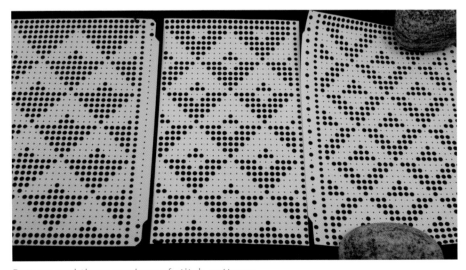

Pattern and three versions of stitch patterns.

and right to left, knit one row, and start the Fairisle rib stitch pattern XOXOXOXOXOXO with the colour in Feeder 1 remaining the same, while the colours in Feeder 2 change every two rows for twelve rows. The tension for the edging is MT-1. Continue to work the Diamond Fairisle stitch pattern as set out.

The armbands and neckband are worked in the same way. Knit one row using a contrasting colour, then remove from the machine using waste yarn, turn round and pick the stitches back up on to the machine. Pick up the stitches from the armhole, knit one row and cast off. The neck rib band was knitted in one piece, and four stitches decreased each end for the front V shaping. Start by picking up the right side of the neck and across the back neck. Place the rest of the needles into HP and knit one row and cast off. Pick up the remaining stitches and continue as before.

The three stitch patterns below illustrate how the Diamond pattern can be altered to make the colour distribution more even. The version used here is sharp and bright with endless colour choice possibilities. The static geometric shape of the diamond appears to swing back and forth across the fabric. The V neck can be altered to start lower down for a more casual look.

Method (Medium Size)

BACK
Cast on 161 sts and either work a 1 x 1 rib for 18 rows or a hem of your choice. RC 000.

Work in patt for 134 rows.

Armhole Shaping
Cast off at the beg of each row 8 sts twice, 6 sts twice, 4 sts twice, 3 sts twice, 2 sts 4 times (25 sts).

Work to RC 220.

Shoulder Shaping
Set carriage to hold and place 7 Ns 4 times into HP and 6 Ns 4 times (26 Ns) for each shoulder. 58 sts rem.

Place each of the two shoulder sections and the back of the neck on to separate lengths of WY.

FRONT
Cast on 161 sts. Rep the same rib or hem choice as the back.

Patt to RC 134.

Armhole Shaping
Rep as for back, at the same time divide for the right or left side, not forgetting to note the row of the patt being used. Place the side not being worked on into HP.

Shape neck edge by dec 1 st on the next row and foll third row until 26 sts rem.

Cont to RC 220. Shape shoulder as back.

Rep to complete the rem side of the sleeveless pullover.

Join shoulders by placing right sides together, k 1 row MT+2 and latch off.

ARMBANDS
Either work a 1 x 1 rib or a smaller hem pattern approx 10 rows in length. 184 sts for a rib but less for a double hem as it will need to be slightly stretched.

Pick up the stitches from the front and back of the waistcoat armhole. K 1 row MT+1 and latch off.

NECKBAND
Approx 186 sts inc 3 sts evenly at each end to mitre the front V. Complete as armband. Pick up the back neck and one front neck section, k 1 row MT+1 and latch off. Pick up the final front

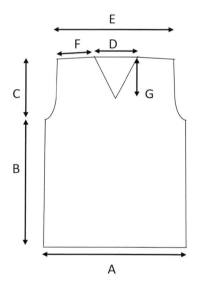

Diagram for V-Neck Sleeveless Pullover.

Materials
Finished weight 250g
Various amounts of colours of your choice. Sample uses Knoll Soft Donegal and Jamiesons of Shetland Spindrift

Measurements
Around chest 86cm, 104cm
Length to shoulder 54cm, 73cm

Tension
33 sts and 36 rows = 10cm
Approx MT 8

Machines
Suitable for standard gauge punchcard and electronic machines

	Small	Medium
A	42cm	52cm
B	29.5cm	39cm
C	24cm	34cm
D	16cm	18cm
E	37cm	47cm
F	10.5cm	11cm
G	18cm	25cm

neck section and k row MT+1 and latch off.

Sew down side seams and join bands. The small size was adapted from the medium-size patt by casting on 130 sts and working to 102 rows before commencing the arm-hole shaping, casting off 6 sts twice, 5 sts twice, 4 sts twice, 2 sts twice and 1 st twice (19 sts). Shape shoulder on RC 180 placing 6 Ns into HP three times, and 5 Ns once. Remove from machine on to WY.

The front is worked as for the back to RC 114 to neck shaping. Dec 1 st on the neck edge every 3rd row until 23 sts rem. Cont as back.

PAISLEY WAISTCOAT

Several stitch patterns were used when designing this front-button waistcoat. The lower hem border is the simple peerie Fairisle Stitch Pattern 3. This was followed by the Vertical Twist pattern, which needed careful colour coordination to enhance the twist, rather than it disappearing into the background, so darker colours in Feeder 1 were required and lighter tones in Feeder 2 with black and white contrast colours at the top.

The third pattern used was the deep Rams Horn Border, which is a formal stylized pattern. The chosen colours are shades of gold in Feeder 1 and highlights of red and cerise in Feeder 2.

The fourth stitch pattern is an adaptation of a Finish Rose pattern, which stands on its own perfectly as a motif.

The final pattern is a Paisley motif, which is worked from the armhole up to the shoulder. The background colours of the waistcoat change in the middle of each Paisley to add interest, and because I did not want any hard-line change of colours. Although each of the separate patterns are unrelated

Paisley Waistcoat.

Paisley Front-Button Waistcoat.

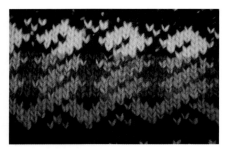

Vertical Twist Fairisle stitch-pattern detail.

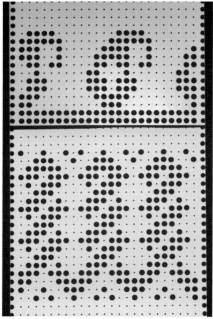

Vertical Twist and Paisley motif stitch pattern.

Materials
Weight when finished: 300g
Various colours Knoll Soft Donegal and Jamiesons of Shetland Spindrift in oil
5 buttons

Measurements
Around chest 102cm
Length to shoulder 58cm

Tension
34 sts – 36 rows = 10cm over Fairisle pattern
MT 8

Machines
Suitable for standard gauge punchcard and electronic machines

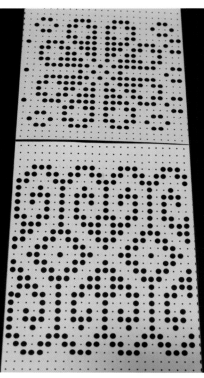

Top to bottom: Finish Rose and Rams Horn border pattern.

they all work together. There are plain stocking-stitch rows knitted between each stitch-pattern band ranging from four to eight rows, so the overall fabric is light and drapes well. The Paisley motif is decorated with Swiss Darning over the middle stitches to add more depth to the pattern.

Decide which ribs or hems to use – the sample shows the small four-row peerie Fairisle Stitch Pattern 3, which I prefer to using a rib, but you need to choose what works best for the pattern you are knitting. For the lower hem note that the stocking-stitch rows are knitted, and then the stitch-pattern rows, so that the Fairisle is the right way round. However, when working the armbands and front bands, start with the Fairisle pattern and complete with the stocking-stitch rows so when picked up, the Fairisle pattern is facing the correct way.

Method
BACK
MT-1 cast on 160 sts and work either a 10-row 1 x 1 rib or 18-row hem peerie Fairisle Stitch Pattern 3.
MT RC 000. Work in chosen patt for 100 rows.

Shape Armholes
Cast off at beg of each row 8 sts twice, 6 sts twice, 3 sts four times and 1 st eight times.
Cont to RC 186.

Shape Shoulder
Place the centre 40 Ns plus the right or left side you are not working on into HP; set carriage to hold and work each side separately. Dec 1 st on the neck edge at the beg of the next 3 rows, and 11 Ns three times HP. K the shoulder sts on to WY and remove from machine. K the centre 40 sts on to WY and remove from the machine.

Rep for the second side reversing shaping.

RIGHT FRONT
Cast on 80 sts and work the rib or hem as for the back.
RC 000 k in pattern to RC 60.

Start Neck Shaping
Dec 1 st at the front edge every 5th row until 23 sts have been dec.
Cont in patt to RC 100.

Shape Armholes
Rep as for right side of back.
Cont to patt RC 186.
Shoulder shaping place 11 Ns into HP on the next 3 alt rows. K the shoulder sts on to WY and remove from the machine.

JOIN THE SHOULDERS
Place the front and back shoulder sts on to the corresponding Ns, k 1 row MT+2 and latch off.

ARMBANDS
Bring forward 150 Ns to WP and cast on using WY, change to MY, work approx 18 row peerie pattern double hem or 1 x 1 rib.
Pick up sts from front and back of waistcoat and k 1 row MT+2, and latch off.

LEFT FRONT BUTTONBAND AND

BACK NECK
Approx 185 sts (50 sts across back neck, 135 sts front left band), and work 10-row rib or 18-row peerie pattern.

RIGHT BUTTONHOLE BAND
Approx 135 sts placing 5 buttonholes from the bottom edge to the start of the V shaping. Rep as button band.

The size can easily be altered – for example for a small size cast on 154 sts and the waistcoat will have narrower shoulders, or cast on 170 sts for a large size and decrease the extra stitches at the armholes.

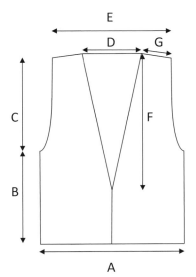

	Medium
A	51cm
B	30.5cm
C	28cm
D	21cm
E	43cm
F	32.5cm
G	14cm

Diagram for Paisley Waistcoat.

WOOD VIOLET WAISTCOAT

Using the same Basic Pattern and working the Wood Violet stitch patterns from the panel cardigan in Chapter 4, a completely different style emerges.

The 1 x 1 bottom rib works through navy and violet colours, with an all-over Spider/Louse pattern (see the Fairisle Tweed Cardigan) placed next, followed by a few rows of stripes and a violet leaf and a further few rows of stripes. Complete three violet plants for the main part of the lower body. A few rows above the armhole shaping repeat the leaf sequence and work the rest of the piece using violet flower heads until the shoulder is reached.

Front view of Wood Violet Waistcoat.

Back view of Wood Violet Waistcoat.

SUNSET SKY BOXY SLIPOVER

Traditional Fairisle patterns are mixed in with a repeated floral scroll. Two peerie patterns and an E wrap braid cast-on rib are used for the edgings. The overall style is for a boxy bold, cropped slipover. This basic shape is very versatile and can be used to design an all-over cable pattern just by adding a few stitches to the width.

The Fairisle stitches in the versions of this pattern are worked in shades of orange, ochre and brown, with blue used as the predominant background colour. However, this is interspersed with dark charcoal, ruby and navy. Small colour variations make for a richer fabric by giving a depth and subtle variety to the overall look. The Floral Scroll pattern is not enclosed with a strong background colour, so appears more fluid and sits lightly and more organically on the surface of the fabric, whereas the Rams Horn stitch pattern has a definite deep band of colour.

When you play with the shapes and styles of the stitch patterns this can test your knowledge as to what will work well from a design viewpoint, and what will not. The more you play with shapes, styles and colours, the more you will learn. It is good practice to try some new ideas in your designs, so you build upon your current knowledge base, rather than remain static in your designs.

Fairisle Stitch Pattern 5 is used for the lower front and back hem, followed by Stitch Pattern 3. Next the Rams Horn border from the previous Paisley waistcoat, Floral Scroll, Stitch Pattern 19, Floral Scroll, Stitch Patterns 12 and 14, Floral Scroll, Rams Horn border, and finally Fairisle Stitch Pattern 5. Two stocking-stitch rows are worked between each stitch pattern.

The neckband is worked using Fairisle Stitch Pattern 1. The armbands are an E wrap braid cast on using two ends of yarn, and OXOXOXOXOXOX Fairisle rib with the colour in Feeder 1 unchanged, and the colours in Feeder 2 changing every two rows.

Sunset Sky Slipover.

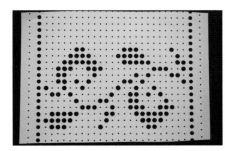

Scroll stitch pattern.

Materials

Finished weight 310g

Variety of colours depending on the chosen Fairisle patterns in Knoll Soft Donegal and Jamiesons of Shetland Spindrift in oil

Measurements

Around chest 102cm
Length to shoulder 48cm

Tension

31 sts – 38 rows = 10cm
MT 8

Machines

Suitable for standard gauge punchcard and electronic machines

Method

BACK

Cast on 164 sts and work bottom border or 1 x 1 rib. RC 000. Work Fairisle patt RC 80.

Armhole Shaping

Cast off 10 sts.

Cont to Fairisle patt to RC 179 and k centre 40 sts on to WY; remove from machine.

Work each side separately. On neck edge dec every foll 5 times at the same time place into HP on shoulder outside edge 11 sts once, 9 sts four times (47 sts). K on to WY, remove from machine.

FRONT

Rep as for back to RC 130.

Neck Shaping

K centre 16 sts on to WY and remove from machine. Work each side separately, dec 1 st on neck edge every foll alt row 17 times.

Cont to RC 179, shape shoulder as back.

Join 1 shoulder seam together by placing right sides together on the knitting machine and picking up the corresponding sts. K 1 row MT+1 and latch off.

NECKBAND

50 sts across back neck, 30 sts down left front, 16 sts centre, 30 sts right front (126 sts).

Cast on and work your chosen border patt or rib. With wrong side facing pick up sts around neck. K 1 row MT+2 and latch off.

Join final shoulder seam.

ARMBANDS

Cast on 110 sts and work your chosen patt or rib, which must be 3cm as this is the depth that needs to fit into the cast-off sts at the armhole. Pick up the front and back on to the Ns and k 1 row MT +2 and latch off. Rep for second side.

MAKING UP

Sew together side seams and join the bottom of the armbands to the armhole cast-off edge.

To k a larger size, cast on 184 sts and incorporate the extra sts into the neck and shoulder shaping.

Boxy Slipover, detail of neckband and armbands.

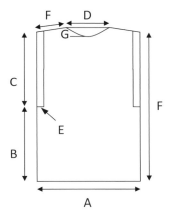

Diagram for Boxy Fairisle Slipover.

		Medium
A		51cm
B		25cm
C		22.5cm
D		20.5cm
E		3.5cm
F		19cm
G		10.5cm

HEATHER FELTED WAISTCOAT

The colours of a Scottish heather moorland are the inspiration for the colours in this waistcoat. The shawl collar is secured with a pin, and the overall shape is boxy. Knitted sideways, this is an easy pattern to follow and to adapt for larger sizes.

The chosen traditional Fairisle stitch patterns are either border or peerie. There are three stocking-stitch rows either side of each Fairisle band. Nine bands were knitted and repeated so they matched at the shoulder seam. A larger band was worked at the centre back for the neck. The Fairisle stitch patterns used in the sample were 20, 3, 4, 5, 6, 7, 11, 12 and 13, and this sequence was reversed for the back to shoulder match. The centre back Fairisle stitch patterns are 3, 19 and 3.

The design is worked in a mixture of yarns to include cashmere, silk and wool. The collar is completed using three ends of fine eco-silk, cashmere, and fine variegated wool.

The garment was placed in the washing machine for 60 minutes, at 40 degrees and 800 spin speed in order for it to felt. It is vital to make a swatch and to felt it before starting to knit. The shrinkage when mixing yarns together must be known if a disaster is to be avoided.

Heather Felted Waistcoat.

Materials
Finished weight 370g
Various colours of your choice

Measurements
Around chest 116cm
Length to shoulder 48cm after felting

Tension
26 sts and 54 rows after felting.
MT 8

Machines
Suitable for standard gauge punchcard and electronic machines

Heather Fairisle before felting.

Method

BASIC PATTERN
E wrap cast on 160 sts using 3 ends of fine yarn. K in st st RC 60.

SHAPE COLLAR
RHS cast off 20 sts and start Fairisle stitch-pattern bands, k 120 rows. RC 180.

SHAPE ARMHOLE
Cast off 70 sts at R. Cast on again over 70 Ns.
  Back k 260 rows RC 440.

SHAPE SECOND ARMHOLE
Cast off 70 sts at R, cast on again over 70 Ns.
  K 120 rows, RC 560.

Heather Fairisle after felting.

SHAPE COLLAR

Cast on 20 sts at RC 160 sts. K 60 rows RC 620 and cast off.

MAKING UP

Join matched shoulder seams, join centre back of collar and sew into place.

Machine wash at 40 degrees, 800 spin speed for 60 minutes. Pull firmly into shape while garment is still damp and malleable. Firm steam press when dry.

BLUE MOON WAISTCOAT

The same Basic Pattern can be used for a variety of stitch patterns. The Blue Moon Waistcoat shows a tuck-stitch version. The collar is worked as before using three ends of a variety of yarns to include wool, eco silk, cotton and linen. It is worth noting that the finished waistcoat weighs less than the previous waistcoat, 270g, because it is worked in tuck stitch and not Fairisle. It also has a lighter feel.

The tuck-stitch bands are all worked using cashmere, and 6 stocking stitch rows worked either side of each tuck-stitch Moon. The stitch pattern is XOOOOOOOXOOOOOOO, tucking for four rows and changing colour, tucking for a further four rows and resuming stocking stitch in MY for six rows.

Once again check your tension swatch carefully after felting, as different sources of cashmere and wool felt more firmly than others.

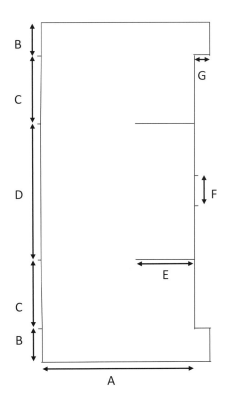

Diagram for Fairisle Felted Waistcoat.

A	50cm
B	12cm
C	24.5cm
D	60cm
E	21cm
F	11cm
G	6cm

Blue Moon Waistcoat.

Back view.

SHAWL COLLAR
WOODLAND WAISTCOAT

The Shawl Collar Waistcoat is an adaptation of the Shawl Collar Jacket in the previous chapter. The armholes are made larger and the shoulders narrower. The overall length was also shortened and the pockets made smaller. The hem was worked with a change of colour when working Stitch Pattern 3.

A small diamond Fairisle stitch pattern was knitted up to the armhole, and various traditional Fairisle stitch patterns worked with four stocking-stitch rows between each band. The stitch patterns featured in the

Woodland Waistcoat are 20, 19, 15, 20, 19 and 27, and for the back of the collar 20 and 5.

Method
BACK
Bring forward 160 sts to WP and cast on using WY. K a few rows and change to col MT -1 k 16 rows MT +2 k 1 row, k 7 rows and work Stitch Pattern 3, complete the hem rows RC 32, pick up hem and MT k 1 row. RC 000. Work the chosen Fairisle pattern to RC 50, inc 1 st each end of every 6th row eight times. 172 sts. RC 112.

Materials
Finished weight 500g

A variety of cols as required using Knoll Soft Donegal and Jamiesons of Shetland Spindrift in oil 6 buttons

Measurements
Around chest 114cm
Length from shoulder to hem 58cm

Tension
32 sts – 38 rows = 10cm over Fairisle
Approx MT 7•

Machines
Suitable for standard gauge punchcard and electronic machines

Shape Armhole
Cast off 14 sts at beg of next 2 rows. Work chosen Fairisle bands at the same time dec 1 st on the armhole edge each alt row until 20 sts have been cast off or dec at each armhole. Cont in patt to RC 220. K on to WY.

POCKET LININGS (MAKE 2)
Bring forward 20 sts to WP and k a few rows WY, change to MY and k 50 rows. K a few rows WY and remove from machine.

LEFT FRONT
Bring forward 82 sts to WP and cast on using WY. Change to col complete hem as back to RC 16, RHS E wrap cast on 32 sts and complete hem. Work to RC 50 and place pocket 28 sts from the LH side edge, cont to RC 100 inc 1 st RHS at the beg of the next row and every alt row. RC 112.

Shape armhole as back cont to inc on RHS as set. 145 sts. RC 220.

Shoulder
Bring forward 100 sts for collar on RHS and place into HP.

Place 45 sts from the back on to the

Shawl Collar Woodland Waistcoat.

Back of Shawl Collar Woodland Waistcoat.

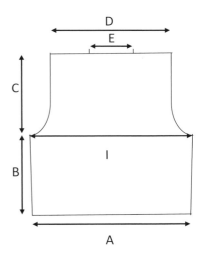

corresponding shoulder sts. K 1 row MT
+ and latch off.

Cont to work on collar sts for 28 rows
and cast off.

RIGHT FRONT

Rep as left front reversing all shaping.
Place the bottom buttonhole 5 rows up
from the bottom and evenly space a
further 5 buttonholes into the front, the
final one on RC 110.

Join right and left collar, cast off
edges together. Fold collar in half and
sew to the back neck.

ARMBANDS

Bring forward 160 NS to WP and k a
few rows WY, change to MY, MT -1 and
k 5 rows, MT k 1 row, MT-1 k 5 rows
and pick up hem, k 1 row MT and pick

up sts around armhole of front and
back pieces. K 1 row MT+2 and latch
off.

Rep for second band.

Fold the facings at the lower edge
and sew into place. Neaten
buttonholes. Sew down pocket and k 6
rows 1 x 1 rib for the pocket top. Sew
on buttons.

A	56cm
B	28cm
C	29cm
D	43.5cm
E	15.5cm
F	30cm
G	28cm
H	16.5cm
I	57cm

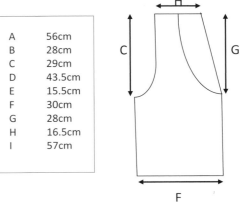

Diagram for Shawl Collar Waistcoat.

CHAPTER 11

CHILDREN'S KNITWEAR

There is something gorgeous about a child wearing an original and custom-made knitted cardigan or sweater. The basic T shape is easy to work and can be adapted using various yarns and stitch patterns. The ribs can be a simple k1, p1 or the textured moss stitch, to add variety. Ribs can be worked either with the use of a garter bar or ribbing attachment, or knitted by hand and the stitches picked up on the machine.

Materials
Approx weights:
Knoll Soft Donegal
Sizes 1 and 2: 200g; sizes 3 and 4; sizes 5 and 6: 350g
2.25mm needles

Measurements
See diagram

Approximate age size:
Size 1: 6–12 months
Size 2: 1–2 years
Size 3: 3–4 years
Size 4: 4–5 years
Size 5: 6–7 years
Size 6: 8–9 years

Tension
26 sts and 40 rows = 10cm over st st
MT 7

Machines
Suitable for standard gauge punchcard and electronic machines

CHILDREN'S BASIC BLOCK

The basic block can be used as a guide to knit a variety of sweaters using either one colour or a variety of stripes. With very little alteration to the instructions the design can be lengthened or shortened, or width added.

Aqua Jumper knitted using Knoll Soft Donegal Shade 5572 Vichy.

Method

BACK
Using MY, cast on 68, 70, 78, 84, 106, 114 sts and work 3, 4, 4, 4, 5, 6cm in moss stitch or k1, p1 rib. K the rib on to WY and pick up the sts back on to the machine increasing evenly across the row to 74, 80, 84, 96, 112, 122 sts.

RC 000.
K 56, 70, 70, 92, 102, 112 rows.

Shape Armholes
Cast off 4, 4, 4, 4, 4, 4 at the beg of the next 2 rows.

For the largest size cast off 2 sts at the beg of the next 2 rows: 66, 72, 76, 88, 104, 110 sts remain.

* Knit a further 50, 56, 56, 56, 68, 70 rows.
RC 108, 128, 128, 146, 174, 184.

Shape Shoulders and Neck
Sizes 1, 2, 3, 4:
K centre 36, 36, 36, 46 sts on to WY and remove from machine.

Working each side separately, k 15, 18, 20, 21 sts on to WY for each shoulder; remove from machine.
Sizes 5, 6:
K centre 48, 50 sts on to WY and remove from machine.

Work each side separately and set the carriage to hold, place 14, 15 Ns into HP. K 1 row.

Place rem 14, 15 Ns into HP and k a few rows on to WY; remove from machine.

Complete the second side.

FRONT
Work as for back to *.
K 36, 36, 36, 34, 46, 48 rows.
RC 94, 108, 108, 124, 152, 162.

Shape Neck
Sizes 1, 2, 3, 4:
K centre 16, 18, 20, 20 sts on to WY.

Work each side separately. Cast off at neck edge on the next and foll alt rows.

5 sts once, 4 sts twice, 4 sts once, 4 sts three times.
2 sts once, 0 sts, 3 sts once, 1 st once.
1 st three times, 1 st once, 1 st once, 0 sts.

Rem sts 15, 18, 20, 21.
Work to RC 108, 128, 128, 146 and k the rem sts on to WY; remove from

machine. Rep for second side.

Sizes 5 and 6:
Knit centre 18, 20 sts on to WY.

Work each side separately, cast off at the neck edge on the next and foll alt rows.

4 sts three times, 2 sts once and 1 st once.

Sts remaining 28, 30.
K to rows 174, 184.

Shape Shoulders
Place 14, 15 Ns into HP, k 1 row, k all sts off on to WY and remove from machine.

SLEEVES
Cast on 32, 32, 44, 44, 46, 52 sts and work the required rib as same as the back.

Place on to WY and inc sts 6, 6, 0, 0, 2, 2 as the rib is picked back up on to the machine.

Total sts 38, 38, 44, 44, 48, 54.
RC 000. K 48, 52, 76, 88, 98, 110 rows and at the same time inc 1 st at each end of every 3rd row until 68, 78, 68, 68, 72, 78 sts.

Sizes 3, 4, 5, 6:
Inc 1 st at each end of every 4th row until 78, 78, 86, 94 sts.

Top of Sleeve
Size 1:
Cast off 4 sts at the beginning of the next 8 rows, cast off rem sts.
Sizes 2, 3, 4:
Cast off at the beg of the next 14 rows 5 sts twice, 4 sts six times, 5 sts six times. Cast off the rem sts.
Sizes 5, 6:
Cast off at the beg of the next 14 rows 6 sts twice, 4 sts ten times. Cast off the rem sts.

NECKBAND
Cast on 86, 100, 102, 110, 112, 116 sts

and work 3cm of rib or moss st.

Pick up the sts or transfer to the machine and k 1 row.

Pick up sts around the sweater neck as follows:
Side neck 17, 23, 23, 22, 23, 23 sts between WY from centre neck 16, 18, 20, 20 18, 20.

Side of neck 17, 23, 23, 22, 23, 23 and across back neck 36, 36, 36, 46, 48, 50.

MT k 1 row, MT+2 k 1 row and latch off loosely.

MAKING UP
Join shoulder seams with right sides together k 1 row MT+ 2 and latch off with wrong sides together with the join seam showing on the outside of the garment.

Set sleeve into armhole. Sew side and sleeve seams together.

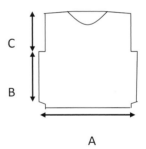

	Size 1	Size 2	Size 3	Size 4	Size 5	Size 6
A	28cm	30cm	32cm	37cm	43cm	47cm
B	17cm	20cm	20cm	26cm	30cm	33cm
C	14cm	15cm	15cm	16cm	17cm	18cm
D	15cm	16cm	22cm	25cm	29cm	30cm

Diagram for children's basic block.

GREY STRIPED SWEATER

The basic pattern can be worked in a variety of stripes. The sweater pictured is worked in ten-row stripes.

The materials used for the Striped Sweater are Knoll Soft Donegal shades 5511 Unshin, 5509 Greese and 5529 Eske. The ribs are k1, p1, cast on using Unshin, k 1 row, Greese k 2 rows, and the remainder of the rib using Eske. Follow the basic block to complete the jumper.

CLOVER PLAIN CARDIGAN

The basic block can be used to make a plain cardigan. The back and sleeves remain the same, and the fronts are approximately half the number of stitches for the back. The front band rib/edging stitches are added, and after the rib/edging is worked, they are placed on a pin to be picked up and the band completed in due course.

Method

LEFT FRONT
Push 42, 43, 47, 50, 61, 65 Ns to WP and work the chosen rib, or hand knit a moss stitch edging 3, 4, 4, 4, 5, 6cm. Wrong side facing, place 8 sts on the right on to a holding needle, for the button band. K off machine on to WY.

Inc row.

Pick up sts inc to 37, 40, 42, 48, 56, 61 sts RC 000.

K to RC 56, 70, 70, 92, 102, 112 rows.

Shape Armholes
Cast off 4, 4, 4, 4, 4, 4 sts at the armhole edge.

For the largest size cast off 2 sts at the beg of the foll two alt rows.

Rem sts 33, 36, 38, 44, 52, 53.

Work to RC 94, 108, 108, 124, 150, 166.

Shape Front Neck
Sizes 1, 2, 3, 4:

Cast off at neck edge on the next and foll alt rows.

8, 9, 10 10 sts once.

5 sts once, 4 sts twice, 4 sts once, 4

Grey Striped Sweater.

Cressida wearing Clover Plain Cardigan.

sts three times.
2 sts once, 0 sts, 3 sts once, 1 st once.
1 st three times, 1 st once, 1 st once, 0 sts.
Rem sts 15, 18, 20, 21. Work to RC 108, 128, 128, 146 and k the rem sts on to WY; remove from machine.

Sizes 5 and 6:
Cast off at the neck edge on the next and foll alt rows.
9 sts once, 10 sts once.
4 sts three times, 2 sts once and 1 st once.
Rem sts 28, 30.
Work to RC 174, 184.

Shape Shoulders
Place 14, 15 Ns into HP, k 1 row, k all sts off on to WY and remove from machine.
Join shoulder seams by picking up the appropriate sts on the machine, k 1 row MT+2 and latch off.

RIGHT FRONT
Rep as for left front, reversing all shaping.

BUTTON BANDS
Pick up the 8 sts held on the pin and cont to knit in chosen pattern to top of neck shaping. Place sts on pin.
Pick up the 8 sts placing buttonholes evenly along the band, note the top buttonhole is placed in the neck band. Work to the top of neck shaping and pick up sts around the neck edge, including the sts from the rem front. Work the rib/edging placing a buttonhole in the appropriate place. K the required length and cast off.

MAKING UP
Set the sleeves into the armholes and sew up sleeve and side seam. Join the bands to the front edge. Sew in ends and sew on buttons.

CHILDREN'S FAIRISLE BASIC BLOCK

Babies and children's heads are large in proportion to their body compared to those of adults, so I make fairly generous neck holes so the child will not be traumatized by pulling and yanking a too small sweater neck hole over their head. If a tighter neck is required then one of the shoulders can be left open, and a placket knitted on either side, one with buttonholes placed for a side opening.

Ribs can be worked either with the use of a garter bar or ribbing attachment, or hand knitted and picked up on the machine.

The shoulder stitches can either be cast off and sewn together right sides facing, or using HP, knitted on to WY and joined together by picking up two sides, knitting one row across both sets of stitches and cast off. Or you can knit the shoulder stitches on to WY on the back, and when the front is completed you will need to pick up the back shoulder stitches on to one of the fronts, knit 1 row T10 and latch off. The

seam stitches will be on the outside.

Use the basic block and work with stitch patterns of your choice to fit with the stitch and row instructions. I have detailed some of the colourways I have

Fairisle children's knitwear.

Fairisle band colour variations.

Materials
Knoll Soft Donegal and Jamiesons of Shetland Spindrift: small amounts of yarn in a variety of chosen colours, finished weight 230g, 250g, 300g, 450g

Measurements
Approximate age size:
Size 1: ages 1–2
Size 2: ages 3–4
Size 3: ages 5–6
Size 4: ages 8–9
See diagram

Tension
30 sts and 39 rows = 10cm over pattern and washed
MT 8 for the main body
MT 7 for the ribs

Machines
Suitable for standard gauge punchcard and electronic machines

used below, but they are all interchangeable. The colourways of the stitch patterns do not need to match front and back, so you can be innovative and change some or all of them. If the same stitch patterns are used, try changing the colours of some of them; an example of this is shown below – it does add interest to the garment and creates a bit of variety and fun.

Method
BACK
Cast on 88, 96, 126, 126 sts for a 1 x 1 rib and work 18 rows, about 6cm.

K rib on to WY, pick up on the machine increasing evenly across the row to 96, 108, 134, 140 sts.

Work in your chosen Fairisle pattern for 92, 104, 116, 132 rows.

Approx measurement from beginning 23, 26, 29, 33cm.

Shape Armhole
Cast off 5, 5, 5 ,6 sts at the beg of the next 2 rows.

86, 98, 124, 128 sts remain.

Cont to k without shaping to rows 148, 160, 180, 200.

Shape Shoulder
Cast off 10, 12, 18, 18 sts at the beg of the next 2 rows.

Cast off 12, 13, 18, 19 sts at the beg of the next 2 rows.

Rem sts 42, 48, 52, 54.

K the rem centre sts on to WY.

FRONT
Work as for back until rows 132, 144, 164, 184.

Approx measurements from beginning 33, 36, 41, 46cm.

Shape Front and Back Neck
Work each side separately. Place centre 24, 28, 28, 28, sts on to WY.

Cast off on the neck edge 5, 5, 5, 5 sts.

K 1 row.

Cast off 4, 4, 4, 4 sts on neck edge.

K 1 row.

Cast off 0, 1, 2, 2 sts on neck edge.

K 1 row.

Cast off 0, 0, 1, 2 sts on neck edge.

Sts remain 22, 25, 36, 37. Cont until front measures the same as the back and work shoulder shaping as specified on back.

SLEEVE
Cast on 46, 46, 54, 56 sts and work 1 x 1 rib 18 rows approx 6cm.

K on to WY and pick up again increasing evenly across the row to 50, 50, 60, 62 sts.

MT 8. Working in Fairisle, inc each end of every row until 90, 90, 102, 106 sts.

Continue without shaping until RC 88, 96, 112, 128.

Shape Top of Sleeve
Cast off 4, 4, 5, 6 sts at the beg of the next 10, 10, 10, 4 rows.

For the larger size only cast off 5 sts at the beg of the next 6 rows.

Cast off the rem 50, 50, 52, 52 sts.

NECKBAND
Cast on 108, 116, 120, 132 sts and work a 1 x 1 rib. Work approx 4cm 8

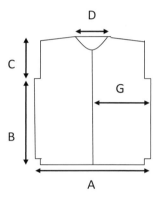

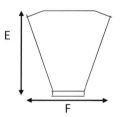

Diagram for the children's Fairisle basic block.

	Caspar Size 1	Storm Size 2	Autumn Size 3	Heather Size 4
A	29cm	36.5cm	38cm	46cm
B	27cm	27cm	28.5cm	42.5cm
C	13cm	14.5cm	15cm	21cm
D	13.5cm	16.5cm	18.5cm	19.5cm
E	28cm	26cm	37.5cm	42cm
F	28.5cm	33.5cm	30cm	40cm
G	14.5cm	18cm	19cm	23cm

rows and either place all sts on to the machine or transfer from the ribber, depending how you have worked the ribs.

K 1 row and with wrong side facing, pick up the sts from the main body of the jumper as follows: left side front 21, 20, 20, 25 sts, centre front sts from WY 24, 28, 28, 28, from right side front 21, 20, 20, 25, and across back neck 42, 48, 52, 54.

K 1 row MT and 1 row MT+2 and latch off.

MAKING UP

Join second shoulder seam. Sew sleeve head into armhole. Sew side seam and sleeve seam together.

Lightly press, but do not press the ribs as this will flatten and stretch them.

CASPAR'S JUMPER

The soft colours of the sea on a summer's day were chosen as the inspiration for this sweater. I wanted to create a soft contrast between the

Caspar's Jumper, knitted size 1, showing the stitch detail.

Caspar's Jumper.

Materials
Knoll Soft Donegal and Jamiesons of Shetland Spindrift: small amounts of yarn in a variety of chosen colours, finished weight 230g, 250g, 300g, 450g

Measurements
Approximate age size:
Size 1: ages 1–2
Size 2: ages 3–4
Size 3: ages 5–6
Size 4: ages 8–9
See diagram

Tension
30 sts and 39 rows = 10cm over pattern and washed
MT 8 for the main body
MT 7 for the ribs

Machines
Suitable for standard gauge punchcard and electronic machines

shades with no one colour dominating. Two plain rows were knitted between each pattern change to create a more intense feel. Small pattern repeats and Fairisle stitch patterns were chosen – the ones in this jumper are 3, 4, 5, 6, 7, 11, 12, 13, 14, 15.

Table 11.1: Stitch and Colour Patterns for Caspar's Jumper

Table 11.1: *Continued*

Rows	Stitch Pattern	Pattern Setting	Feeder 1	Feeder 2
2		Knit	Gara	
2	3	Fairisle	Gara	Unshin
2	3	Fairisle	Boyne	Swilly
2		Knit	Boyne	
2	4	Fairisle	Boyne	Moy
1	4	Fairisle	Finn	Swilly
2	4	Fairisle	Gara	Moy
2		Knit	Gara	
2	5	Fairisle	Gara	Malone
2	5	Fairisle	Boyne	Finn
2	5	Fairisle	Silver	Vichy
2		Knit	Silver	
2	6	Fairisle	Silver	Finn
2	6	Fairisle	Swilly	Malone
2	6	Fairisle	Annalee	Finn
2		Knit	Annalee	
2	7	Fairisle	Annalee	Gara
3	7	Fairisle	Eske	Vichy
2	7	Fairisle	Annalee	Gara
2		Knit	Annalee	
3	11	Fairisle	Annalee	Boyne
3	11	Fairisle	Swilly	Vichy
3	11	Fairisle	Silver	Boyne
2		Knit	Silver	
3	12	Fairisle	Silver	Vichy
3	12	Fairisle	Swilly	Moy
3	12	Fairisle	Silver	Vichy
2		Knit	Silver	
3	13	Fairisle	Silver	Boyne
3	13	Fairisle	Swilly	Gara
3	13	Fairisle	Eske	Boyne
2		Knit	Eske	
2	14	Fairisle	Eske	Finn
2	14	Fairisle	Swilly	Malone
1	14	Fairisle	Gara	Vichy

Rows	Stitch Pattern	Pattern Setting	Feeder 1	Feeder 2
2	14	Fairisle	Swilly	Malone
2	14	Fairisle	Eske	Malone
2		Knit	Eske	
2	15	Fairisle	Eske	Unshin
3	15	Fairisle	Vichy	Unshin
1	15	Fairisle	Annalee	Malone
3	15	Fairisle	Vichy	Unshin
2	15	Fairisle	Moy	Unshin
2		Knit	Moy	
2	3	Fairisle	Moy	Boyne
2	3	Fairisle	Malone	Gara
2		Knit	Malone	
2	4	Fairisle	Malone	Finn
1	4	Fairisle	Swilly	Gara
2	4	Fairisle	Malone	Finn
2		Knit	Malone	
2	5	Fairisle	Malone	Unshin
2	5	Fairisle	Annalee	Boyne
2	5	Fairisle	Eske	Finn
2		Knit	Eske	
2	6	Fairisle	Eske	Vichy
2	6	Fairisle	Swilly	Moy
2	6	Fairisle	Eske	Vichy
2		Knit	Eske	
2	7	Fairisle	Eske	Gara
3	7	Fairisle	Swilly	Vichy
2	7	Fairisle	Eske	Gara
2		Knit	Eske	
3	11	Fairisle	Eske	Unshin
3	11	Fairisle	Swilly	Vichy
3	11	Fairisle	Eske	Unshin
2		Knit	Eske	
2	5	Fairisle	Eske	Vichy
2	5	Fairisle	Annalee	Malone
2	5	Fairisle	Eske	Gara

STORM JUMPER

Darker, deeper colours with highlights of bright green and peacock make up the colours of a boiling sea scape.

The yarns used were a combination of Knoll Soft Donegal and Jamiesons of Shetland Spindrift – any combination of yarn of the same weight can be used in the following colours: Bright Blue, Purple, Peacock, Mid Blue, Green, Turquoise, Charcoal, Pale Blue, Cream, Lime Green, Chestnut, Dark Brown, Pale Grey, Dark Purple, Yellow, Silver, Deep Blue and Dark Grey.

The ribs are striped in a k1, p1 rib; the colour sequence is as follows: cast on in Bright Blue and knit one row,

then two rows of each of the following colours: Purple, Peacock, Mid Blue, Turquoise, Green, Charcoal, Purple, Peacock and Mid Blue.

The neck rib colour sequence is Bright Blue, Purple, Peacock, Mid Blue, Green and Charcoal, and cast off in pattern.

Four plain rows are knitted between most of the patterns, and the background-coloured stripes add to the overall pattern and the colour changes after each Fairisle coloured band. It is easy to alter the length of the colour charts – either knit two plain rows or add six plain rows between the Fairisle bands.

Storm Jumper detail.

Table 11.2: Stitch Pattern and Colour Sequence for the Storm Jumper

Rows	Stitch Pattern	Pattern Setting	Feeder 1	Feeder 2
2		Knit	Mid Blue	
2	3	Fairisle	Mid Blue	Pale Blue
2	3	Fairisle	Purple	Cream
4		Knit	Purple	
2	4	Fairisle	Purple	Lime
1	4	Fairisle	Deep Blue	Chestnut
2	4	Fairisle	Brown	Lime
4		Knit	Brown	
2	5	Fairisle	Brown	Turquoise
2	5	Fairisle	Chestnut	Peacock
2	5	Fairisle	Deep Blue	Silver
4		Knit	Deep Blue	
2	6	Fairisle	Deep Blue	Pale Grey
2	6	Fairisle	Mid Blue	Cream
2	6	Fairisle	Dark Purple	Silver
4		Knit	Dark Purple	
2	7	Fairisle	Dark Purple	Chestnut
3	7	Fairisle	Brown	Turquoise
2	7	Fairisle	Dark Grey	Chestnut
4		Knit	Dark Grey	
3	11	Fairisle	Dark Grey	Yellow
3	11	Fairisle	Purple	Lime
3	11	Fairisle	Deep Blue	Yellow
4		Knit	Deep Blue	
3	12	Fairisle	Deep Blue	Peacock
3	12	Fairisle	Chestnut	Turquoise
3	12	Fairisle	Charcoal	Peacock

Table 11.2: *Continued*

Rows	Stitch Pattern	Pattern Setting	Feeder 1	Feeder 2
4		Knit	Charcoal	
3	13	Fairisle	Charcoal	Green
3	13	Fairisle	Yellow	Turquoise
3	13	Fairisle	Mid Blue	Green
4		Knit	Mid Blue	
2	14	Fairisle	Mid Blue	Cream
2	14	Fairisle	Deep Blue	Silver
1	14	Fairisle	Purple	Chestnut
2	14	Fairisle	Deep Blue	Silver
2	14	Fairisle	Mid Blue	Cream
4		Knit	Purple	
2	15	Fairisle	Purple	Peacock
3	15	Fairisle	Chestnut	Turquoise
1	15	Fairisle	Cream	Green
3	15	Fairisle	Chestnut	Turquoise
2	15	Fairisle	Deep Blue	Peacock
4		Knit	Deep Blue	
2	19	Fairisle	Deep Blue	Pale Blue
3	19	Fairisle	Silver	Green
3	19	Fairisle	Cream	Peacock
3	19	Fairisle	Silver	Green
2	19	Fairisle	Mid Blue	Pale Blue
4		Knit	Mid Blue	
2	3	Fairisle	Mid Blue	Pale Blue
2	3	Fairisle	Purple	Cream
4		Knit	Purple	

If you are making a larger size then add more Fairisle stitch patterns.

HIGHLAND HEATHER JUMPER

The Highland Heather Jumper is worked in pink, blue and green and is inspired by the Scottish glens covered with heather with the sea in the distance. Larger Fairisle patterns can be used as the sweater is larger and the design is capable of absorbing them.

Table 11.3 shows the stitch pattern settings and colour sequence for the Highland Heather Jumper.

Materials
Small amounts of Knoll Soft Donegal were used in the following shades: 5566 Fuchsia (cerise), 5536 Killalla (green), 5527 Roe (dark blue), 5507 Swilly (cream), 5572 Vichy (turquoise), 5515 Finn (mid blue), 5528 Beltra (greeny blue), 5564 Peacock (peacock), 5504 Annalee (pale grey blue), 5565 Deep Blue (deep blue), 5514 Glyde (navy), 5550 0'Byrne (lime green), 5535 Rea (pink), 5526 Liscannor (clover), 5511 Unshin (dark grey), 5508 Silver Mist (grey), 5532 Dariana (purple), 5520 Sheelin (charcoal), 5548 Malone (pale blue)

Two plain rows are knitted between the Fairisle stitch-pattern bands, and you may find it easier to punch the cards in the sequence you are going to use

The ribs are knitted in k 1, p 1 rib casting on using Fuchsia, and k 1 row, k 2 rows green and the remainder using Deep Blue

The sleeves work through the stitch charts, although the colours change in some instances as this is a useful device and adds interest and surprises to the design – try changing just the middle Feeder 2 rows, or blues to greens. For example, the Fairisle Stitch Pattern 22 at the top of the sleeve becomes the sequence as shown in Table 11.4.

Highland Heather Jumper.

Table 11.3: Stitch Pattern and Colour Sequence for the Highland Heather Jumper

Rows	Stitch Pattern	Pattern Setting	Feeder 1	Feeder 2
2		Knit	Roe	
3	18	Fairisle	Roe	Swilly
3	18	Fairisle	Finn	Vichy
3	18	Fairisle	Malone	Beltra
3	18	Fairisle	Annalee	Peacock
2		Knit	Annalee	
3	20	Fairisle	Annalee	Deep Blue
3	20	Fairisle	Cream	Glyde
1	20	Fairisle	Fuchsia	Dariana
3	20	Fairisle	Swilly	Glyde
3	20	Fairisle	Annalee	Deep Blue
2		Knit	Annalee	
1	2	Fairisle	Annalee	Fuschia
1	2	Fairisle	O'Byrne	Fuchsia
1	2	Fairisle	Roe	Fuchsia
2		Knit	Roe	
2	19	Fairisle	Roe	Swilly
3	19	Fairisle	Peacock	Rea
3	19	Fairisle	Vichy	Liscannor
3	19	Fairisle	Peacock	Rea
2	19	Fairisle	Roe	Swilly

Rows	Stitch Pattern	Pattern Setting	Feeder 1	Feeder 2
2		Knit	Roe	
2	5	Fairisle	Roe	Fuchsia
2	5	Fairisle	Unshin	Rea
2	5	Fairisle	Silver	Dariana
2		Knit	Silver	
3	21	Fairisle	Silver	Peacock
3	21	Fairisle	Unshin	Vichy
1	21	Fairisle	Sheelin	Killala
3	21	Fairisle	Unshin	Vichy
3	21	Fairisle	Silver	Peacock
2		Knit	silver	
2	5	Fairisle	Silver	Dariana
2	5	Fairisle	Unshin	Rea
2	5	Fairisle	Deep Blue	Fuchsia
2		Knit	Deep Blue	
3	17	Fairisle	Deep Blue	Killala
2	17	Fairisle	Peacock	O'Byrne
1	17	Fairisle	Dariana	Swilly
2	17	Fairisle	Peacock	O'Byrne
3	17	Fairisle	Deep Blue	Killala
2		Knit	Deep Blue	
2	14	Fairisle	Deep Blue	Swilly
2	14	Fairisle	Finn	Annalee
1	14	Fairisle	Unshin	Fuchsia
2	14	Fairisle	Finn	Annalee
2	14	Fairisle	Deep Blue	Cream
2		knit	Deep Blue	
3	8	Fairisle	Deep Blue	Killala
1	8	Fairisle	Sheelin	Rea
3	8	Fairisle	Dariana	Killala
2		Knit	Dariana	
3	22	Fairisle	Dariana	Silver
3	22	Fairisle	Liscannor	Unshin
1	22	Fairisle	Fuchsia	Sheelin
3	22	Fairisle	Liscannor	Unshin
3	22	Fairisle	Dariana	Silver
2		Knit	Dariana	
1	2	Fairisle	Dariana	Swilly
1	2	Fairisle	Sheelin	Swilly
1	2	Fairisle	Peacock	Swilly
2		Knit	Peacock	
3	17	Fairisle	Peacock	Swilly
2	17	Fairisle	Roe	Vichy
1	17	Fairisle	Sheelin	Killala
2	17	Fairisle	Roe	Vichy
3	17	Fairisle	Peacock	Swilly
2		Knit	Peacock	

Table 11.3: *Continued*

Rows	Stitch Pattern	Pattern Setting	Feeder 1	Feeder 2
2	3	Fairisle	Peacock	Dariana
2	3	Fairisle	Malone	Killala
2		Knit	Malone	
3	21	Fairisle	Malone	Glyde
3	21	Fairisle	Unshin	Swilly
1	21	Fairisle	O'Byrne	Fuchsia
3	21	Fairisle	Unshin	Swilly
3	21	Fairisle	Malone	Glyde
2		Knit	Malone	
2	3	Fairisle	Malone	Killala
2	3	Fairisle	Roe	Fuchsia
2		Knit	Roe	
7	9	Fairisle	Roe	Annalee
2		Knit	Roe	
2	3	Fairisle	Roe	Fuchsia
2	3	Fairisle	Finn	Peacock
2		Knit	Finn	
3	22	Fairisle	Finn	Swilly
3	22	Fairisle	Roe	Silver
1	22	Fairisle	Dariana	Killala
3	22	Fairisle	Roe	Silver
3	22	Fairisle	Finn	Swilly
2		Knit	Finn	
2	6	Fairisle	Finn	O'Byrne
2	6	Fairisle	Fuchsia	Killala
2	6	Fairisle	Vichy	O'Byrne
2		Knit	Vichy	
2	5	Fairisle	Vichy	Sheelin
2	5	Fairisle	Vichy	Dariana
2	5	Fairisle	Vichy	Killala
2		Knit	Vichy	

Table 11.4: Top of Sleeve Fairisle Stitch Pattern 22 Sequence

Rows	Stitch Pattern	Pattern Setting	Feeder 1	Feeder 2
2		Knit	Silver	
3	22	Fairisle	Silver	Peacock
3	22	Fairisle	Unshin	Vichy
1	22	Fairisle	Sheelin	Fuchsia
3	22	Fairisle	Unshin	Vichy
3	22	Fairisle	Silver	Peacock
2		Knit	Silver	

AUTUMN SWEATER

Method

The ribs are knitted in k1, p1 rib, casting on using Ochre and k 1 row, Gold k 2 rows; for the remainder of the rib use Dark Brown.

The neckband is knitted by casting on using Ochre k 1 row, Gold k 2 rows, Dark Brown k 6 rows, then transfer sts to the back bed. K 1 row Ochre and pick up the sts around the neck, joining at the shoulder; k 1 row MT + 2 and latch off.

K 2 st st rows between each Fairisle band.

Materials

A variety of spinner's yarns were used in this design. Although all are of similar weight, they range from Knoll Soft Donegal, Jamiesons of Shetland wool, through to cashmere – they were chosen purely for their colour

Small quantities of the following colours were used: Dark Brown, Ochre, Gold, Yellow, Olive, Dark Green, Green, Cream, Chestnut, Bright Blue, Mid Brown, Pale Grey, Dark Red and White

Wulfie wearing the Autumn Sweater.

Table 11.5: Autumn Jumper Stitch Pattern Chart and Colour Sequence

Table 11.5: Continued

Rows	Stitch Pattern	Pattern Setting	Feeder 1	Feeder 2
2		Knit	Dark Brown	
2	28	Fairisle	Chestnut	Dark Brown
1	28	Knit	Chestnut	
2	28	Fairisle	Gold	Chestnut
1	28	Knit	Gold	
2	28	Fairisle	Olive	Gold
1		Knit	Olive	
2	27	Fairisle	Olive	Pale Grey
3	27	Fairisle	Dark Green	Cream
1	27	Fairisle	Green	Chestnut
3	27	Fairisle	Dark Green	Cream
2	27	Fairisle	Olive	Pale Grey
1		Knit	Olive	
2	28	Fairislea	Gold	Olive
1	28	Knit	Gold	
2	28	Fairisle	Chestnut	Gold
1	28	Knit	Chestnut	
2	28	Fairisle	Dark Brown	Dark Red
3		Knit	Dark Brown	
3	8	Fairisle	Dark Brown	Olive
1	8	Fairisle	Dark Red	Bright Blue
3	8	Fairisle	Dark Brown	Olive
3		Knit	Dark Brown	
2	3	Fairisle	Dark Brown	Gold
2	3	Fairisle	Cream	Chestnut
3		Knit	Cream	
3	21	Fairisle	Cream	Dark Green
3	21	Fairisle	Mid Brown	Dark Brown
1	21	Fairisle	Yellow	Green
3	21	Fairisle	Mid Brown	Dark Brown
3	21	Fairisle	Cream	Dark Green
3		Knit	Cream	
2	5	Fairisle	Cream	Chestnut
2	5	Fairisle	White	Gold
2	5	Fairisle	Dark Green	Yellow
3		Knit	Dark Green	
3	17	Fairisle	Dark Green	Olive
2	17	Fairisle	Mid Brown	Green
1	17	Fairisle	Chestnut	Green
2	17	Fairisle	Mid Brown	Green
3	17	Fairisle	Dark Green	Olive
3		Knit	Dark Green	
2	5	Fairisle	Dark Green	Dark Red
2	5	Fairisle	Mid Brown	Yellow
2	5	Fairisle	Dark Red	Bright Blue
3		Knit	Dark Red	
3	22	Fairisle	Dark Red	Olive
3	22	Fairisle	Dark Brown	Cream
1	22	Fairisle	Green	Gold
3	22	Fairisle	Dark Brown	Cream
3	22	Fairisle	Dark Red	Olive
3		Knit	Dark Red	
2	4	Fairisle	Dark Red	Gold
1	4	Fairisle	Dark Brown	Bright Blue
2	4	Fairisle	Mid Brown	Gold
3		Knit	Mid Brown	
3	13	Fairisle	Mid Brown	Dark Brown
3	13	Fairisle	Green	Dark Green
3	13	Fairisle	Mid Brown	Dark Brown
3		Knit	Mid Brown	
3	12	Fairisle	Mid Brown	White
3	12	Fairisle	Gold	Bright Blue
3	12	Fairisle	Dark Brown	White
3		Knit	Dark Brown	

HEARTS FAIRISLE CARDIGAN

The basic sweater pattern can be altered to make a cardigan – the back and sleeves remain the same and the front is half of the back – all other shaping remains the same. If the measurements you need to knit fall between any of the basic pattern sizes simply add or take off a few stitches or rows.

Method

ALL RIBS

The ribs are E wrap braid cast on using two ends of COL Moy and Greese: wind clockwise round the Ns and then anti-clockwise. K 2 rows Malone.

Stitch chart XOXOXOX Fairisle. Keeping Malone in Feeder 1 and changing the colours in Feeder 2 to the

Materials
Finished weight 250g

Small quantities of Jamiesons of Shetland Spindrift: 633 Jupiter (lilac), 186 Sunset (mid pink)

Small quantities of Knoll Soft Donegal 5548 Malone (pale blue), 5582 Purple Heart (mid purple), 5541 Ahearne (pale pink), 5526 Liscannor (clover), 5527 Vichy (turquoise), 5507 Swilly (cream), 5509 Greese (grey), 5535 Rea (pink), 5550 O'Byrne (lime green), 5571 Hickory (yellow), 5519 Moy (aqua), 5529 Eske (dirty white) 5518 Boyne (light brown)

Cressida wearing the Hearts Cardigan.

Hearts Cardigan detail.

foll sequence, k 2 rows each of Purple Heart, Ahearne, Swilly, Liscannor, Greese, Vichy, Jupiter, Eske.

The button bands have fewer rows and end with the Liscannor. K 1 row Purple Heart and pick up the front or neck edge/using Malone k 1 row MT + 2 and latch off.

BACK

The Hearts Cardigan was knitted by completing a braid E wrap on using two ends of yarn winding clockwise and then anti-clockwise. MT 7 k 1 row and complete a 1 x 1 rib or use the Stitch Pattern Chart X0X0X0X0X locked on the row. Keeping the C in

Feeder 1 the same, change the colour in Feeder 2 every 2 rows for 16 rows. K on to WY and pick up again on the machine complete inc row MT 8. Foll instructions for basic Fairisle sweater.

FRONT

Push half the number of Ns as required for the back to WP and rep the E wrap braid cast on and rib as for the back. Cont as for right or left side of back. Join shoulders by picking up the sts on the machine and k 1 row MT+2 and latch off.

SLEEVES

As basic pattern.

BUTTON BANDS

Push required Ns to WP and work the rib as set for 8 rows, at the same time dec 4 sts evenly at the top of the neck. This will form a mitre with the rib from the back neck.

Knit the button band placing five buttonholes evenly down the front, noting that the top buttonhole is in the mitre at the top neck. K 1 row Malone. Pick up front edge of cardigan k 1 row

MT+2 and cast off.

Rep for rem button band reversing all shaping.

NECKBAND

Push the required Ns to WP and make the rib as set, at the same time dec 4 sts at each end of the band.

MAKING UP

Set sleeve into armhole. Sew down side and sleeve seams. Join mitres, leaving a small gap for the button hole. Sew in ends. Sew on buttons. Wash and press.

Table 11.6: Hearts Cardigan Stitch Pattern Chart and Colour Sequence

Rows	Stitch Pattern	Pattern Setting	Feeder 1	Feeder 2
2		Knit	Greese	
3	18	Fairisle	Greese	Liscannor
3	18	Fairisle	Vichy	Jupiter
3	18	Fairisle	Annalee	Rea
3	18	Fairisle	Swilly	Sunset
4		Knit	Swilly	
2	3	Fairisle	Swilly	Hickory
2	3	Fairisle	Greese	O'Byrne
4		Knit	Greese	
3	23	Fairisle	Greese	Liscannor
3	23	Fairisle	Malone	Purple Heart
1	23	Fairisle	O'Byrne	Sunset
3	23	Fairisle	Malone	Purple Heart
3	23	Fairisle	Eske	Liscannor
4		Knit	Eske	
2	5	Fairisle	Eske	Ahearne
2	5	Fairisle	Moy	Jupiter
2	5	Fairisle	Vichy	Rea
4		Knit	Vichy	
3	27	Fairisle	Vichy	Swilly
2	27	Fairisle	Greese	O'Byrne
1	27	Fairisle	Hickory	Ahearne
2	27	Fairisle	Greese	O'Byrne
3	27	Fairisle	Moy	Swilly
4		Knit	Moy	

Table 11.6: *Continued*

Rows	Stitch Pattern	Pattern Setting	Feeder 1	Feeder 2
2	5	Fairisle	Moy	Jupiter
2	5	Fairisle	Greese	Liscannor
2	5	Fairisle	Annalee	Sunset
4		Knit	Annalee	
2	6	Fairisle	Annalee	Hickory
2	6	Fairisle	Boyne	O'Byrne
2	6	Fairisle	Greese	Hickory
4		Knit	Greese	
2	19	Fairisle	Greese	Purple Heart
3	19	Fairisle	Annalee	Liscannor
3	19	Fairisle	Swilly	Rea
3	19	Fairisle	Annalee	Liscannor
2	19	Fairisle	Greese	Purple Heart
4		Knit	Greese	
3	13	Fairisle	Greese	Vichy
3	13	Fairisle	Swilly	O'Byrne
3	13	Fairisle	Annalee	Vichy
4		Knit	Annalee	
2	14	Fairisle	Annalee	Purple Heart
2	14	Fairisle	Vichy	Liscannor
1	14	Fairisle	Hickory	Sunset
2	14	Fairisle	Vichy	Liscannor
2	14	Fairisle	Greese	Purple Heart
4		Knit	Greese	

CHAPTER 12

ACCESSORIES

SCARVES

Scarves are an adaptable accessory, can be worn all the year round, and are therefore excellent value for money. Depending on the choice of yarn and size they can be light and diaphanous and can soften a neckline while adding a splash of colour. A large scarf can become a wrap and be worn in place of a jacket.

Consider the type of scarf that you want to make and how the scarf is to be worn and tied, as this will dictate what size it will need to be knitted – if you make it too short it won't fold over and be capable of being looped around

the neck. A further golden rule is that if in doubt about sizing, then knit a size up, as a too fitted scarf appears skimpy and uncomfortable and does not allow the knitted shape to drape – a stretched stitch pattern is ugly when under stress and does not lie naturally. If you make your scarf too thick and bulky, then it is difficult to wrap around the head. So consider what your expectations are for how your scarf design will be worn – should it be worn as a muffler? Should it be long and thin? Should it be an elongated triangle? Should it be oblong and thick? Should it be skinny and short? Should it be square? And so on.

All the following scarves use a similar technique yet create a variety of results by changing the yarn weight or the pattern setting from slip stitch to tuck stitch. I have been exploring this technique for years and used it hundreds of times, and know there are a myriad of variations I have yet to discover and develop.

Scarf selection.

PEACOCK SCARF

The Peacock Scarf was inspired by the fabulous colours of the male peacock tail and used the circular shape of the eye in the tail feather as the main motif. I found that the slip stitch technique worked perfectly for this design, and the subtle colour changes within the circle created the desired effect.

The slip stitch pattern is

Materials
Finished weight 70g

2/28s, 1 ply weight, small amounts of the following colours: Mustard, Purple, Pink, Orange, Lime Green, Lilac, Mauve, Emerald Green, Leaf Green, Denim Blue, Bright Blue, Pale Blue, Dark Red, Bright Red, Grey, Dark Green, Navy, Olive Green

Measurements
Width 26.5cm

Length 148cm

Tension
30 sts – 36 rows = 10cm over sl st pattern
MT 7

Machines
Suitable for standard gauge punchcard and electronic machines

XX0000000000 repeated for ten rows, knit two rows stocking stitch, offset the next repetition.

Method

Bring forward to WP 100 Ns E wrap hand cast on. Follow the pattern sequence as set out in Table 12.1.

Peacock Scarf.

Table 12.1: Pattern Sequence for Peacock Scarf

Rows	Stitch	Colour
2	Knit	Mustard
2	Knit	Purple
2	Knit	Pink
*4	Slip	Orange
4	Slip	Mustard
2	Slip	Lime Green
2	Knit	Lime Green
4	Slip	Lilac
4	Slip	Mauve
2	Slip	Purple
2	Knit	Purple
4	Slip	Olive Green
4	Slip	Emerald Green
2	Slip	Leaf Green
2	Knit	Leaf Green
4	Slip	Denim Blue
4	Slip	Bright Blue
2	Slip	Pale Blue
2	Knit	Pale Blue
4	Slip	Dark Red
4	Slip	Bright Red
2	Slip	Pink
2	Knit	Pink
4	Slip	Grey
4	Slip	Dark Green
2	Slip	Navy
2	Knit	Navy

Repeat from * until length required. Cast off.

BEE DANCE SCARF

The Bee Dance Scarf is a variation of the stitch pattern used when knitting the Peacock Scarf. The hexagon shape created by the slip stitch mirrored a bee honeycomb, to capture the spirit of the bees in the summer, dancing from flower to flower – this mirrored my own joy at observing them and acknowledging that they are very welcome and vital visitors to the gardens and orchards in and around my home.

The three colourways create three different dances: the right one combines the floral colours, the centre one creates the colours of the bees, and the left design shows a combination of the previous two versions.

The slip stitch pattern is XX0000000000 repeated for ten rows, knit two rows stocking stitch, offset the next repetition. This combination of colour changes creates a very different effect to the previous Peacock Scarf.

Materials
Finished weight 90g

2/28s, 1 ply weight. Small amounts of the following colours: Bright Pink, Lime Green, Emerald Green, Turquoise, Lemon, Mustard, Mauve, Red, Bright Purple

Measurements
Approximate width 26.5cm

Length 148cm

Tension
30 sts – 36 rows = 10cm over slip stitch pattern
MT 7

Machines
Suitable for standard gauge punchcard and electronic machines

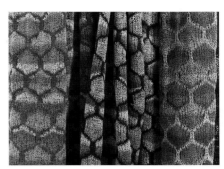

Bee Dance Scarves.

Table 12.2: Pattern Setting and Colour Sequence for the Bee Dance Scarf

Rows	Pattern Setting	Feeder 1
2	Knit	Bright Pink
*4	Slip	Lime Green
4	Slip	Emerald Green
2	Slip	Turquoise
2	Knit	Bright Pink
4	Slip	Lemon
4	Slip	Mustard
2	Slip	Mauve
2	Knit	Bright Pink
4	Slip	Emerald Green
4	Slip	Turquoise
2	Slip	Lime Green
2	Knit	Bright Pink
4	Slip	Mustard
4	Slip	Mauve
2	Slip	Lemon
2	Knit	Bright Pink
4	Slip	Lime Green
4	Slip	Emerald Green
2	Slip	Turquoise
2	Knit	Red
4	Slip	Mauve
4	Slip	Lemon
2	Slip	Mustard
2	Knit	Red

Rep from *. Continue to work through the colours. Repeat the knit row colours five times and change colour working through Bright Pink, Red and Bright

Method

Bring forward to WP 100 Ns E wrap hand cast on.

For the version on the left follow the pattern and colour chart sequence in Table 12.2.

BEE SONG SCARF

The Bee Song Scarf is a further progression using the same stitch pattern but a different sequence for the colours and row combinations and four knit rows between each slipstitch pattern. The differences are further enhanced by a change in yarn quality.

The design uses a thicker weight silk 2/20s, 2-ply yarn for the knit rows and a fine weight 2/28s 1-ply yarn for the slip stitch rows.

See Bee Dance Scarf (previous pattern) for approximate weights of yarn, sizing and method.

Bee Song Scarves.

Materials

Colours in fine yarn slip stitch rows are Mustard, Lime Green, Denim Blue, Bright Purple, Purple, Bright Green, Blue, Turquoise, Rust, Leaf Green, Olive Green, Forest Green, Beige, Terracotta, Brown

Colours in a thicker yarn for the knit rows are Maroon, Navy, Purple

Method

Table 12.3: Colour Sequence and Row Combinations for Bee Song Scarf

Rows	Pattern Setting	Feeder 1
4	Knit	Maroon
4	Slip	Mustard
4	Slip	Lime Green
2	Slip	Denim Blue
4	Knit	Navy
4	Slip	Bright Purple
4	Slip	Purple
2	Slip	Bright Green
4	Knit	Purple
4	Slip	Blue
4	Slip	Turquoise
2	Slip	Rust
4	Knit	Maroon
4	Slip	Leaf Green
4	Slip	Olive Green
2	Slip	Forest Green
4	Knit	Navy
4	Slip	Beige
4	Slip	Terracotta
2	Slip	Brown

Repeat from the beginning for the required length.

HYDRANGEA SCARF

The Hydrangea Scarf uses a smaller, more intricate slip-stitch pattern. The petal and leaf shape of the hydrangea is mirrored in the shape of the slip-stitch pattern and the colours chosen. Bright purple and emerald green are colours that always bounce off and enhance each other, creating a sense of movement. The blue hydrangeas have a huge variety of shades from navy through to pale blue within each separate flower.

The slip-stitch pattern X00000X00000X00000 is slipped for twelve rows and knit two rows, the repetition is offset.

Hydrangea Scarf.

Materials

Finished weight 100g 2/28s 1 ply

Small amounts of colour: Lemon, Purple, Olive Green, Turquoise, Grey, Emerald Green, Bright Purple, Leaf Green, Mustard, Navy, and Denim Blue

Measurements

Width 30cm

Length 180cm

Tension

27 sts – 52 rows = 10cm
MT 7

Machines

Suitable for standard gauge punchcard and electronic machines

Old Rose version of Hydrangea scarf.

Table 12.4: Pattern and Colour Sequence for Hydrangea Scarf

Rows	Pattern Setting	Feeder 1
2	Knit	Lemon
*2	Slip	Olive
10	Slip	Purple
2	Knit	Purple
2	Slip	Turquoise
10	Slip	Grey
2	Knit	Grey
2	Slip	Emerald
10	Slip	Bright Purple
2	Knit	Bright Purple
2	Slip	Leaf Green
10	Slip	Mustard
2	Knit	Mustard
2	Slip	Navy
10	Slip	Denim
2	Knit	Denim

Rep from * cont to work through the colours and pattern as set until required length. Cast off.

Method

Bring forward 90 Ns to WP E wrap hand cast on. Follow the pattern and colour sequence as set out in Table 12.4.

Change colours completely for soft greys and beige, and pink and lilac for a more muted version of the same stitch pattern.

CHINA SCARVES

One stitch pattern can create a huge variety of changes depending how you are inspired to use it. This simple stitch pattern has been used hundreds of times before, yet there is always a new colour combination or yarn you can use, which will totally change the character of the pattern.

The standard Card Three from the Silver Reed stitch patterns can be used for this design. X000X000X000 any repeat is offset.

A tuck stitch is used and the colour changed every fourth row. The colour inspiration for the design came from studying the colours of Chinese textiles. I looked at the colours and the use of combinations on the borders of long flowing garments, and these were transferred into the colours I had available in the workroom – I then simply worked through them. Four different colourways were worked out, and these were all interchangeable by using a different combination for either end of a scarf and the main block.

Quing with Tang Border Scarf.

The colours chosen for each group were as follows:

Quing: Navy, Denim, Purple, Blue, Forest Green, Mustard and Brown.

Celadon: Mint Green, Bright Green, Forest Green, Sage Green, Lime Green, Red, Maroon and Mustard.

Tang: Lime Green, Mustard, Sage Green, Bright Pink, Brown, rep Lime Green, Olive Green, Forest Green.

Phoenix: Emerald Green, Leaf Green, Mustard, Terracotta, Forest Green, Maroon, Denim Blue, Rust.

Famille Rose: Red, Maroon, Mustard, Leaf Green, Bright Purple, Blue, Navy, Beige, Dark Purple, Lime.

Materials
100g 1 ply 2/28s weight in colours of whichever two groups are being worked

Measurements
46 x 168cm

Tension
20 sts x 36 rows = 10cm over tuck st pattern
Approx MT 7•

Machines
Suitable for standard gauge punchcard and electronic machines

Method

Decide which colour combinations you intend to use for the deep border block at either end of the scarf and the main block.

Bring forward 100 sts to WP and E wrap cast on with Col k 2 r st st change Col RC 000.

Start tuck pattern changing colour every fourth row RC 60.

Change to the main colour sequence of your choice and work RC 400.

Return to the colours used for the deep border block at the beginning of the scarf and work a further 60 rows. K 2 rows st st and cast off.

Sew in ends and press very lightly – do not flatten the stitch.

CHINA CARDIGANS

The colours worked out for the scarves were then transferred into a cardigan design and the pattern setting changed to a slip stitch. To produce a firmer fabric two ends of yarn were used.

The left cardigan uses Tang borders with Quing for the main body. The top right cardigan uses Quing borders with Phoenix for the main body. The one at lower right uses Celadon for the borders and Famille Rose for the body.

Famille Rose with Celadon borders.

China cardigans.

Materials

Finished weight 430g 1 ply 2/28s, two ends of the yarn used

Tension

MT 8

Machines

Suitable for standard gauge punchcard and electronic machines

Method

Follow the instructions for the basic sideways knitted Fairisle jacket. Decide which two-colour colourways to use, one for the collar and the lower part of the sleeve, and one for the left front, back and right front and main part of the sleeve.

CHINA SCARF – COTTON YARN VARIATION

Knitting with sewing cotton creates a complete change in texture when juxtaposed with cashmere or wool. There is always sewing thread left over after any project and I wanted to use some of the lovely fine colours that had been languishing in a box for far too long. I chose colours that I thought went well together to create bright and happy scarves. The colours used at each end were darker, and the lighter, more subtle shades were placed in the middle of the scarf. The aim was to create colour interest and contrast when the scarf was folded and worn.

The work needs to be carefully weighted with claw weights as you knit to prevent the fine cotton yarn jumping off the needles when working the tuck stitch.

Detail of China variation.

Method

Bring forward 100 Ns to WP E wrap cast on and work two small 4-row picot hems for the bottom border.

Col 1* k 2 rows transfer every alternate stitch to the N on the right, k 2 rows and pick up the sts from the first row using Col 1*.

Col 2, rep fom *to* RC 000 Col 3 start tuck stitch pattern and change col every fourth row RC 760; rep the two small picot edges and k 2 rows MT+2 and latch off.

Materials

Finished weight 110g 2/20s 2 ply

Quantity of sewing cotton and wool of your colour choice

Measurements

Width 37cm
Length 152cm

Tension

36 sts – 44 rows = 10cm over tuck stitch pattern
Approx MT 7•

Machines

Suitable for standard gauge punchcard and electronic machines

China variation scarf.

CORNISH SUN AND MOON SCARVES

When working on the Cornish Sun and Moon designs I sketched out many combinations of colours, circles and stripes based on what I was observing in the sky at that time.

Small and large moons were created by using varying tuck stitch patterns such as XOOOOO and tuck for eight rows, XOOOOOOO and tuck for eight rows, XOOOOOOOOOOO and tuck for ten rows. Some of the moons change colours midway, and the stripes between the moons vary in width and texture by using yarns of various weights and blended together with a mixture of colours and strands.

All the scarves were knitted using cashmere and lightly felted in the washing machine at 40 degrees, and 800 spin speed for 60 minutes. You will need to check the result that your washing machine creates.

Many different sketches were drawn and coloured, and when I sat down to knit I kept them in front of me, and I worked directly from them when knitting. Having completed one sketched page I then turned to another, and altered the sequence the colours came in to create a different effect. I continued to work directly from the sketches and did not refer back to what I had knitted previously, preferring to look afresh at each sketch. Using this way of designing on the knitting machine directly from sketches, different colour changes occurred, and some stripes came to the fore while others receded. Some of the yarns that I knew felted more densely squashed the small circles to create oblongs.

Try designing and knitting together yourself, as it is a lovely and invigorating way to knit and one that I find energizing. If you are knitting a

Sketches and Cornish Sun and Moon Scarves.

Cornish Sun and Moon Scarves.

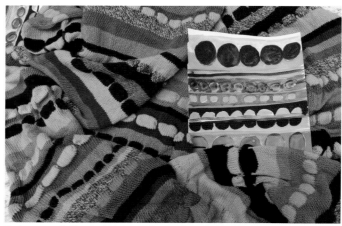

Colour variations Autumn Song Scarf.

Materials
Finished weight 200g 2/28s 1ply
through to 2/10s 4 ply yarns

Measurements
Width 32cm
Length 165cm

Tension
35 sts – 34 rows = 10cm after felting
MT 7•

Machines
Suitable for standard gauge punchcard
and electronic machines

scarf with no shaping to consider then
there is nothing else to focus on except
the pattern and the colours – so have
an invigorating experience creating
your own colour combinations and
patterns directly on to the finished
scarf.

Method

Bring forward 100 Ns to WP and E wrap
cast on. Work following sketches and
creating your own version of tuck stitch
circles and stripes until approx RC 800
cast off.

DIAGONAL REDS SCARF

Knitting on the diagonal creates an
uneven lower edge, which becomes
part of the design. This looks
particularly effective when colours are
gently merged to create a wave effect.
Skinny scarves can be made by using
fewer stitches and adding to the
length.

Method

Bring forward 70 sts to WP E wrap; cast
on at the far right side of the machine.

Diagonal Reds Scarf.

Materials
Finished weight 200g

Knoll Soft Donegal in equal amounts of
the following colours: 5530 Clare, 5503
Forbes, 5566 Fuchsia, 5516 Dingle,
5567 Cardinal

Measurements
Width 20cm
Length 222cm

Tension
28 sts – 48 rows = 10cm
MT 8

Machines
Suitable for standard gauge and
electronic machines

K 12 row stripes working through the
colour palette.

Every fourth row inc 1 st ff on the
right and dec 1 st ff on the left. As the
increases and decreases take place the
scarf will move along the machine so
eventually you will be required to run
the sts off on to WY and pick up again
on the RHS, and continue to
completion.

Cont for as many rows as required.
Approx 732 rows.

WORCESTER BLUE SCALE, SPRIG AND FANTASY BIRD SCARVES

All three scarves use the same basic
instructions. The finished piece is folded
in half and stitched together.

Method

BLUE SCALE SCARF
See the stitch patterns inspired by Royal
Worcester porcelain in the *Painting with
Yarn* chapter.

Bring forward 100 Ns to WP E wrap
cast on and commence to k the
Malvern Scroll, followed by the Floral
stitch patt and repeat a Malvern Scroll
stitch patt. RC 000 work the Blue Scale

Materials
Finished weight = 210g of a variety of
yarn colours 2/20s 2 ply

Measurements
Width 14cm
Length 160cm

Tension
38 sts – 37 rows = 10cm
MT 7••

Machines
Standard-gauge punchcard and
electronic machines

this scarf was made in the same way as the previous one, with the bird being placed between two scroll borders from the Malvern Cardigan.

Swiss embroidery was added to create a landscape scene.

SPRIG

Some of the border patterns from the Malvern Cardigan were used to decorate the ends of the final scarf and add a new stitch pattern. The perky sprig creates a fresh and quirky variation – texture was added to the border with the addition of a gold chenille and soft cream for the main part of the scarf to create a crisp clean contrast.

Worked to the same method as the Blue Scale Scarf.

Worcester scarves Fantasy Bird, Sprig and Blue Scale.

SHIVER SCARF

The yarns placed in Feeder 1 (cashmere, alpaca, lambswool, Donegal wool and Shetland wool) are all felted to some degree, whereas the yarns in Feeder 2 (raw silk, cotton, eco silk and mulberry silk) do not felt due to the

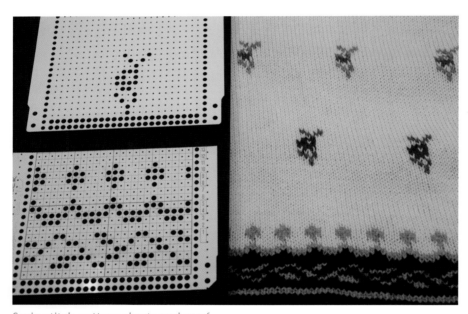

Sprig stitch pattern charts and scarf.

Materials
Finished weight 250g
Small amounts of a variety of cream colours in felting yarns 2 ply, 2/20s
Small amounts of a variety of cream colours in non-felting yarns. Fine 1 ply 2/34s

Measurements
25cm at the widest point
Length 266cm

Tension
Approx 22 sts – 40 rows = 10cm
MT 7••

Machines
Suitable for standard gauge punchcard and electronic machines

stitch patt RC 460 rows, rep the Scroll/Floral/Scroll stitch patt, and cast off.

Note when working the scarf reverse the stitch patt at the base of the second half and reverse the colour chart

sequence so it appears the correct way up when worn.

FANTASY BIRD
Inspired by the paintings on the porcelain from the Worcester factory,

Shiver Scarf.

Method

Bring forward 110 Ns to WP E wrap, cast on Col 1 and k 2 rows. Commence the Fairisle stitch patt with felting yarns in Feeder 1 and non-felting yarns in Feeder 2, work each deep block of 30 or 40 rows and change colours. Work approx 850 rows k 2 rows st st and cast off.

Sew in ends and felt in the washing machine.

Press lightly.

Any of the samples that have been knitted can also be used as scarves. This Fairisle version was knitted to experiment and develop various peerie stitch patterns.

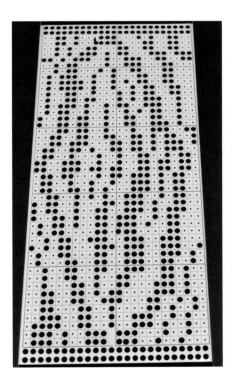
Shiver Scarf detail.

inherent properties of the yarn. The colours used were cream, white, off white and pale blue, to represent the colours of snow and ice.

The scarf was knitted and then placed in the washing machine for 60 minutes at 40 degrees, 800 spin speed. Some of the wools felted firmly, pulling in and constricting the fabric, while others felted more loosely. The stitch pattern enhanced this effect by creating thick and thinner lines that expanded and contracted, and the overall effect of this was to create a visual shiver.

Stitch pattern for Shiver Scarf.

Peerie Fairisle pattern scarf.

GLOVES

A glove is a garment covering the hand, and it usually has a separate sheath for each finger and the thumb. Gloves that cover the entire hand or fist, but do not have separate finger sheaths, are called mittens. Gloves, as well as being attractive outerwear, protect and comfort hands against cold, heat, damage by friction, abrasion, chemicals or disease.

Cave paintings suggest that humans wore simple mittens, possibly knitted, as far back as the Ice Age, but the oldest known glove in existence today was found in the tomb of Tutankhamun, and dates from between 1343 and 1323BC.

Gloves started to come to the forefront of fashion between the twelfth and sixteenth centuries in Europe and the British Isles. Early gloves were offered in two styles, three-fingered and five-fingered, three-fingered gloves only being worn by working-class men and never by women. Up to the fifteenth century

Short finger gloves.

there are few depictions of anyone wearing five-fingered gloves, but in the sixteenth century gloves become a fashionable accessory for both men and women – see the leather gloves held by Queen Elizabeth I of England in the Ditchley portrait of 1592.

In the sixteenth century gloves were transformed into a highly decorated accessory embellished with slashing, gems, pearls, lace, embroidery, tabs, ribbons and elaborate cuffs, and became part of the identifying insignia of emperors and kings. In the 1700s short sleeves came into fashion and women began to wear long gloves reaching halfway up the forearm. By the 1870s wearing gloves in public was seen by the upper classes as being as mandatory as wearing shoes, and different gloves were available for casual and formal settings – buttoned kid, silk or velvet gloves were worn with evening or dinner dress, and long suede gloves were worn during the day and when having tea. This was not just a social convention, but also to help stop the spread of contagious diseases.

Gloves played an important role in 1950s fashion, and by the late 1950s stylish women wore long white gloves when they wanted to look ultra-fashionable and glamorous, a look that was popularized by Audrey Hepburn in the film *Breakfast at Tiffany's*. Today we wear various styles of gloves with long and shorter cuffs, mittens, fingerless mittens and wrist warmers, for both utilitarian and fashionable reasons.

Here are a few examples of gloves that I have made and which you can adapt to create a new and exciting design of your own by using the basic pattern and adding various modes of decoration – either embellished with Swiss Darning or Fairisle, slip or tuck stitch, each with its own distinctive character. The pattern can easily be altered slightly to add width or length.

BASIC PATTERN FOR GLOVES

Two sizes.

Method (Two Sizes)

Decide which rib or top edging you are going to use, either a knitted 1 x 1 rib or an E wrap braid cast on (using two ends of yarn, wrap around the needles clockwise and anti-clockwise, break off yarn) and use Fairisle stitch pattern OXOXOXOXO locked; keeping the same col in Feeder 1, change the Col in Feeder 2 every 2 rows.

Materials
Knoll Soft Donegal in various colours

Finished weight 60g

Measurements
See diagram

Tension
32 sts – 40 rows = 10cm
MT 7••

Machines
Suitable for standard gauge punchcard and electronic machines with or without a ribber

For machines without a ribber, either work a mock rib, or drop the stitch down and latch up, hand knit or design a pattern that does not require a rib

Grey Gloves.

RIGHT GLOVE

Push 32, 34 Ns to left 0 (centre) and 32, 34 to right 64, 68 sts in total.

Work 31 rows 1 x 1 rib. CAL.

RC 000 ** k 22, 24 rows. CAL.

Mark thumb opening.

Set carriage to Hold, leave 11 Ns at left edge in WP, push all rem Ns to HP.

Using length of nylon cord, k 1 row over sts at left.

Using WY, k 5 rows.

Using another length of nylon cord, k 1 row.

Using WY, k 5 rows.

Using third length of nylon cord, k 1 row. CAR reset RC 22, 24.

Cancel hold. Using MY cont over all sts. K until RC 42, 46.

Place a marker on the first st at left of centre 0. Rep over the first st at right of centre 0.

Using nylon cord k 1 row.

Using WY, k several rows and remove from machine. Do not remove WY until all fingers have been completed.

Little Finger

Push 8, 8 Ns at left and right of 0 to WP 16, 16 Ns in total.

With wrong side facing, place the marked sts on the centre Ns, pick up 16, 16 sts from the last completed row in MY. Mark the st on the edge N on both sides. RC 000.

K 26, 28 rows.

Shape top * dec 4 sts evenly along the row. Move sts to fill empty Ns 12, 12 sts rem. K 2 rows.

Cut yarn and thread through rem sts, remove from machine, pull sts together and fasten off*.

Third Finger

Push 18, 18 Ns at centre of 0 to WP. With wrong side facing and placing the marked sts from the little finger on to the 2 centre Ns, pick up 8 sts either side of the little finger on to the rem Ns.

18, 18 sts.

Mark the st on the edge Ns at each side.

RC 000. Using MY k 32, 34 rows.

Shape Top

Rep as for little finger *to*.

Middle Finger

Push 18, 20 Ns at centre of 0 to WP. With wrong side facing and placing the marked sts on to the centre Ns, pick up 8, 9 sts from each side of the third finger on to the rem Ns. Mark the edge Ns.

RC 000. K 34, 36 rows.

Shape top rep from *to*.

First Finger

Push 18, 20 Ns to WP. Place the marked sts, the edge sts from the second finger, on to the centre Ns, and 8, 9 sts from each side of the second finger on to the rem Ns.

RC 000 k 30, 32 rows.

Shape top rep *to*.

Thumb

Push 23, 25 Ns to WP at centre 0. Remove the cord between the WY sections. With wrong side facing, pick up the sts between the WY, inc 1 st at the cent.

RC 000 k 26, 28 rows.

Shape top rep *to*.

LEFT GLOVE

Knit as for right, but start to shape the thumb on row 21, 23 so reversing to the right side.

MAKE UP

Sew up fingers, sew up thumb, palm and cuff.

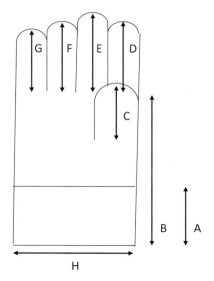

Diagram for Plain Gloves.

A	9cm	9cm
B	19cm	19cm
C	7cm	7.5cm
D	6.5cm	7.8cm
E	9cm	9.5cm
F	7.5cm	8cm
G	6cm	7cm
H	11cm	12cm

FAIRISLE GLOVES

The Fairisle stitch pattern will require extra stitches being added to the width, as the finished fabric will be firmer and denser and therefore slightly smaller.

All-over stitch patterns can be used with different coloured fingers; a smaller pattern is best as there will inevitably be floats on the inside, and if long, these can get caught up in fingers when the gloves are being put on. Also make sure that you make a note of the punchcard stitch-pattern row when the thumb opening is worked.

If you are using a traditional Fairisle stitch pattern choose a smaller stitch pattern such as peerie or border, which will be easier to match at the seams.

Fairisle Zigzag Gloves.

SHORT FINGER GLOVES

Have fun when designing. There is no reason why both ribs have to be identical, so change the striped sequence. However, if certain elements remain the same, such as the braid cast on and certain stripes and colour palette, then the gloves or fingerless gloves appear as a pair.

The method is to follow the basic glove pattern but to alter the length of the fingers. For example, I knitted eight rows and cast off loosely for the little finger. For the third finger knit twelve rows and cast off, for the middle finger knit twelve rows and cast off, first finger knit ten rows and cast off, and for the thumb knit eight rows and cast off.

WRIST WARMERS

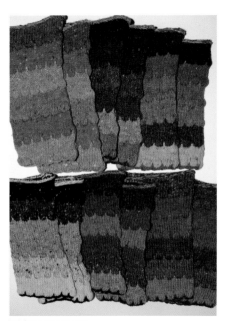

Wrist warmers.

Short finger gloves.

Materials
Any fine 3-ply yarn, Nm 3.8/1 Knoll Soft Donegal
Six colours
Finished weight 48g

Measurements
Length 20cm

Tension
32 sts – 40 rows = 10cm
MT 8

Machines
Suitable for standard gauge punchcard and electronic machines

Detail of wrist warmers.

Method (knit two alike)

Tuck stitch pattern: X000X000X000.
Bring forward 56 Ns to WP and E wrap
braid cast on using three ends of
contrasting coloured yarn. Using one
end of col 1,* k 10 rows st st, inc 1 st at
each end of next row. Change pattern
setting to tuck k 6 rows*, rep from * to
* three more times, changing col each
time.

Lengthen by adding extra pattern
rows here.

*Inc 1 st at each end of row. Change
col, k 10 rows st st. K 6 rows tuck st.*

Rep from * to * k 1 row contrast col
MT+2 and latch off.

MAKING UP

Join the seam leaving a 3.5cm gap;
3cm from the top, cast off the edge.

HATS

A hat can be worn for many different
reasons: safety, protection from the
weather, religious, ceremonial, or as a
fashion accessory. Hats can denote
status, or being part of a gang, tribe or
pressure group – for example, the
Pussyhat Project for advancing
women's and human rights created a
political statement out of the wearing
of a pink knitted hat.

Some people insist that hats don't
suit them, but as there are so many
different styles and shapes of hat, I
really believe that there is a hat
somewhere to suit everybody. Most of
the following hats are versions of the
knitted beanie seamed cap, in as much
as they fit closely and follow the shape
of the head and are shaped by
decreasing or gathering in stitches. The
first documented hat of this type is the
Monmouth cap that was knitted in
Monmouth, Wales, from the fifteenth
to the eighteenth centuries. It was a
practical accessory as it was warm,
knitted with wool, and felted to make it
weatherproof, with the basic shape
being adopted by the military,

Beret worn with Cornish Sun Scarf.

Paisley and Plaid Hats.

fishermen and outdoor workers.
Embellishments were later added such
as pompoms, or ear flaps with ties
under the chin.

The traditional use of a beanie hat is
to keep the head warm in cold
weather, but today beanies have
become a fashion staple for the winter,
as well as being a way to show off your
individuality with various colours,
design flourishes and additions. For
those affected with hair loss from
chemotherapy, alopecia or ageing,
beanies are a great option as they are
soft against the head, provide warmth,
and have a timeless yet casual look.
Beanie hats are also used in hospitals to
help keep premature babies warm.

The basic patterns can be made
longer, shorter, or with a larger

Materials
Finished weight approx 60g. Various
colours of Knoll Soft Donegal and
Jamiesons of Shetland Spindrift

Measurements
Medium: Circumference 51cm, depth
including crown 18cm

Tension
26 sts and 38 rows = 10cm
MT 8

Machines
Suitable for standard gauge punchcard
and electronic machines

circumference, just by adding a few extra stitches or rows.

Hats are a great way to use up small quantities of yarn.

Method

BASIC HAT PATTERN FOR CAT, ZIGZAG, PAISLEY AND RAMS HORN HATS

The basic pattern can be tweaked to accommodate any Fairisle stitch pattern so that the join is well matched. But choose the stitch pattern carefully as smaller patterns are easier to match at the seams. If the repeated stitch pattern is slightly larger than the basic instructions add a few more stitches or rows.

Push 140 Ns to WP and cast on using WY, k a few rows with the carriage on the left, k 1 row using the nylon cord. Insert required punchcard and lock on first row.

RC 000. Using MT and col 1, k 6 rows. Make a piping hem by placing the loops from the first row on to the corresponding Ns.

RC 000. Using col 2, k 2 rows. Release the punchcard and start to Fairisle patt approx 36 rows. Remove card and k 36 rows in MY. Make a hem by placing the loops from the first row on to the corresponding Ns. Insert required card and lock on first row. K 28 rows RC 106 approx. Release punchcard and cont in Fairisle pattern for 36 rows RC 146.

Divide for Crown Shaping

Set carriage to Hold. Push 105 Ns to HP. Cont on remaining 35 sts *. Dec 1 st at each end of the next 17 rows. Fasten off the rem st.* Using transfer tool push 35 Ns at right from HP to WP. Rep from * to *. Using transfer tool, push the rem 35 Ns from HP to WP. Rep from * to *.

Sew in ends and join seams.

CAT HAT

Cat Hats.

Materials
Small amounts of 4ply 2/10s yarn in A Black, B Yellow, C Grey, D Blue, E Ochre, F Brown, G Orange, plus an oddment of Yellow for the eyes

Finished weight 75g

Measurements
Large size Cat Hat:

Circumference 54cm, depth inc crown 18cm

Punchcard Stitch Patterns

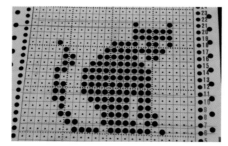
Cat stitch pattern chart.

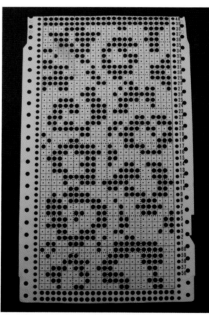
Cat fur stitch pattern chart.

Diagonal stripe.

Method

Push 144 Ns to WP. Using MT and WY cast on and k a few rows ending with the carriage on the left. Using the nylon cord, k 1 row. Carriage at right. Insert Diagonal Stripe card and lock on row one. RC 000.

Using MT and B, k 6 rows. Make a piping hem by placing the loops from the first row worked in B on to the corresponding Ns.

RC 000. Using A, k 1 row. Release card and cont in Fairisle pattern. K 4 rows A/E and 2 rows A/F. Remove card. Cont in st st. Using A, k 1 row. Insert Cat punchcard and lock on first row. Using C, k 2 rows. Release card and cont in Fairisle. K 5 rows C/A and 11 rows D/A. Remove card. Cont in st st. Insert Diagonal card and lock on the first row. Using D, k 2 rows. Using A, k 1 row. Release card and cont in Fairisle. K 3 rows A/B and 3 rows A/E. Remove card. Cont in st st. Using A, k 1 row. Using C, k 1 row. Using MT+1 and A, k 1 row. Using MT, k 36 rows. Make a hem by placing the loops from the first row worked in A on to the corresponding Ns. Insert Cat Fur card and lock on any row. K 6 rows in a contrasting colour. K 22 rows. RC 102. Release card and cont in Fairisle Cat Fur pattern. K 28 rows. RC 130.

SHAPE CROWN

Set carriage to Hold. Push 108 Ns to HP. Cont on rem 36 sts.* Using A/E throughout, dec 1 st at each end of the next 18 rows. Fasten off rem st. Do not rewind card, cont in Fairisle: this gives a random effect.*

Using a transfer tool, push 36 Ns from HP to WP. Rep from * to *. Using a transfer tool, push 36 Ns from HP to WP. Rep from * to *. Using a transfer tool, push the rem Ns from HP to WP. Rep from * to *.

Swiss darn cat's eyes in yellow. Sew in ends and join seams.

ZIGZAG HAT

Method

Push 140 Ns to WP. Using MT and WY, cast on and k a few rows. Using nylon cord k 1 row. Insert Zigzag card and lock on first row. RC 000 using MT and col 1 k 6 rows. Make a piping hem by placing loops from the first row on to the corresponding Ns. Set RC 000. Using col 1, k 1 row. Release the card and cont in Fairisle patt. K 36 rows changing colours in Feeder 1 and 2 every 6 rows.

Lock card on first row. Cont in st st. Using M +1, k 1 row. Using MT k 36 rows. Make a hem by placing loops from the first row worked on to the corresponding Ns. K 32 rows. RC 106. Release card and cont in Fairisle patt changing the colours every 6 rows. K 24 rows. RC 130.

Note punchcard patt row.

SHAPE CROWN

Set carriage to Hold, push 105 Ns to HP. Cont on rem 35 sts,* cont in patt and dec 1 st at each end of the next 17 rows. Fasten off rem st.* Reset the punchcard to the first patt row required and lock and memorize row. Release card. Push 35 Ns from HP to WP and cont rep *–*. Rep for the next two sections of hat crown.
Join seams and sew in ends.

Zigzag Hats – Bright, Blue and Woodland.

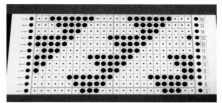

Zigzag stitch pattern.

WOODLAND COLOURWAY

Knitted using small amounts of Jamieson and Smith Spindrift 998 Autumn, 226 Thyme, 423 Burnt Ochre, 261 Paprika, 231 Bracken, 241 Tan Green, 198 Peat, 237 Thistledown, 318 Woodgreen, 118 Moorit Shaela, 230 Yellow Ochre, 230 Grouse.

It is interesting to note that the Zigzag stitch pattern can change course depending on the colour mix. The overall appearance can be one travelling up and across the fabric, or this can change into an S shape. This is can be seen very clearly in the bright coloured hat. Either way the use of stitch pattern and colour can be dynamic.

Table 12.5: Stitch Pattern and Colourway for Zigzag Hat

Rows	Stitch Pattern	Pattern Setting	Feeder 1	Feeder 2
6	Zigzag	Fairisle	Moorit Shaela	Autumn
6	Zigzag	Fairisle	Thyme	Yellow Ochre
6	Zigzag	Fairisle	Thistledown	Burnt Ochre
6	Zigzag	Fairisle	Paprika	Bracken
6	Zigzag	Fairisle	Tan Green	Peat
6	Zigzag	Fairisle	Grouse	Woodgreen

Rep from beginning.

PAISLEY HAT

For measurements and materials see previous Basic Pattern.

Knitted using Jamiesons of Shetland Spindrift and a small amount of navy chenille.

Small amounts of the following colours were used: A 101 Black, B 259 Leprechaun, C 226 Thyme, D 1290

Paisley Hat colourway Hydrangea.

Loganberry, E 929 Aqua, F 286 Moorgrass, G 231 Bracken, H 633 Jupiter, I 525 Birch, J 423 Burnt Ochre, K 676 Sapphire, Navy chenille.

Many of the hats are knitted with a chenille crown, which gives a soft, textured and rich feel to the hat.

Follow the basic pattern for making a piping hem using Moorgrass, RC 000, k 2 rows Black, cont see Table 12.6.

MAKING UP

Sew seams and Swiss Darn centre of Paisley with contrasting colour.

This basic hat pattern has been adapted hundreds of times, making a variety of motifs fit. It is incredibly versatile as stitch patterns used in many other designs can be utilized and adapted.

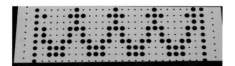

1 U stitch pattern chart.

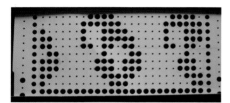

2 Paisley stitch pattern chart.

3 Peerie stitch pattern.

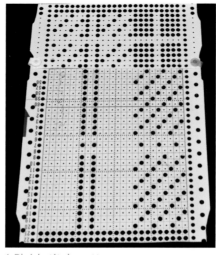

4 Plaid stitch pattern.

Autumn Gold Paisley and Plaid Hat.

Table 12.6: Stitch Pattern and Colour Sequence for Paisley Hat

Rows	Stitch Pattern	Pattern Setting	Feeder 1	Feeder 2
2	1	Fairisle	Black	Leprechaun
3	1	Fairisle	Black	Thyme
3	1	Fairisle	Loganberry	Aqua
1		Knit	Loganberry	
2		Knit	Moorgrass	
10	2	Fairisle	Moorgrass	Burnt Ochre
2		Knit	Moorgrass	
2		Knit	Loganberry	
3	1 Upsidedown	Fairisle	Loganberry	Aqua
3	1	Fairisle	Black	Thyme
2	1	Fairisle	Black	Jupiter
1		Knit	Black	
3	3	Fairisle	Birch	Sapphire

Using Leprechaun k 38 rows and pick up hem. RC 76, k 6 rows. Change col to Birch, k RC 106, follow Table 12.7 for Plaid stitch pattern.

Table 12.7: Plaid Stitch Pattern and Colour Sequence

Rows	Stitch Pattern	Pattern Setting	Feeder 1	Feeder 2
12	Plaid	Fairisle	Loganberry	Moorgrass
1	Plaid	Knit	Leprechaun	
1	Plaid	Fairisle	Jupiter	Moorgrass
1	Plaid	Knit	Leprechaun	
12	Plaid	Fairisle	Loganberry	Moorgrass
5	Plaid	Fairisle	Birch	Bracken
1	Plaid	Knit	Birch	
5	Plaid	Fairisle	Birch	Bracken

K 1 row in any contrasting colour.

RC 141, divide for crown shaping and use one col Navy chenille, Black or a different col for each section.

HARE AND STARS

This hat uses the U pattern border from the previous Paisley design, incorporating a running hare into the centre section, followed by the U pattern again. The main section of the hat uses the Star stitch chart knitted using shades of blue in Feeder 1, and gold, ochre and off white in Feeder 2.

Hare and Stars Hat.

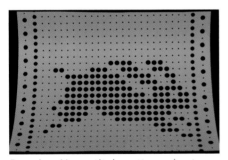

Running Hare stitch pattern chart.

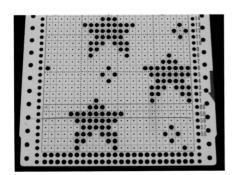

All-Over Star stitch pattern chart.

STARRY NIGHT HAT

The stitch pattern used is the Spit Star. It is used throughout with no piped edging. The crown is knitted in Navy Blue chenille.

The basic pattern can be used to make a traditional Fairisle version. The stitch patterns used for this were 10, 22, 10 for the turn-back brim, and 17, 3, 22 for the main section, with the crown XOXOXOXO.

Starry Night Hat.

Traditional Fairisle variation.

PATCHWORK HAT AND SCARF

Patchwork Scarf and Hat.

Materials
Hat and scarf approx 20g each of 2 ply 2/20s yarn in 16 different colours: A, B, C, D, E, F, G, H, I, J, K, L, M, N, O, P

8 beads

Hat: Finished weight 95g

Scarf: Finished weight 115g

Measurements
Hat: Circumference around head 49cm, depth 22cm with brim turned back and including crown

Scarf: 25.25 x 137cm

Tension
26 sts and 38 rows to 10cm
MT 8

Method

HAT
Knit 8 strips.

First Strip
Push 18 Ns to WP. Using A E wrap cast on. RC 000. Using MT k 60 rows. Using B k 20 rows. Using C knit 20 rows. Using D knit 80 rows. Using A knit 20 rows. RC 200.

Shape Crown
Using B, dec 1 st at left edge of next 17 rows, fasten off rem sts.

Berry Patchwork Scarf and Hat.

PAISLEY AND STAR PATCHWORK HATS AND SCARFS

Hats

The Paisley and Star Patchwork hats are variations of the *Patchwork Hat*. Table 12.8 shows where the Paisley and Star motif should be placed.

Using sixteen colours as before, start the second strip using the same colours in a different place, for example, start with B and run through the four colours. The star* in Table 12.8 denotes where the motif should be placed.

For the Paisley and Star Hats cast on twenty stitches for each strip. Follow the Patchwork pattern for all other shaping.

The colour of the Paisley motif changes each time with five rows of

Make one more strip using the same colours but starting with B and running through the rest of the colours.

Make 2 more strips using E, F, G, H.

Make 2 more strips using I, J, K, L reversing crown shaping reading right for left.

Make 2 more strips using M, N, O, P.

MAKING UP

Join straight sides together alternating colours, then join seams with the shaped crown. Sew in the ends. Turn up to cast on edge to inside of hat to first row of shaping, and hand slip stitch into place. Turn up brim.

Paisley and Star Patchwork Hats.

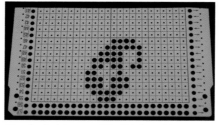

Single Paisley motif stitch pattern chart.

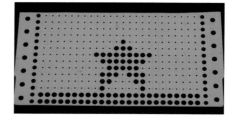

Star Single Motif stitch pattern chart.

Table 12.8: Colour Sequence for the Paisley and Star Motif

Rows	Strip 1 Col	Strip 2	Strip 3	Strip 4	Strip 5	Strip 6	Strip 7	Strip 8
60	A	E	I	M	B	F	J	N
20	B*	F	J*	N	C*	G	K*	O
20	C	G*	K	O*	D	H*	L	P*
80	D	H	L	P	A	E	I	M
20	A*	E	I*	M	B*	F	J*	N
20	B	F	J	N	C	G	K	O

each colour in Feeder 2. The sixteen main hat colours are dark, with the motif using brighter colours as a contrast. The centre stitches are Swiss Darned with bright red to offer a highlight.

The Star motif is knitted using varying shades of gold and ochre, with the main body of the hat knitted using sixteen shades of blue, grey and black.

Scarfs

METHOD

Knit 4 strips.

Push 2 Ns to WP. Using A cast on E wrap method. RC 000.

Using MT, inc 1 st at beg of the next 16 rows. 18 sts k 4 rows RC 20 rows.

Cont in blocks of 20 rows each in B, C, D, rep from A and through the 4 colours until RC 500. Dec 1 st at beg of next 16 rows. Fasten off rem 2 sts. Don't cut the end too short as this will be used to sew a bead in place.

Make another strip using E, F, G, H, and another I, J, K, L, and another M, N, O, P. Join seams together. Sew in ends and sew beads on to the points of the scarf.

IVY LEAF HAT

A further variation of a warm double fabric hat for extra cold days. This hat would work well with all-over designs such as the Zigzag or Diamond Trellis stitch patterns.

Method

Push 146 Ns to WP, cast on WY, k a few rows, change to MY and follow Table 12.9.

SHAPE CROWN

Divide into four equal sections, work on one section at a time. Place rem Ns into

Ivy Leaf Hat.

HP. Using Navy chenille dec 1 st at each end of every row until 0 sts. Rep for next section, cont until all sections have been completed.

MAKING UP

Sew side seam and join crown sections.

Materials

Finished weight 150g
Small amount Jamiesons of Shetland Spindrift, 261 Paprika.
Small amounts Knoll Soft Donegal 5548 Malone (pale blue), 5580 Silver Mist (pale grey), 5509 Greese (grey) , 5524 Abbert (dark red), 5519 Moy (aqua), 100g 5539 Sheridan (dark navy)
Navy chenille for crown

Measurements

Circumference 55cm
Depth 23cm

Tension

25 sts – 44 rows = 10 cm
MT 7••

Machines

Suitable for standard gauge punchcard and electronic machines

Table 12.9: Stitch Pattern and Colour Sequence for Ivy Leaf Hat

Rows	Stitch Pattern	Pattern Setting	Feeder 1	Feeder 2
58		Knit	Navy	
1		Knit	Paprika	
1*		Knit	Navy	
3	Rope	Fairisle	Navy	Pale Blue
3	Rope	Fairisle	Red	Grey
3	Rope	Fairisle	Navy	Pale Grey
1*		Knit	Navy	
1		Knit	Paprika	
1		Knit	Navy	
26	Large Leaf	Fairisle	Navy	Aqua
1		Knit	Navy	
1		Knit	Paprika	
Rep *to*				
1		Knit	Paprika	
Rep *to*				
1		Knit	Paprika	
76		Knit	Navy	
10	Small Leaf	Fairisle	Navy	Paprika
1		Knit	Navy	
1		Knit	Paprika	
Rep*to*				
1		Knit	Paprika	

Pick up sts from the first row, k 1 row Navy.

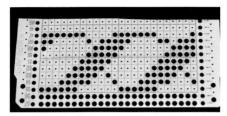
A: Rope stitch pattern chart.

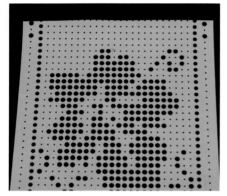
B: Large Ivy Leaf stitch pattern chart.

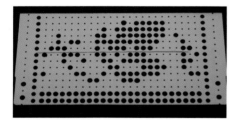
C: Small Ivy Leaf stitch pattern chart.

KEP

This pattern is based on a traditional Fairisle hat known as a Kep; it is usually hand knitted in the traditional style by the Fairisle knitters of the Shetland Isles.

Method

PUNCHCARDS
Mock Rib Stitch Pattern XX00XX00. Fairisle Stitch Patterns 2, 25, 27, 3.

BASIC PATTERN
Push 146 Ns to WP and using three different coloured ends of yarn, wrap clockwise from left to right and anti-

Traditional Fairisle Kep.

Materials
Finished weight 60g
Small amounts of a variety of cols
Jamiesons of Shetland, Spindrift

Measurements
Circumference 56cm
Length to crown 14cm

Tension
31 sts – 38 rows = 10cm
MT 7••

Machines
Suitable for standard gauge punchcard and electronic machines

clockwise from right to left to make a braid edging.

Lock the Rib punchcard.
RC 000.
K 2 rows.

Keeping the punchcard locked and working in patt setting Fairisle, k 2 rows each in col A/B, A/C, A/D, A/E.

Remove the Rib punchcard and replace with Pattern 2. K 1 row and start Fairisle patt. Complete and change stitch patt to 25, and then work stitch patt 27 and stitch patt 3. Finally replace the Rib chart and use this for the crown shaping. Work through the colours as for the lower edge rib.

SHAPE CROWN
Divide evenly into four equal sections, placing three sections of NS into Hold. Set the carriage to Hold and work the section remaining in WP, dec 1 st at each end of the row until 2 sts remain. Fasten off.

Bring the next section into WP and rep. Cont until all four sections have been knitted.

MAKING UP
Join side seams and crown seams together and sew in ends.
Wash and press firmly.

AUTUMN KEP

Change some of the stitch patterns and the colour palette to create a hat of different character.

This basic pattern can easily be made larger by adding more sts. However, it is worth bearing in mind that it will look better if the pattern matches at the sides. The Kep can also be made longer by adding extra rows and finishing off with a pompom.

Image of hat with 3 Rams Horn repeats (stitch pattern 25 and rep off set) and colourway from the Turquoise

Autumn Fairisle Traditional Kep.

Traditional Fairisle Variation Kep.

Stripe Fairisle Jacket in a previous chapter.

The above basic pattern can be further changed to make a reversible hat, replacing the crown shaping by simply gathering in the stitches at the top of the crown.

REVERSIBLE HAT

The reversible hat can be made using blocks of colour and a striped brim. Follow the pattern below but just add stripes for the twenty rows to make the brim. Tighten the tension for the brim rows, and revert to MT for the main part of the hat.

Reversible hat with striped brim.

Fairisle Variation Reversible Hat

The inside of the hat is a different colour to the outside, and the brim consists of a Fairisle stitch pattern that complements the main block of colour. The Fairisle stitch patterns chosen amounted to twenty rows each side. It is not necessary to tighten the tension for the brim as this will happen automatically when knitting the Fairisle pattern.

The brim is turned up, so this must be remembered when knitting, and use the correct colours and pattern for the main part of the hat. If you are using bright blue on one side and brown on the other the brim pattern will be the one that corresponds to the other colour.

The sequence will be ninety rows

Fairisle brim of reversible hat.

bright blue in stocking stitch, twenty rows brown Fairisle stitch pattern, twenty rows bright blue Fairisle stitch pattern, ninety rows stocking stitch.

Method

SHORT VERSION

Push 144 Ns to WP cast on WY and k a few rows; k 1 row using nylon cord. RC 000, using MY k 90 rows st st.

Brim

20 rows first Fairisle stitch pattern of your choice.

20 rows second Fairisle stitch pattern.

K 90 rows st st using a contrasting colour.

Materials
Variety of yarns 3 ply, 2/14s
Finished weight:
Short version: 80g with pompom
Long version: 90g with pompom

Measurements
Short version: circumference 56cm, depth 19cm
Long version: circumference 56cm, depth 23cm

Tension
MT 7••

Machines
Suitable for standard gauge punchcard and electronic machines

Completed hat with blue right side.

Completed hat with brown right side.

K 1 row nylon cord.
K a few rows with WY.
Remove from machine.
Sew down the side seam.
Sew in ends.
Thread a needle with strong thread and pick up all the sts from the first row, remove the nylon cord and pull the sts together firmly and fasten off. If a hole is left, stitch together using the appropriate yarn.

Rep for the other end. Wash at 30 degrees. Make a pompom for the hat if required.

LONGER VERSION

A longer version of the hat can be made by knitting 110 rows st st in the plain colours. The Fairisle brim can also be lengthened.

HATS MADE OVER A FORM

Great fun can be had by knitting a length of fabric and placing it over a felt block. You can use the fact that a knitted fabric is stretchy, and distort the fabric to create new patterns. The resulting hat will be more formal in style. It is also possible to use an old, tired hat and upcycle it by adding knitted fabric.

The basis for the hat was a millinery felt wool hood blocked over a wooden beret-shaped form. The knitted fabric is tucked and glued or stitched down underneath the base which will make

the overall fit smaller, so bear this mind when deciding on sizing.

Method

Pin and trim the knitted fabric to the underside of the block. Ease and adjust, glue or stitch in place. Keep checking that the fabric is even all the way round the block to avoid pleating and gathering.

Leave to dry, and trim any further excess fabric. Sew Petersham hat ribbon, which has been curved around the turnback. This must be neat, as it

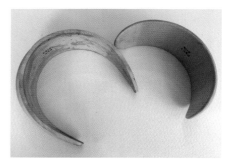

Halo block.

Hats made over a form.

will work as the hat band, and do not pull too tight as this will alter the overall size of the hat.

Various hat blocks can be used as bases – for example, a headband can be made from a halo block shape with the knitted fabric tucked inside and stitched together. A small metal headband can then be covered with velvet ribbon and sewn to the underside to cover the join.

Materials

Block, a millinery wool felt hood: this can be purchased from a millinery supplier

Textile glue: this is needed to attach the knitted fabric to the underside of the hat

2.5cm width millinery Petersham hat ribbon with cotton content (note, not synthetic, as the ribbon will not curve when ironed to fit the inside of the hat)

To curve the ribbon, cut the required length and lay it out flat on an ironing board. Hold the ribbon in one hand and follow it with the iron in the other hand following the curve. Continue to repeat this process until you have achieved the shape of the blocked hat. This length of ribbon is sewn to the underside of the hat to cover the join between the felt and the knitted fabric

Knitted fabric: finished weight 40g of fine yarn in various colours

The fabric was knitted using a fine silk marl yarn using a slip stitch Card 3 pattern from the Silver Reed basic pack. The main tension is approximately at 5 with the colours changing every four rows

Depending how open the knit is, the colour of the felt can show through – however, this only adds to the design. When easing and gently pulling the knitted fabric it can create patterns of its own as some stitches are closer and others stretched to show the base felt. The resulting fabric was fine and stretchy. You will need enough fabric to be placed over the block and under the rim – approximately 130 sts and 280 rows

Halo Hat in the making.

Beret in reds.

Halo Hat.

188/189

TURBAN

The basic felt block is a dome. Use either a shallow dome or for a deeper version, cut a soft curved V out of the centre front (as shown in the image). Knit two pieces of fabric 50cm wide by 60cm long.

Fold the two lengths of fabric in half, then thread the one half through the middle of the other half and pin in place just below the crown at the front of the form. Arrange the fabric around the block, gently easing and pinning to the lower edge. Leaving approx 4cm around the edge to turn under, glue or stitch in sections around the inside. Ease into place making sure the block is completely covered. Sew the ironed Petersham hat ribbon around the inside edge, pleating to fit, and cover the join between the fabric and the felt block.

Turban Hat.

SOFT TURBAN OR HEADBAND

Knit two pieces of fabric 60cm long by 18cm wide.

Fold one piece in half and sew together leaving a gap of 4cm in the middle. Thread the second length of fabric through the gap, so that it is in the middle. Fold the length in half and sew down the side seam. Make sure the two ends are not twisted in any way, and join the two lengths together at the back.

Soft Headband.

Soft Headband as a Turban.

Thread a needle with a strong thread and stitch small running stitches down the back seam. Gather up and pull tightly, fasten off securely.
Sew in the ends.

SOCKS

There is evidence that socks were worn by the Egyptians, the first known example dating from 1500BC. Socks grew into stockings, and have been a popular accessory throughout history. They were the catalyst for the development of the first knitting machine invented by William Lee in 1589, as speed was required to make hosiery in larger numbers. There is something very comforting about a pair of warm and cosy socks, and there is nothing nicer than a present of homemade socks.

The basic sock pattern can be altered by adding a few rows and stitches to change the sizing.

Method
RIGHT SOCK
Bring 70 Ns to WP and E wrap braid cast on by winding yarn clockwise and then anti-clockwise around the Ns. MT-1 k 1 row commence mock rib Fairisle stitch pattern XX00XXOOXXOO for 10 rows, or work a 2 x 2 rib for the required rib length and transfer stitches to the main bed.

Grey Diamond Socks.

Materials
MY suitable 3 ply

Measurements
To fit women's shoe size 6, 7, 8, 9, 10, 11

If knitting a Fairisle pattern as a general rule I knit a size up. However, it is always best to check your tension, and the size required. See sizing chart

Tension
32 sts and 42 rows = 10cm
MT approx 6

Machines
Suitable for standard gauge punchcard and electronic machines

Grafting in progress.

RC 000, k 3 rows. Dec 1 st at each end of the next and every foll 15th row until 60 sts remain.

RC 64

Alter length here as required.

Shape Heel
*Push 30 sts at opp end to carriage to HP. Cont on the rem 30 sts, k 2 rows. Push 1 N at opp end to carriage to HP on the next 14 rows, remembering to wrap the yarn around the end needle to prevent holes. Push 1 N at opp end to carriage from HP to UWP on the next 14 rows. Push all rem Ns to UWP. K 1 row *. K 80, 82, 84, 88, 92, 96 rows.

Alter foot length here as required.

Shape Toe
Work as for heel from * to *.

Using WY, k the 30 sts and remove from machine. K the rem 30 sts on to WY and release from machine.

LEFT SOCK
Work as for right sock, reversing the shaping.

Graft sts tog under foot. Join side seams.

GRAFTING
Grafting is used when an invisible join is required. Thread a tapestry needle with the same yarn as used when knitting and insert the needle into the two top loops and down into the corresponding bottom loops. Continue to repeat this process.

FAIRISLE SOCKS

Check your tension and alter the basic pattern to your own required measurements. Decide which Fairisle patterns are suitable for the socks, avoiding large floats, and complete a stitch pattern before the heel and toe shaping.

Decide which rib or top edging you are going to use, either a knitted 1 x 1, 2 x 1, 2 x 2 rib, or use an E wrap braid cast on and use stitch pattern OXOXOXOXOXOX or 00XX00XX00XX locked; keeping the same colour in Feeder 1, change the colour in Feeder 2 every two rows.

Many stitch patterns work well with socks, and you can also add an extra

Fairisle Socks.

fine thread to the main yarn for the heel and toe shaping to reinforce these areas, as this is where the main wear and tear occurs.

This pattern can also be used to make slouchy socks – simply use the larger size.

Explore the possibilities of knitting a cable into the rib or the top of the sock. Plait cables would certainly lend themselves to this. I keep the heel and toe shaping without a stitch pattern, however a small repeat pattern would work just as well, and act as a reinforcement.

Diamond pattern Autumn Socks.

SLIPPERS

These slippers are based on a 1940 December *Stitchcraft* magazine pattern that my grandma used to make. They are easy to complete and many adaptations can be configured to produce larger, smaller, plain and patterned variations. They are called

Slipper socks in red and white cashmere.

Materials
Any 3 ply, 2/14s suitable yarn in two colours
3mm crochet hook
Weight when finished 65g

Measurements
One size: length 21cm, width 12cm

Tension
32 sts – 37 rows = 10cm over Fairisle pattern
MT 7

Machines
Suitable for standard gauge punchcard and electronic machines

This pattern uses two colours only and resembles some of the stitch chart patterns from the Scandinavian countries

Original 1940 pattern and slipper.

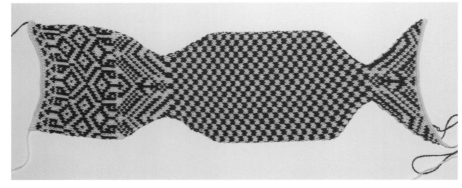

Slipper before sewing up.

bedroom slippers but have been used by my family as travel slippers, presents and stocking fillers!

Method

UPPER FRONT
Place the stitch chart pattern for the upper into the machine and lock on first row.
    Bring forward 40 Ns to WP and using MY E wrap cast on by hand. K 2 rows. Start to Fairisle pattern and work 36

rows, dec 1 st at beg of the next and every foll row until 22 sts remain.

SOLE SHAPING
Change stitch pattern to sole pattern. Inc 1 st at the beg of the next and every row until 40 sts, cont to K without shaping for 56 rows.

HEEL SHAPING
Dec 1 st at each end of the next and every foll row until 12 sts remain.
    Change stitch pattern, use the

opposite end of the upper pattern. Inc 1 st at each end of the next and every foll row until 42 sts remain. K 1 row MY, k 1 row MT+2 and latch off.

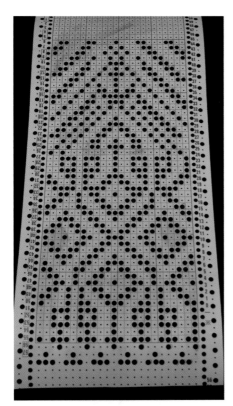

Stitch pattern chart for upper front; for the heel reverse the chart.

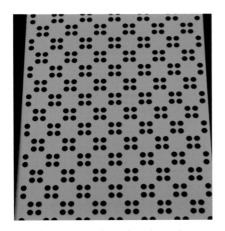

Stitch pattern chart for the sole.

TO MAKE UP

Fold the upper back over the sole and join the sloped side of the toe with the corresponding slopes of the sole. Rep with the heel. Sew in the ends and single crochet three rows around the top in alternating MY and col 1.

FLEUR DE LYS SLIPPERS

The basic slippers can be made more elaborate by using several colours and adding a cuff around the top.

The floats on the Fleur de Lys pattern are quite long so you may wish to add a few infill stitches to the pattern. If you use a Shetland or similar hairy yarn this does help to bind the floats to the surface of the accompanying yarn so it is not entirely necessary to do this.

The Fleur de Lys are knitted in shades of gold, ochre and yellow chenille, with the colours in Feeder 1 being shades of red, ruby and maroon. The colours are

changed every two, four and six rows and rep. The sole and heel stitch patterns are worked in ruby and red. The cuff stitch pattern is a small Fairisle stitch pattern knitted using ruby and red with a flash of gold through the centre. (*See* Figure-of-Eight stitch pattern on page 250.)

Follow the instructions for the previous two-colour slippers, changing stitch pattern as required.

Method

THE CUFF

Bring forward to WP 72 Ns, work a few rows using WY. Change to MY, MT-1 k 2 rows, and k the 5-row Fairisle cuff patt, k 2 rows st st, k 1 row MT+1 in contrasting yarn for the fold. MY and MT -1 k 9 rows and pick up sts of the first row to make a hem. Remove WY and k 1 row in contrast yarn. Pick up the sts around the top of the slipper. K 1 row MT, k 1 row MT+2 and latch off.

Fleur de Lys Slippers.

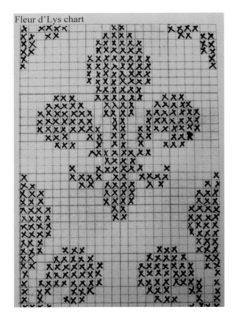

Fleur d'Lys chart

Fleur de Lys stitch patterns chart.

There are endless stitch pattern variations that can be adapted and worked into slippers. The Zigzag pattern from the hat section was used for the slippers below.

A variety of slippers.

WOMEN'S SOCK SIZES

Table 12.10 shows approximate comparison sizes and measurements for women's socks.

Table 12.10: Women's Sock Sizes

UK Size	US	Euro	Foot Length cm	Foot Circumference	Instep	Heel
2	3	34	22.2	20.5	21	32.5
2.5	4	35	22.8	21	21.5	33
3.5	5	36	23.4	21.5	22	33.5
4	6	37	24	22	22.5	34
5	7	38	24.6	22.5	23	34.5
5.5	8	39	25.2	23	23.5	35
6.5	9	40	25.8	23.5	24	35.5
7	10	41	26.4	24	24.5	36
8	11	42	27	24.5	25	36.5

Table 12.11: Men's Sock Sizes

UK Size	US	Euro	Foot Length cm	Foot Circumference	Instep	Heel
6	7	39	24.6	23.3	25.5	37
7	8	40	25	23.8	26	38
8	9	42	26	24.8	26.5	38
9	10	43	27	25.3	27	40
10	11	44.5	27.9	25.8	27.5	41
11	12	46	28.8	26.3	28	42
12	13	47	30	26.8	28.5	43
13	14	48	30.5	27.3	29	44
14	15	49	31.4	27.8	29.5	45

Foot length: measure from the outer part of the heel to the longest toe on the foot.
Foot circumference: measure around the ball of the foot to the widest part of the foot.
Instep circumference: measure the highest part of the foot around the centre of the instep (arch).
Heel circumference: measure from the base of the heel to the front of the foot where it bends.

MEN'S SOCK SIZES

Table 12.11 shows approximate comparison sizes and measurements for men's socks.

CHRISTMAS STOCKING

This pattern is basically a very large version of the sock pattern that lends itself to traditional Fairisle patterns, Christmas designs, and even lettering for names. The heel and toe are left plain but use different colours. Many of the traditional Fairisle stitch patterns are ideal for the stockings, especially when knitted in bright jewel colours.

The stocking at the right uses bright reds and greens and a variety of traditional Fairisle stitch patterns – the ones I used are 2, 23, 2, 20, 3, 22, 5, 19, 8, 17, 3, 15, 12, 14 with three to four stocking stitch rows between each pattern band.

The middle stocking uses the all-over stitch pattern 25 with turquoise, greens and blue colours in Feeder 1, and shades of red, orange and pink in Feeder 2.

The left-hand stocking is knitted in shades of brown and green with highlights of red. The Fairisle stitch patterns used for this version are 15, 5, Holly, 3, 22, 3, 21, 8, 23, 1, 6, 3, 25, 2.

Materials
Each requires differing amounts, but as a rough guide the finished weight is 130g to 150g

Measurements
Each one is different as the rows and top rib vary
Approx 57cm in height

Tension
32 sts – 36 rows over the Fairisle pattern
MT 8

Machines
Suitable for standard gauge punchcard and electronic machines

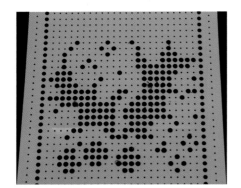

Holly stitch pattern chart.

Method

The stocking is knitted from the top down, so bear this in mind if any of the patterns you are using needs to be the correct way up, such as the holly design. When choosing stitch patterns make sure they fit into the overall length and width, and if not then add on a few rows and stitches. Try and match up as best as you can down the side seams.

Bring forward 112 Ns to WP E wrap braid cast on using two ends of yarn. K 2 rows MT – 1 using XOXOXO stitch pattern and keeping MY in Feeder 1 and changing the col in Feeder 2 every 2 rows work 30 rows (or fewer) MT start Fairisle pattern of your choice. RC 000.

Work to row 128, COR adjust length if required. Set carriage to partial knitting, always wrap the yarn around the last needle to prevent holes. Push 90 Ns at opp end to carriage to HP on the next row.

K 1 row. Push 5 Ns at opp end to carriage to HP on next row, k 1 row. Push 4 Ns at opp end to carriage to HP, k 1 row. Push 3 Ns at opp end to carriage to HP and on next and every foll alt row 3 times, k 1 row. Push 2 Ns at opp end to carriage to HP on next row, k 1 row. Push rem Ns to HP.

Cut yarn. Take carriage to opp side of work. Push 78 Ns at opp end to carriage from HP to UWP. K 2 rows. Push 5 Ns at opp end to carriage to HP on next row, k 1 row. Push 4 Ns at opp end to carriage to HP, k 1 row. Push 2 Ns at opp end to carriage to HP.

Stockings hung from the mantelpiece.

HEEL SHAPING

*Push 1 N at carriage end to HP on next 22 rows**. Push 1 N at carriage end to HP on next 2 rows, k 1 row. ** Rep ** to ** 4 times.*** Push 1 N at opp end to carriage from HP to UWP on next 2 rows, k 1 row ***Rep from *** to *** 4 times. Push 1 N at opp end to carriage from HP to UWP on next 22 rows*.

COL. Push 2 Ns at opp end of carriage from HP to UWP on next and foll alt row, k 1 row. Push 3 Ns at opp end to carriage from HP to UWP on next and every foll alt row 3 times, k 1 row. Push 4 Ns at opp end of carriage from HP to UWP on next row, k 1 row. Push 5 NS at opp end to carriage from HP to UWP on next row, k 1 row. Cut yarn. COR.

Push all Ns to HP, push 2 Ns opp carriage from HP to UWP on next and foll alt row, k 1 row. Push 3 Ns at opp end to carriage from HP to UWP on next and foll alt row 3 times, k 1 row. Push 4 Ns at opp end to carriage from HP to UWP on next row, k 1 row. Push 5 Ns at opp end to carriage from HP to UWP on next row, k 1 row. Push all rem Ns to UWP. K 46 rows.

TOE SHAPING

Push 56 Ns at left to HP. Rep as for heel shaping * to *, remove from machine on to WY.

K rem sts off machine on to WY.

MAKING UP

Graft stitches under the foot. Sew the side seam. Make a loop and tassel and attach to the top back of the stocking to hang from the mantelpiece.

CHRISTMAS BAUBLES

Method

Work the middle Fairisle section first. Choose a Fairisle pattern. The examples use 15, 19, 20 or 23.

Cast on 50 sts using WY and k a few rows. Change to MY, k 3 rows st st.

K the chosen Fairisle stitch pattern. MY k 3 rows st st.

Remove from the machine WY.

TOP PART

**Pick up sts from WY on to N I* VIIVII rep from * ending with I.

K 1 row.

K a few rows WY, remove from machine.

Rep previous 2 rows.

Pick up sts from WY on to Ns IVIV rep to end.

K 1 row, k a few rows WY, remove from machine.

Pick up sts on to NS VVV rep to end.

K 1 row, k a few rows WY, remove from machine. Rep last two rows **
until 3 sts remain.

K an I cord for 9cm. Break yarn leaving a long end to sew up side seam.

Materials
10g of assorted colours Knoll Soft Donegal and Jamiesons of Shetland Spindrift
Cotton ball 18.50cm circumference or filling

Measurements
19cm circumference

Tension
32 sts – 36 rows = 10cm
MT 8

Machines
Standard gauge punchcard and electronic machines

Abbreviations
I = pick up one st on to the N
V = pick up two sts on to the N

Thread yarn through 3 sts and pull to tighten.

For lower part rep from ** to ** until 2 sts remain, break yarn and thread through rem sts.

Either wrap around cotton ball and sew down side seam, tucking in loose ends as you go, or stuff with filling as side seam is sewn up.

Christmas baubles.

CHAPTER 13

INTERIORS

Throws can aesthetically enhance a room, placed over the arm of a sofa or draped on a bed and used to add extra warmth on cold winter nights. There is real comfort to be had in wrapping yourself in a throw while relaxing. This is handmade soft furnishings at its very best. If you enjoy the process of knitting this throw, and carry on knitting, it will develop into a blanket – since a throw is a kind of blanket usually smaller in size and just right to grab and create an extra layer.

LOG CABIN THROW

The process and making up of the Log Cabin Throw design lends itself to knitting, as well as quilting and patchwork, as repeated squares and oblongs are easy to knit. The design has its origins firmly in the thrifty quilt field, which used up fabric oddments and worn-out clothing. Small amounts of yarn that you have left over from another project can be used when making these designs, and while the idea behind the design of this throw was to use up every scrap of material, this is even more important today with the waste and excesses as practised by our disposable culture acting against the spirit of sustainability that we discussed earlier.

The origin of the design I am interpreting to use in the throw design is incredibly ancient, with similar design motifs being found in Egyptian tombs.

Antique Log Cabin Throw.

According to Janet Rae in *Quilts of the British Isles,* the dark and light pattern used can be traced back to tenant farmers of the Middle Ages, who were given a dry and a wet portion of land to cultivate, and the ploughing of these fields made what were known as '*run rigs*', patterns of light and dark in the soil. A quilt dated before 1830 that was made in England shows this design quite clearly.

The real popularity of the throw started in America in the 1860s during the Civil War, and as with many other heritage crafts, the designs made in this period are steeped in symbolism. Traditionally made, they used half dark and half light colours, with either a red centre symbolizing the home hearth, or a yellow centre representing a welcoming light in the window. And the light build-up of oblongs along one side represents the light shining on one side of the home or cabin, while the dark colours on the other side represent the shadows on the other side of the home or cabin.

These designs embodied the pioneering spirit of early America. During the American Civil War folklore has it that if a quilt hanging on the line had a black centre it meant it was a safe stop on the underground railway (a route used by enslaved African Americans to escape into the free states and Canada). The Union army raised funds by raffling off quilts of this kind.

While it is always interesting to delve into the history of heritage crafts, it very often raises more questions than answers. There is no doubt, however, that it is a popular pattern in use today with some contemporary innovative and original designs, and its versatility ensures that it will be in use as a design source for many centuries to come.

The knitted Antique Log Cabin Throw comprises four large squares sewn together – once you start to work and develop more designs you will discover that this is a rich seam for many pattern variations based on the log cabin formula.

Keep the yarn you are using the same weight, as this will help prevent uneven squares that will not fit together neatly.

Materials
A variety of colours using Knoll Soft Donegal, and Jamiesons of Shetland Spindrift in oil
The finished throw with four squares is equal to 800g

Measurements
Each single square measures 61cm. The completed throw with four squares sewn together and a crochet edging measures 127cm square

Tension
32 sts – 36 rows = 10cm
MT 8

Machines
Suitable for standard gauge punchcard and electronic machines

Method

The log cabin throw is made up of four large squares knitted half with dark colours and half using a lighter palette, to create the distinctive pattern that is so characteristic of the old log cabin quilted blankets.

The interest is further enhanced by working larger and smaller Fairisle stitch patterns alternately. The centre block, numbered 1 on the diagram, uses the same colours and stitch pattern but it would certainly be an interesting exercise to alter the stitch pattern for each square. However, the squares should remain the same size, so careful choice of patterns would be required.

To make the throw you will need to make two completed squares, containing twenty-five blocks, turning to the left, and two turning to the right.

When knitting the Fairisle pattern make sure the end stitches are not loose thereby causing holes, so wrapping the end needles with the

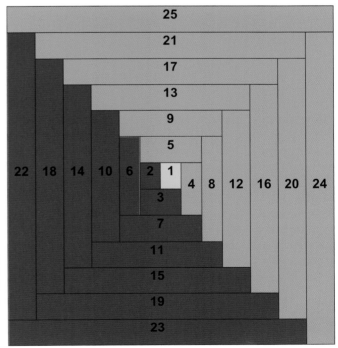

Diagram showing numbered blocks and numbered sequence.

Blocks 1, 2 and 3.

Block 4 added.

Block 5 added.

yarn and gently tightening ends.

Do not pull or stretch the work when picking up the stitches as this will distort the finished square.

BLOCK 1
Bring forward 30 Ns to WP using MC E wrap cast on. K 3 rows using Fairisle Stitch Pattern 25, complete the 23 rows in colours of your choice. MC k 2 rows st st, k 1 row MT+2 and latch off.

BLOCK 2
With wrong side facing, pick up 26 sts along right side of Block 1. Using a dark palette k 2 rows st st. Using Fairisle Stitch Pattern 8, k the 7 rows of patt, K 2 rows st st, k 1 row MT+2 and latch off.

BLOCK 3
Turn right and pick up along the edge of Block 1 and the extra stitches from the previous Block 2. Using Stitch Pattern 8 and a different set of dark colours, k 2 rows st st, k 7 rows Fairisle pattern, k 2 rows st st, k 1 row MT + 2 and latch off.

FURTHER BLOCKS 4 AND 5
Continue to turn the work right; using Fairisle Stitch Pattern 8 and two sets of lighter shades and adding the extra stitches as required, knit the blocks.

Blocks 6 and 7: Continue to turn right and pick up stitches along the required edge without stretching the work; using dark colours and Stitch Pattern 21, knit the blocks.

Blocks 8 and 9: Using light colours and Stitch Pattern 21, knit the blocks.

Blocks 10 and 11: Using dark colours and Stitch Pattern 22, knit the blocks.

Blocks 12 and 13: Using light colours and Stitch Pattern 22, knit the blocks.

Blocks 14 and 15: Using dark colours and Stitch Pattern 17, knit the blocks.

Blocks 16 and 17: Using light colours and Stitch Pattern 17, knit the blocks.

Blocks 18 and 19: Using dark colours and Stitch Pattern 25, knit the blocks.

Blocks 20 and 21: Using light colours and Stitch Pattern 25, knit the blocks.

Blocks 22 and 23: Using dark colours and Stitch Pattern 8, knit the blocks.

Blocks 24 and 25: Using light colours and Stitch Pattern 8, knit the blocks.

Repeat the twenty-five block square.

Make another two twenty-five block squares, turning the work to the left for the mirror image.

Completed twenty-five block square.

The dark colours joining in the centre.

MAKING UP

Before the Antique Throw is sewn together you can decide if you prefer the dark colours in the middle of the throw or the light colours. My preference was for the light colours.

Sew the squares together. Sew in the ends. Crochet a border, or knit a small border of your choice.

LOG CABIN CUSHION COVER

If you have knitted a square and decided that enough is enough, you can always turn it into a cushion cover. Knit one twenty-five block square and make a cushion cover.

The reverse of the cushion cover was

Antique Log Cabin Cushion Cover.

The reverse of the Cushion Cover.

Method

Following the diagram, knit the first quarter:

Block 1: Col 1. Bring forward 20 Ns to WP and E wrap cast on k 32 rows. K 1 row MT+1 and cast off.

Block 2: Col 2. Pick up 20 sts from the side of the first square and k 12 rows. K 1 row MT+1 and cast off.

Block 3: Col 2. Pick up 26 sts along the required edge of Blocks 1 and 2. K 12 rows. K 1 row MT+ 1 and cast off.

Block 4: Col 1. Pick up 26 sts along the

worked using a Fairisle all-over stitch pattern and two complimentary colours, mid green and clover, using Shetland wool.

QUARTERED LOG CABIN THROW

The following throw uses the same principles of building up a square, but this time square one is placed in the corner, and blocks two, three, four and five are worked round two sides. An unseen surprise result having knitted these squares was that an optical illusion was created in that the outlined square appears to float in front of the knitted background colour.

This again is an easy throw to knit, yet the colour combinations create a real impact. The throw was worked using a random colour choice with a variety of colours that I had on the shelf, to create a happy, vibrant fabric. You could restrict the colour choice to blues and greens, or blues and reds, or orange pinks and reds – either way they would all be successful.

Four smaller squares make up one larger, and it is up to you how large the throw/blanket is going to be.

Quartered Log Cabin Throw.

Materials

Each square made up of four quarters requires 35g of yarn
The throw shown is made up of twenty-five squares, the finished weight 900g
A variety of colours in a fine 3-ply yarn, Knoll Soft Donegal and Jamiesons of Shetland Spindrift in oil
Two colours are required for each quarter, eight for each completed square
3mm crochet hook

Measurements

Each square of four quarters measures 26.5 x 26.5cm
The throw shown measures 148sq cm

Tension

24 sts – 28 rows = 10cm over st st
Approx MT 8

Machines

Suitable for standard gauge punchcard and electronic machines

required edge of Blocks 2 and 3. K 12 rows. K 1 row MT+1 and cast off.
Block 5: Col 1. Pick up 34 sts along the required edge of 3 and 4, k 12 rows, k 1 row MT+1 and cast off.

Make three more, taking care to follow the diagram and pick up the correct edges so they all fit together. Sew together and make as many more as required.

FINISHING OFF

Lay out all your squares and arrange and rearrange them to obtain the best colour mix. Sew all squares together. Wash and press. Finish the edge with either a single row of crochet or a knitted edging.

COURT HOUSE STEPS MARAZION FAIRISLE THROW

This vibrant throw uses another technique by adding borders to a central block. The centre block uses Stitch Pattern 25 throughout. Each centre block is worked in shades of blue. Blocks 2 and 3 are worked in shades of red, Blocks 4 and 5 in shades of blue, Blocks 6 and 7 in shades of red, Blocks 8 and 9 in shades of blue, Blocks 10 and 11 in shades of red, and Blocks 12 and 13 in shades of blue.

Make two identical completed blocks and then change the colours for the next two.

Diagram showing Quartered Log Cabin numbered sequence.

Marazion Court House Steps Throw.

Materials

The finished weight of the completed throw is 850g

12 blocks each weighing approx 70g, each in a variety of colours of fine 4-ply Knoll Soft Donegal and Jamiesons of Shetland Spindrift in oil

Measurements

Each block is 42 x 42cm; the throw consists of twelve completed blocks

The completed blanket is 173 x 128cm including the crochet edging

Tension

32 sts – 36 rows = 10cm
MT 8

Machines

Suitable for all standard gauge punchcard and electronic machines

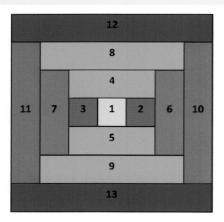

Diagram showing Marazion Court House Steps Throw numbered

Method

Block 1: Bring forward 30 Ns to WP and E wrap cast on. Using shades of blue colours, K 3 rows st st, work the Fairisle Stitch Pattern 25, k 2 rows st st, 1 row MT+2 and latch off.

Block 2: Worked to the left and right of the previous block. Working with shades of red and using Fairisle Stitch Pattern 9. With wrong side facing pick up 26 sts from LHS. K 2 rows st st, work the Fairisle stitch pattern, k 2 rows st st, k 1 row MT +1 and latch off. Rep for **Block 3** on RHS.

Blocks 4 and 5: Use the same stitch pattern but in shades of blue. Pick up approx 48 sts.

Blocks 6, 7, 8, 9: Cont to build up the blocks as set using Fairisle Stitch Pattern 20.

Squares 5 and 6 showing colour changes.

Squares 1 and 2 showing colour changes.

Squares 7 and 8 showing colour changes.

Squares 3 and 4 showing colour changes.

Squares 9 and 10 showing colour changes.

Squares 11 and 12 showing colour changes.

Blocks 10, 11, 12, 13: As set in using Fairisle Stitch Pattern 19.

Complete twelve squares in total. When all the twelve squares have been knitted, lay them out and decide which ones compliment the adjacent ones best. You could place all the blue borders together, which will give an hour-glass shape to the colours, and also keeps the blocks uniform. I decided to twist the adjacent block through 180 degrees and therefore an adjacent red border was placed next to a blue one.

Block, press and sew the squares together. Sew in ends.

Single crochet and edging, completing three rounds of the throw using contrasting colours, or knit a garter stitch border.

All the blocks placed the same way. Note the hour-glass shape to the coloured blocks.

Court House Steps Fairisle Throw completed.

TARGET SQUARE THROW

Single colours can have a real visual impact when placed next to other colours that can make them 'pop', and this was the case with the Target Throw. Single coloured squares are built up using the Court House Steps technique, and four graded, coloured floating squares enclose a central square in a contrasting colour. Sixteen squares make up the finished blanket. This technique is also known as a target, for obvious reasons.

Follow the instructions for the previous throw but use only a variety of contrasting single colours.

Method

Block 1: Bring forward 24 Ns to WP and Col 1 E wrap cast on. K 32 rows, MT+1 k 1 row, latch off.
Blocks 2 and 3: Worked to the left and right of the previous block. Using Col 2* pick up the edge stitches from the right or left side, without stretching the

Target Square Throw.

Twelve squares sewn together make an oblong Target Throw.

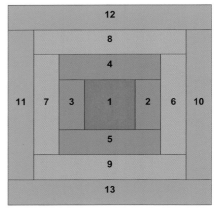

Diagram showing Court House Steps Target Throw numbered sequence.

previous block. K 10 rows, k 1 row MT+1, latch off.
Blocks 4 and 5: Col 2. Pick up along the edge of Blocks 2, 1 and 3 and work

10 rows and k 1 row MT+1 latch off.*
Blocks 6, 7, 8, 9: Rep from * to * using Col 3.
Blocks 10, 11, 12, 13: Rep from * to * using Col 4.
Blocks 14, 15, 16, 17: Rep from * to * using Col 5.

Make fifteen more squares using varying sets of colours. Block and press each square and sew together.

Materials
Finished weight 650g

Variety of colours of Knoll Soft Donegal and Jamiesons of Shetland Spindrift in oil

Measurements
Each square 30 x 30cm

Completed blanket of sixteen squares 140 x 140cm

Tension
32 sts – 36 rows = 10cm
Approx MT 8

Machines
Suitable for all standard gauge punchcard and electronic machines

PORTAL BLANKET

The Portal Blanket is a variation on the previous pattern, and the choice of colours makes this eye catching as colours are graded and shaded to create a contrast and each works as a catalyst for the next one chosen. There is an extra set of blocks – 14, 15, 16 and 17 – so it is larger in size. The colours used were inspired by the artist Victor Vaserely, who was a master at mixing bright shades together.

Method

Follow the basic instructions for the previous throw, and knit the first central square.

Block 1: Bring forward 24 Ns to WP and Col 1 E wrap cast on and k 32 rows MT+1 k 1 row, latch off.

The surrounding blocks all consist of twelve rows plus the final row MT+2 latch off row. However, these are broken down into four rows of three colours.

Blocks 2, 3, 4, 5: K 4 rows each of three contrasting colours.

Blocks 6, 7, 8, 9: K 3 rows each of 4 colours.

Blocks 10, 11, 12, 13: Rep the cols and

Materials
650g of assorted colours Knoll Soft Donegal and Jamiesons of Shetland Spindrift

Measurements
Each square is 34.5cm

Twelve squares sewn together make 165 x 111cm

Tension
32 sts – 36 rows = 10cm
MT 8

Machines
Suitable for all standard gauge punchcard and electronic machines

Square 1.

Square 4.

Square 2.

Square 5.

Square 3.

Square 6.

Square 7.

Square 9.

Square 11.

Square 8.

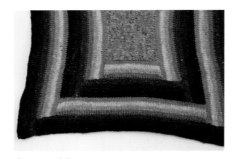

Square 10.

Square 12.

rows worked in 2, 3, 4, 5.

Blocks 14, 15, 16, 17: Rep the cols and rows for 6, 7, 8, 9.

Square 1: Block 1 is Blue. Blocks 2, 3, 4, 5 and 10, 11, 12, 13 worked in 3 rows each of Cerise, Orange, Pink and Red.

Blocks 6, 7, 8, 9 and 14, 15, 16, 17 worked in 4 rows each of Purple, Emerald and Yellow.

Square 2: Centre square is Dark Red. Blocks 2, 3, 4, 5 and 10, 11, 12, 13 worked in 3 rows each of Light Brown, Ochre, Gold and Yellow. Blocks 6, 7, 8, 9 and 14, 15, 16, 17 worked in 4 rows each of Orange, Turquoise and Emerald Green.

Square 3: Centre square Pale Blue. Blocks 2, 3, 4, 5 and 10, 11, 12, 13 worked in 3 rows each of Peacock Blue,

Mid Blue, Turquoise and Bright Blue. Blocks 6, 7, 8, 9 and 14, 15, 16, 17 worked in 4 rows each of Purple, Charcoal and Mauve.

Square 4: Centre square Dark Grey. Blocks 2, 3, 4, 5 and 10, 11, 12, 13 worked in 3 rows each of Dark Purple, Dark Red, Purple, and Lavender. Blocks 6, 7, 8, 9 and 14, 15, 16, 17 worked in 4 rows each of Cerise, Mauve and Pale Pink.

Square 5: Centre square Pale Turquoise. Blocks 2, 3, 4, 5 and 10, 11, 12, 13 worked in 3 rows each of Cream, Silver, Aqua and Pale Grey.

Blocks 6, 7, 8, 9 and 14, 15, 16, 17 worked in 4 rows each of Grey, Dark Grey and Black.

Square 6: Centre square Bright Blue. Blocks 2, 3, 4, 5 and 10, 11, 12, 13 worked in 3 rows each of Red, Maroon, Purple and Black. Blocks 6, 7, 8, 9 and 14, 15, 16, 17 worked in 4 rows each of Red, Bright Red and Orange.

Square 7: Centre square Mid Blue. Blocks 2, 3, 4, 5 and 10, 11, 12, 13, worked in 3 rows each of Purple, Bright Blue, Peacock Blue and Turquoise. Blocks 6, 7, 8, 9 and 14, 15, 16, 17 worked in 4 rows of Orange, Bright Red and Cerise.

Square 8: Centre square Red. Blocks 2, 3, 4, 5 and 10, 11, 12, 13 worked in 3 rows each of Yellow, Lime, Emerald and Grass Green. Blocks 6, 7, 8, 9 and 14, 15, 16, 17 worked in blocks of 4 rows of Cerise, Purple and Maroon.

Square 9: Centre square Pink. Blocks 2,

Portal Blanket completed.

uses Fairisle Stitch Pattern 26, the large snowflake, and the throw is made up of twelve squares. The Fairisle stitch pattern enclosing the centre is 17, followed by 21 and finally 22, with three stocking stitch rows beginning and completing each block. The same Fairisle stitch patterns are used throughout, although the colours are

Materials
Finished weight 900g
Each single square 75g
A variety of colours of Knoll Soft
Donegal and Jamiesons of Shetland
Spindrift

Measurements
Each square approx 38 x 39cm
Completed twelve-square throw 177 x
125cm

Tension
32 sts – 36 rows = 10cm
MT 7••

Machines
Suitable for all standard gauge
punchcard and electronic machines

3, 4, 5 and 10, 11, 12, 13 worked in 3 rows each of Bright Blue, Maroon, Purple and Cerise. Blocks 6, 7, 8, 9 and 14, 15, 16, 17 worked in 4 rows each of Orange, Dark Green and Ochre.

Square 10: Centre square Grey. Blocks 2, 3, 4, 5 and 10, 11, 12, 13 worked in 3 rows each of Ochre, Pale Green, Lime and Grass Green. Blocks 6, 7, 8, 9 and 14, 15, 16, 17 worked in 4 rows each of Green, Forest Green and Dark Green.

Square 11: Centre square Purple. Blocks 2, 3, 4, 5 and 10, 11, 12, 13 worked in 3 rows each of Peacock Blue, Bright Pink, Aqua and Pink. Blocks 6, 7, 8, 9 and 14, 15, 16, 17 worked in 4 rows each of Lime, Orange and Yellow.

Square 12: Centre square Silver. Blocks 2, 3, 4, 5 and 10, 11, 12, 13 worked in 3 rows each of Dark Grey, Rust, Black and Terracotta. Blocks 6, 7, 8, 9 and 14, 15, 16, 17 worked in 4 rows each of Orange, Grey and Bright Orange.

When each of the squares has been completed, block and press. Place them together and rearrange them for the best colour combination. Sew together and work an edging of your choice.

ORKNEY FAIRISLE THROW

This intricate and cosy throw is based on the target patterns of the original antique American quilts. The effect relies on the squares around the central square alternating light to dark to allow the pattern to appear to recede and advance in turn. The central square

Orkney Throw.

changed with each square to create a vibrant and elaborate fabric.

The twelve squares are shown below in detail, but customise and choose your own colour palette from an inspiration which excites. This is a good exercise to knit spontaneously and mix colours – so group together the light and dark colours as this will help speed things up. Return to your sketch book for colour or pattern combinations.

Square 1.

Square 5.

Method

Follow the diagram for the Target Throw.

Bring forward to WP 26 sts E wrap cast on k 3 rows, complete the Snowflake Fairisle Stitch Pattern 26, k 3 rows k 1 row MT+1 and latch off.

Blocks 2, 3: With wrong side facing pick up 26 sts along the edge k 3 rows, complete Stitch Pattern 17, k 3 rows, k 1 row MT+1 latch off.

Blocks 4, 5: With wrong side facing pick up 50 sts and rep previous blocks.

Blocks 6, 7: Pick up 52 sts k 3 rows complete Stitch Pattern 21, k 3 rows, k 1 row MT+1 latch off.

Blocks 8, 9: Pick up 76 sts rep previous two blocks.

Blocks 10, 11: Pick up 78 sts k 3 rows, complete Stitch Pattern 22, k 3 rows k 1 row MT+1, latch off.

Blocks 12, 13: Pick up 108 sts, rep previous 2 blocks.

Block and press each square and sew in the ends.

Lay out the completed squares and move them around to work out which sit well together and then sew together, three squares by four squares.

Crochet or knit an edging. Wash and press.

Square 2.

Square 6.

Square 3.

Square 7.

Square 4.

Square 8.

Square 9.

Square 10.

Square 11.

Square 12.

PEBBLES THROW

The Court House Steps pattern lends itself to producing squares, which can be seen in some of the previous throws. With this in mind and having researched the work of Josef Albers and his *Homage to The Square* I wanted to work my own homage. Josef Albers produced hundreds of variations on the basic compositional scheme of three or four squares set inside each other using different colour palettes and different orders of colours with the squares slightly gravitating towards the bottom edge, so revealing an extraordinary perceptual complexity inside what appears to be a very narrow conceptual framework.

The way that he designed this series of work was that each square was placed within another, and the distances between the squares were rigorously adhered to. The square was not placed in the middle but nearer the base to create a squeezing tension within the square. The width of the outer blocks, to the left and right of the central square, are half the width of the centre. The top dimensions are three times those of the bottom. Whether using a three square or four square design, the ratios remained the same, and knowing this, it is very easy to create your own versions scaling up and down to create larger and smaller squares.

The choice of colour is important to create the effect you require. A dark middle square recedes while a light one advances. The surrounding colours on some of the squares are graded within the same colour, while others are chosen to compliment.

Each central square of the Pebbles Throw is surrounded on all four sides by two more squares and uses all the subtle colours of a pebble beach – grey, aqua, beige and cream. An attempt

Pebbles Throw.

Materials
Various colours of your choice of fine Knoll Soft Donegal and Jamiesons of Shetland Spindrift

Weight of each square 25g; scale up for the size you require

The Pebbles Throw uses 30 squares, 750g in total

Measurements
Each single square measures 23 x 23cm

Finished throw 116 x 146cm

Tension
26 sts – 44 rows = 10cm
MT 7••

Machines
Suitable for all standard gauge punchcard and electronic machines

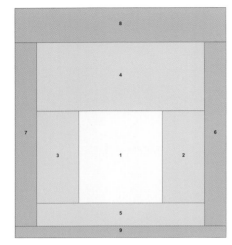

Diagram showing the numbered sequence for the Pebbles Throw.

Pebbles Throw: the inspiration for this throw was found on the banks of Kinloch Rannoch in Scotland.

was made to capture not only the colours of the pebbles and sand, but also the light breeze and quiet contemplation which is present when sitting and watching the waves gently ebb and flow.

Method

Worked in st st throughout.

Refer to the blocks on the diagram and work in sequence 1–9:

1: Col 1 bring forward 24 Ns to WP and using Col 1 E wrap cast on k 30r, *k 1 row MT+2 cast off* rep *–* at the end of every block.
2: Col 2 pick up 24 sts k 18 rows.
3: Col 2 pick up 24 sts k 18 rows.
4: Col 2 pick up 42 sts k 26 rows.
5: Col 2 pick up 42 sts k 10 rows.
6: Col 3 pick up 50 sts k 10 rows.
7: Col 3 pick up 50 sts k 10 rows.
8: Col 3 pick up 62 sts k 14 rows.
9: Col 3 pick up 62 sts k 6 rows.

Sew in ends, block and press the squares, sew together.

EQUAL AND UNEQUAL THROW

Following on from the Pebbles Throw, the Equal and Unequal Throw consists of four squares; the formula is the same as the Pebbles Throw, but adding an extra square and using a greater variety of colours creates a very different character.

Equal and Unequal Throw.

Materials

A single square weighs 30g; the throw is made up of twenty-five squares so the finished weight is 750g

Collect together a variety of colours of fine 3-ply 2/14s weight

Measurements

A single square measures 26 x 26cm

The finished throw is 140 x 140cm washed and lightly pressed

Tension

26 sts – 44 rows = 10cm
MT 7••

Machines

Suitable for all standard gauge punchcard and electronic machines

Method

Refer to the blocks in the diagram and work 1–13.

Block 1: Col 1 bring forward 24 Ns to WP E wrap cast on k 28 rows, *k 1 row MT+2 and cast off* rep * to * complete all the blocks.

Block 2: Col 2 pick up 22 sts k 12 rows.
Block 3: Col 2 pick up 22 sts k 12 rows.
Block 4: Col 2 pick up 36 sts k 16 rows.
Block 5: Col 2 pick up 36 sts k 8 rows.
Block 6: Col 3 pick up 38 sts k 12 rows.
Block 7: Col 3 pick up 38 sts k 12 rows.
Block 8: Col 3 pick up 50 sts k 16 rows.
Block 9: Col 3 pick up 50 sts k 8 rows.
Block 10: Col 4 pick up 51 sts k 12 rows.
Block 11: Col 4 pick up 51 sts k 12 rows.
Block 12: Col 4 pick up 61 sts K 16 rows.
Block 13: Col 4 pick up 61 sts k 8 rows.
Sew in ends, block and press. Sew squares together.

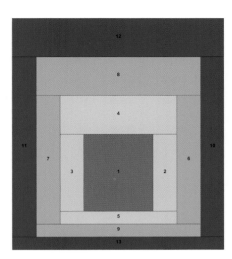

Diagram showing the numbered sequence for the Equal and Unequal Throw.

VARIATIONS

There are many other variations on this theme, as can be seen below. Use the diagrams and work through the blocks and make oblongs or squares either in stocking stitch or Fairisle variations. It is a great way to use up small quantities of yarn. Scale them up or down and make blankets, throws or cushion covers.

BASKET WEAVE CUSHION

Basket Weave Cushion.

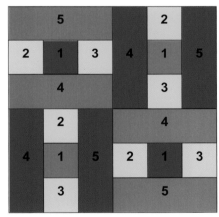

Diagram showing Fairisle numbered sequence.

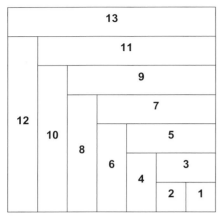

Diagram showing the numbered sequence for the Log Cabin variation.

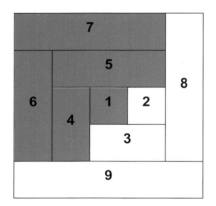

Diagram showing the numbered sequence for the Red and Gold Log Cabin Square variation.

Red and Gold Log Cabin Square variation.

Log Cabin variation.

FAIRISLE AND PLAID CUSHION COVERS

Cushions appear to make a chair or sofa cosier and more inviting, and encourage you to put your feet up. They are also a relatively quick and easy way to reinvigorate a tired room as they can add a splash of intense colour to neutral surroundings and create a real focal point. Ideally you need about five cushions for a sofa, and a variety of sizes and shapes help when arranging them, with the larger more subtle tones are placed at the back and the smaller, vibrant statements at the front. The traditional Fairisle cushion designs will add interest to any room, and can be finished with a complimentary traditional herringbone pattern on the reverse.

The smaller cushions use the Plaid stitch pattern on one side and the Fairisle border and peerie stitch patterns on the other. Using either side would create a statement, and makes for a versatile cushion, which can be turned round to ring the changes.

Always make a cover smaller than the cushion pad to make sure it appears plump and comfy rather than flat and thin.

A pile of cushions.

Lewis Mist Cushion.

Materials
Finished weight 260g; various colours of yarns in the chosen palette

Knoll Soft Donegal and Jamiesons of Shetland Spindrift

Measurements
Cushion pad 62 x 42cm

Tension
32sts – 36rows = 10cm
MT 8

Machines
Suitable for all standard gauge punchcard and electronic machines

Method
Choose whichever peerie traditional Fairisle stitch patts fit into the 142 row sequence. The ones chosen for the samples were 21, 3, 25, 5, 23, 2, 15, 3, 22, 5 and 19, with 3 st st rows between each patt band.

The Plaid Stitch Pattern can be found with the Paisley Hat in the Accessories chapter. Turn it upside down to knit the pattern.

Table 13.1: Plaid Fairisle Pattern Stitch and Colour Sequence

Rows	Stitch Pattern	Pattern Setting	Feeder 1	Feeder 2
5	Plaid	Fairisle	Col 1	Col 2
1	Plaid	Knit	Col 3	
5	Plaid	Fairisle	Col 1	Col 2
12	Plaid	Fairisle	Col 4	Col 5
1	Plaid	Knit	Col 6	
1	Plaid	Fairisle	Col 7	Col 8
1	Plaid	Knit	Col 6	
12	Plaid	Fairisle	Col 9	Col 10

Rep from beginning using a different combination of colours.

HEBRIDEAN WINTER CUSHION COVER

Method
Note the pattern blocks are not the same size – the Fairisle block is larger.

FAIRISLE BLOCK
Bring forward 92 Ns to WP, E wrap cast on and work the Fairisle patt bands to RC 142, cast off.

PLAID BLOCK
Bring forward 70 Ns to WP, E wrap cast on and work the Plaid stitch patt to RC 142 cast off.

Sew the two blocks together using mattress stitch for a neat join.

HERRINGBONE BACK
The Herringbone stitch pattern can be found in the Panelled Coats and Jackets chapter.

Bring forward 150 Ns to WP E wrap cast on and pattern to RC 142 cast off.

MAKING UP
Sew the pieces together leaving a gap to insert the cushion pad. Sl st closed.

Hebridean Winter Cushion.

IONA BLUE CUSHION

Fairisle and Plaid Block:
E wrap cast on 80 sts and work Plaid pattern to RC 142, cast off.

E wrap cast on 80 sts and work the traditional Fairisle pattern bands to RC 142 and cast off.

Rep herringbone stitch pattern back as Brown version.

Iona Cushion.

HARRIS RED AND LEWIS MIST CUSHION COVERS

Method

The front side of the cushion is knitted with peerie and border traditional Fairisle stitch patts and the reverse

Materials
The finished weight is 160g, so gather together various small amounts of yarn in the required colour palette

2/14s, fine 3-ply

Measurements
Cushion pad 45 x 45cm

Tension
32 sts – 36 rows = 10cm
MT 8

Machines
Suitable for all standard gauge punchcard and electronic machines

knitted using the Plaid Fairisle stitch patt. I used a different sequence of Fairisle patts for each cushion with 2 st st rows between each patt band. The stitch patts chosen were 19, 2, 23, 5, 28, 27, 28, 22, 5, 20, 3, 15, 6 and 3. But choose your own and alter the sequence and colour choice.

FAIRISLE FRONT BLOCK
Bring forward 110 Ns to WP, E wrap cast on and work 142 rows. Cast off.

PLAID BACK BLOCK
Rep as for front block.
Sew front and back together leaving a space to insert the cushion pad. Hand sl st closed.

Front of Harris Red and Lewis Mist cushions.

Plaid reverse side of the cushions.

BEE DANCE LARGE CUSHION

This bright and cheerful cushion cover followed the stitch pattern instructions for the Bee Song Scarf, however the fine silk yarn was replaced with a 4-ply wool yarn, using similar colours. The cover was knitted in one piece and folded over.

Materials
Finished weight 260g
Various bright coloured yarn of your choice, fine 4-ply, 2/10s weight

Measurements
Large cushion: 62 x 42cm

Small cushion: 30 x 30cm

Tension
32 sts - 36R = 10cm over st st
MT 7••

Machines
Suitable for all standard gauge punchcard and electronic machines

Method

Bring forward 138 Ns, E wrap cast on and work the sl st patt as instructed in the silk Bee Song Scarf.

Complete approx 360 rows ending with a complete hexagon. Pick up the first row knitted, k 1 row MT+ 2 and latch off.

Sew together one side seam, insert cushion pad, hand sl st the second side seam together.

For the smaller cushion cover 30 x 30cm bring forward 68 Ns E wrap cast on and work 216 rows using Bee Song sl st patt and complete as for previous cushion cover.

Bee Dance Cushions.

OTHER CUSHION DESIGN IDEAS TO TRY YOURSELF

All the stitch patterns in this book can be used to knit a cushion cover; the Fleur de Lys is worked knitting a central block, enclosed with a small six-row hem. A border pattern is then worked and mitred at the corners. A further small six-row hem is worked. This creates the front of the cushion; the reverse side is either worked in stocking stitch or a two-colour all-over Fairisle stitch pattern.

Refer back to the Log Cabin and Court House Steps throws and blankets

Fleur De Lys cushion detail.

and work the Fairisle Basket Pattern. Blocks 1, 2, 3 used the Finnish Rose Stitch Pattern and Stitch Pattern 20 for the surrounding Blocks 4 and 5. Make four squares and sew them together to make a cushion cover.

Basket Weave Cushion.

CHAPTER 14

CABLE DIRECTORY

The Aran Islands in Galway Bay, Ireland, consist of three islands, Inishmore, Inishmaan and Inisheer, and although the history of Aran knitting is relatively recent, it has proved problematic to try and pin down actual dates through lack of firm evidence and the muddying of waters by fanciful tales that are repeated as fact by lazy authors both online and in print.

There is clear evidence to show that Aran sweaters were available to purchase in the 1930s. Two of the most enduring myths associated with the Aran sweater, constructed purely by conjecture and with no real supporting evidence, are these:

* That the Irish fishermen on the Aran Islands had specific cable patterns associated with different villages or clans, so that if ever a body washed ashore after a boat wreck the other villagers would identify the victim by his sweater.
* That there is a direct and religious relationship between the complex cables in Aran sweaters and the Celtic knots carved in stone centuries before, which leads to the conclusion that the Aran fisherfolk must have been knitting their sweaters since time immemorial.

Examples of a variety of stitches can be found in *Mary Thomas's Book of Knitting Patterns* published in 1943, and several other publications show various examples of cabling and textured stitch patterns. Their emphasis has been on the variety of stitches and how to execute them, rather than the history. Some state that the cable sweater was a version of the fisherman's gansey. However, what is indisputable is that the National Museum of Ireland has a small collection of exquisite and some extremely competently knitted Aran sweaters donated and dated from 1937 onwards through to the 1940s and 1950s.

ARAN AND CABLES

Cable stitch patterns always appear better on a plain background, as the intricate patterns are more visible. Once you get to grips with a few basic techniques it is easy to make up your own examples.

Think about creating a pattern with a series of interlocking organic shapes, which interpenetrate but at the same time share a common contour. With the clever use of cables, a whiplash-like line can be made thicker and then thinner, sharpened then made to disappear completely, weaving in and out, appearing and disappearing. The cables do not have to follow any structure – the lines can dart and skip, collide and flow into one another, creating a formal or an informal overall textured pattern.

While cables can be planned out on paper, it is by knitting them and feeling them as they twine and glide their way up a sweater that you really get to know what is possible. Some cables create an optical image and appear to snake under and over, but this can be a deception, as in the mock cables. The use of hand and mind come into play here with the making of the pattern and the visual tactile result. Designing your own cable combinations is fun. Hundreds of variations can be produced – light, open work, lacy panels can be mixed with chunky cables, and intricate cables with all-over patterns.

When deciding which patterns to use for a panel always work from the centre out, whether you are designing a sweater or a throw. The stitch patterns themselves will dictate how many stitches are required, and how many will fit into a sweater front and back. A central, wide pattern of, say, sixteen stitches can be flanked either side by a narrower one of nine stitches. Build up another panel of cable stitches on each side of those, and so on until you have the required width. There are no rules – use whichever ones appeal to you most, and your own creativity will show through your unique design – sticky notes are useful tools to keep to the correct pattern row.

When knitting a cable stitch, the knitted fabric will be less stretchy, so extra stitches will need to be added to the required width or length, so work a tension swatch for each stitch chosen and piece them together like a jigsaw. A tension swatch is vital when working a large panel of cables, and add extra stitches if the required width is not met. Open work and lacy stitches will inevitably make the knitted fabric looser. As you work the tension square you will get a feel for the fabric you are making and may need to add a few extra rows between each cable to extend the length. Only by playing and experimenting will you get to know what is possible and so broaden your knowledge.

Cables can also be added in small panels, for example as decoration to the back of gloves, top of socks, or as an all-over pattern. Intricate or chunky cables can be worked together in panels to create an almost sculptural effect. To accentuate the cable you can undo the stitches on each side of the cable and reform them to make a knit stitch.

A great variety of intricate cables can be made using the knitting machine. Many years ago I translated some cable stitches from hand knitting patterns, but found the diagrams a little difficult to follow so I devised a method that I found easier to follow. The basic information needed is how many stitches are required to produce a repeat, and how many rows in total produce the pattern. Use the numbering ruler on the machine bed as this makes it easy to keep the pattern in line.

Read the instructions carefully. The first numbers mentioned are the stitches that are moved first, so they will be placed under the second stitches mentioned – for example 123 under 456, so using a three transfer tool to transfer the stitches from Ns 123 on to the transfer tool, and using another three transfer tool the stitches from Ns 456 and place 123 on to the empty

456 Ns and on to the empty 123 Ns place 456 – therefore 123 is under or at the front of the work on the right side. This is also known as C3R – cable three stitches right.

I have divided the various cables into sections: simple cables, spiral cables, plaits, butterfly and lobster variations, honeycomb variations, bobbles and cables and finally decorative cables.

SIMPLE CABLES

Seed Cable

This is a small, delicate cable that can be used as decoration on a rib or in blocks for surface decoration. If you require a small textured surface pattern this little stitch will break up large plain areas. It is also useful for rib decoration.
Pattern over 2 sts and 3 rows:
*1 under 2 k the row.
  K 2 rows*.
  Rep. from * to *.

The number or rows between each crossover can vary depending how dense you require the cable.

Small Snake Cable

This version keeps the cable at the front of the fabric and it appears to snake its way up a panel.

Seed Cable and Snake Cable.

Simple Cable 2x2.

Pattern over 2 sts and 6 rows:
*1 under 2 k the row.
  K 2 rows.
  2 under 1, k the row.
  K 2 rows* rep from * to *.

Simple Cable 2x2

Pattern over 4 sts and 5 rows:
*1,2 under 3,4 k the row.
K 4 rows* rep from * to *.

To keep the cable at the front of the work and make a larger Snake cable:

*1,2 under 3,4.
  K 4 rows.
  3,4 under 1,2 k the row.
  K 4 rows*.
  Repeat from *to*.

Three Cable

Pattern over 6 sts and 10 rows:
*1, 2, 3 under 4, 5, 6. K the row.

Three Cable.

Ribbon Waved Cable or Snakey Cable.

Knit 4 rows* rep from * to *.
Altering the number of rows between each transfer can create a tighter or looser cable.

Snakey Cable or Ribbon Waved Cable

Pattern over 6 sts and 10 rows:
*1,2,3 under 4,5,6 k the row.
  K 4 rows.
  4,5,6 under 1,2,3 k the row.
  Knit 4 rows*.
  Rep from * to *.

SPIRAL CABLES

Any of the following cables lend themselves to a braid edging.

Corded Cable

Pattern over 6 sts and 5 rows:
  K 4 rows.

Corded Cable.

Sand Pattern.

4,5,6 under 1,2,3 k the row.
Rep these five rows.

Sand Pattern

Pattern over 12 sts and 8 rows:
*K 3 rows.
  1,2,3 under 4,5,6 k the row.
  K 3 rows.
  10,11,12 under 7,8,9 k the row*.
  Rep from *to*

Spiral Cable Left.

Spiral Cable Right

Pattern over 9 sts and 10 rows:
*K 4 rows.
  1,2,3 under 4,5,6 k the row.
  K 4 rows.
  4,5,6 under 7,8,9*.
  Rep from *to*

This stitch lends itself to be used as a decorative braid.

Spiral Cable Left

Pattern over 9 sts and 10 rows:
*K 4 rows.
  4,5,6 under 1,2,3 k the row.
  K 4 rows.
  7,8,9 under 4,5,6* k the row.
  Rep from *to*.

Spiral Cable Right.

PLAITS

These cables are some of the most successful worked on a machine and create intricate, decorative surface decoration that is highly adaptable for use on furnishings and garments.

Single Plait

Pattern over 6st and 6 rows:
*K 2 rows.
   1,2 under 3,4 k the row.
   K 2 rows.
   5,6 under 3,4 k the row *.
   Rep from * to *.

Three Plait

Pattern over 9 sts and 10 rows:
  *K 4 rows.
   1,2,3 under 4,5,6 k the row.
   K 4 rows.
   7,8,9 under 4,5,6   k the row *.
   Rep from * to *.

Four Plait

Pattern over 12 sts and 12 rows:
*K 4 rows.
   1,2,3 under 4,5,6 k the row.
   K 1 row.
   7,8,9 under 10,11,12 k the row.
   K 4 rows.
   7,8,9 under 4,5,6 k the row *.
   Rep from * to *.

Four Plait.

Table 14.1: Pattern over 14 sts and 30 Rows Chart

Rows	Transfer Stitches
*1	knit
2	8,9 under 6,7
3	knit
4	4,5 under 6,7
5	knit
6	8,9 under 6,7
7	knit
8	4,5 under 6,7
9	knit
10	8,9 under 6,7
11	knit
12	6,7 under 5. 8,9 under 10.
13	knit
14	5,6 under 4. 9,10 under 11
15	knit
16	4,5 under 3. 10,11 under 12
17	knit
18	3,4 under 2. 11,12 under 13
19	knit
20	3,2 under 1. 12,13 under 14
21	knit
22	1,2 under 3 . 13,14 under 12
23	knit
24	2,3 under 4. 12,13 under 11
25	knit
26	3,4 under 5. 11,12 under 10
27	Knit
28	4,5 under 6. 10,11 under 9
29	Knit
30	5,6 under 7. 9,10 under 8
Rep from*	

Single Plait.

Three Plait.

Plaited Braid Cable.

Plaited Braid Cable

Trellis Plait

Pattern over 18 sts and 16 rows:
*K 4 rows.
   1,2,3 under 4,5,6 13,14,15 under
16,17,18 k the row.
   K 2 rows.
   7,8,9 under 10,11,12   k the row.
   K 4 rows.
   7,8,9 under 4,5,6   k the row.
   K 2 rows.
   13,14,15 under 10,11,12   k the row.
   Rep from *.

Ear of Wheat Plait

This is a small plait.
Pattern over 3 sts and 2 rows:
   *2 under 1   k the row.
   2 under 3   k the row *.
   Rep from * to *.

Plaited Basket Stitch

Pattern over 7 sts and 4 rows:
*K 1 row.
   2 under 1   4 under 3   6 under 5   k
the row.
   K 1 row
   2 under 3   4 under 5   6 under 7   k
the row*.
   Rep from * to *.

Double Plaited Basket Stitch

Pattern over 14 sts and 6 rows:
*K 2 rows.
   3,4 under 5,6   7,8, under 9,10
11,12 under 13,14   k the row.
   K 2 rows.
   3,4 under 1,2   7,8 under 5,6
11,12 under 9,10   k the row*.
   Rep from * to *.

Trellis Plait.

Ear of Wheat Plait.

Plaited Basket Stitch.

Double Plaited Basket Stitch.

Zigzag Plait.

Zigzag Plait

When four rows are knitted between
transfers the pattern becomes less
dense and fluid.

Pattern over 14 sts and 10 rows:
*K 4 rows.
   3,4 under 5,6   7,8 under 9,10
11,12 under 13,14   k the row.
   K 4 rows.
   3,4 under 1,2   7,8 under 5,6
11,12 under 9,10   k the row*.
   Rep from * to *.

Shadow Plait

Pattern over 16 sts and 10 rows:
*K 4 rows.
   3,4 under 1,2   11,12 under 9,10   k
the row.
   Knit 4 rows.

Shadow Plait Cable.

5,6 under 7,8   13,14 under 15,16   k the row*.

Rep from * to *.

V Stitch, also known as Wide Plait Cable

Pattern over 14 sts and 13 rows:
K 1 row.
6,7 under 8,9   k the row.
K 1 row.
6,7, under 5   8,9, under 10   k the row.
K 1 row.
*5,6 under 4   9,10   under 11   k the row.
K 1 row.
4,5 under 3   10,11 under 12   k the row.
K 1 row.
3,4 under 2   6,7 under 8,9   11,12 under 13   k the row.

V Plait, also known as Wide Plait Cable.

K 1 row.
3,2 under 1   6,7 under 5   8,9 under 10   12,13 under 14   k the row.
K 1 row*.
Rep from * to *.

BUTTERFLY AND LOBSTER CABLES

It is easy to see why these cables are called this as the shape is indicative.

Arrow Cable

You may need to loosen the tension for this stitch as it is quite a stretch for the stitches.
Pattern over 8 sts and 5 rows:
*K 4 rows.
1,2 under 3,4   7,8 under 5,6   k the

Arrow Cable.

row*.
Rep from * to *.

The sample shows that by altering the number of rows between each cable transfer different results can be achieved.

Horseshoe, also known as Double Cable

Pattern over 12 sts and 7 rows:
This cable will require a strong yarn with lots of stretch. You may decide to place the outside Ns into NWP.

HORSESHOE CABLE
*K 6 rows.
4,5,6 under 1,2,3   7,8,9 under

Horseshoe and Inverted Horseshoe.

10,11,12 k the row*.
    Rep from *–*.

INVERTED HORSESHOE CABLE

*K 6 rows.
    1,2,3 under 4,5,6   10,11,12 under
7,8,9 k the row*.
    Rep from * to *.

Butterfly or Wishbone Cable.

Butterfly Cable, also known as Wishbone Cable

Pattern over 8 sts and 5 rows:
*K 4 rows.
    4 under 1,2,3   5 under 6,7,8   k the
row*.
    Rep from * to *.

LOBSTER AND VARIATIONS

Lobster Claw Cable

This represents the bounty of the sea.
Pattern over 7 sts and 3 rows:
*K 2 rows.
    3 under 1,2   5 under 6,7   k the
row*.
    Rep from *–*.

Lobster Claw.

Fancy Strip

This is a pretty variation on the Lobster
Claw and works well on smaller
garments, adding little pulses of
textural interest.
Pattern over 6 sts and 12 rows:
*K 5 rows.
    3 under 1,2   4 under 5,6 k the row.
    K 2 rows.
    3 under 1,2   4 under 5,6 k the row.
    K 2 rows.
    3 under 1,2   4 under 5,6 k the
row*.
    Rep from *to*.

Fancy Strip.

Large Lobster Claw

Pattern over 10 sts and 6 rows:
*K 1 row.
   1,2 under 3   6,7, under 8   k the row.
   K 1 row.
   3,4 under 2   7,8 under 9   k the row.
   K 1 row.
   2,3 under 1   8,9 under 10   k the row*.
   Rep from * to *.

Hearts.

Large Lobster Claw.

Hearts

This is a variation of the large lobster claw, and with a few changes can become a heart design.

Pattern over 12 sts and 11 rows:
K 1 row.
   5,6 under 4   7,8 under 9   k the row.
   K 1 row.
   *4,5 under 3   8,9 under 10   k the row.
   K 1 row.
   3,4 under 2   9,10 under 11   k the row.
   K 1 row.

   2,3 under 1   10,11 under 12   k the row.
   K 1 row.
   1,2 under 3   5,6 under 4   7,8 under 9   11,12 under 10   k the row.
   K 1 row*.
   Rep from * to *.

HONEYCOMB AND VARIATIONS

Honeycomb Cable

Pattern 8 sts over 10 rows:
*K 4 rows.
   3, 4 under 1,2   5,6 under 7,8   k the row.
   K 4 rows
   1,2 under 3,4   7,8 under 5,6   k the row*.
   Rep from *to*.

Honeycomb Cable.

Large Honeycomb Cable

This cable is quite a stretch for the sts, so not transferring N7 can make a small difference.

Large Honeycomb Cable.

Pattern over 13 sts and 14 rows:
*K 6 rows.
   4,5,6 under 1,2,3   8,9,10 under
11,12,13   k the row.
   K 6 rows.
   1,2,3 under 4,5,6   11,12,13 under
8,9,10 k the row*.
   Rep from * to *

Honeycomb Panel

This panel looks complicated but once
you start you will get the rhythm of it
and realize that it's quite easy.

Pattern over 24 sts and 14 rows:
*K 6 rows.
   3,4 under 1,2   5,6 under 7,8
11,12 under 9,10   13,14 under 15,16
19,20 under 17,18   21,22 under
23,24 k the row.
   K 6 rows.
   1,2 under 3,4   7,8 under 5,6   9,10
under 11,12   15,16 under 13,14
17,18 under 19,20   23,24 under 21,
22   k the row *.
   Rep from * to *.

Honeycomb Panel.

Laced Honeycomb

Pattern over 8 sts and 9 rows:
*K 1 row.
   3,4 under 12   5,6 under 7,8   k the
row.
   K 1 row.
Transfer 5 on to 6 k the row.
   K 1 row.
Transfer 4 on to 3 k the row.
   K 1 row.
   Transfer 5 on to 6 k the row.
   K 1 row.
   1,2 under 3,4   7,8 under 5,6*.
   Rep from * to *.

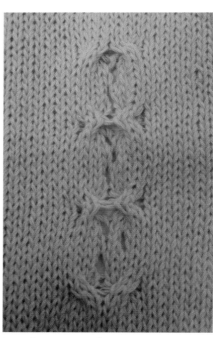

Laced Honeycomb.

Noughts and Crosses Cable

It is an interesting exercise to alter the
number of rows between each transfer,
for example four rows, eight rows and
six rows, and then back to four. The
cable appears textured and the crosses
appear highlighted.

Pattern over 8 sts and 20 rows:
*K 4 rows.
   3,4 under 1,2   5,6 under 7,8   k the
row.
   K 4 rows.
1,2 under 3,4   7,8 under 5,6   k the
row.
   K 4 rows.
   1,2 under 3,4   7,8 under 5,6   k the
row.
   K 4 rows.
   3,4 under 1,2   5,6 under 7,8 k the
row*.
   Rep from * to *.

Noughts and Crosses Cable.

Olympic Rings Cable Panel

Pattern over 24 sts and 30 rows:
*K 4 rows.
  11,12 under 9,10   13,14 under 15,16 k the row.
  K 4 rows.
  7,8 under 5,6   9,10 under 11,12 15,16 under 13,14   17,18 under 19,20 k the row.
  K 4 rows.
  3, 4 under 1,2   5,6 under 7,8 11,12 under 9,10   13,14 under 15,16 19,20 under 17,18   21,22 under 23,24 k the row.
  K 4 rows.
  1,2 under 3,4   7,8 under 5,6   9,10 under 11,12   15,16 under 13,14 17,18 under 19,20   23,24 under 21,22 k the row.
  K 4 rows.
  5,6 under 7,8   11,12 under 9,10 13,14 under 15,16   19,20 under 17,18 k the row.
  K 4 rows.
  9,10 under 11,12   15,16 under 13,14 k the row*.
  Rep from * to * as required.

Olympic Rings Honeycomb.

Bobbles integrated into a cable pattern add real interest and texture. An ordinary wavy line can be enhanced decoratively when bordered by a bobble.

Bobble 1

This bobble looks most like a hand-knitted one.
  Pattern over 3 sts and 6/8 rows:
With a separate length of yarn for each bobble, manually knit the 3 bobble sts for 6/8 rows, transfer the left and right outside stitch on to the centre N. Pick up the 2 outer sts of the first row and place on to the empty Ns.
Cont to knit as required.

Bobble 2

This bobble looks more like a small tuck but can be useful when adding texture and surface interest.
  Pattern over 5 sts and 6/8 rows:
Place all Ns not being used for the bobble into HP. Using a separate length of yarn, k the bobble sts back and forth for 6/8 rows. With a transfer tool pick up the first knitted row. Place all Ns back to WP and k the row.
Rep as required.

Bobble 1 and 2.

Heavy Cable with Bobbles

The bobble is made using a separate length of yarn over 3 stitches and manually knitting 8 rows picking up the two side stitches to the centre stitch and the two outer stitches on the first row on to the empty Ns.
  Pattern over 7 sts and 14 rows:
*K 4 rows.
  1,2,3 under 5,6,7 k the row.
  K 4 rows.
  1,2,3 under 5,6,7 k the row.
  K 4 rows.
  Make bobble over 3,4,5 and 8 rows*.
Rep from * to *.

Heavy Cable with Bobbles.

Diamond and Bobble Cable

Pattern over 10 sts and 39 rows:
*K 2 rows.
  4,5 under 6,7 k the row.
  K 2 rows.
  4,5 under 3 6,7 under 8 k the row.
  K 2 row.
  3,4 under 2 7,8 under 9 k the row.
  K 2 rows.
  Make bobble on 4,5,6 k the row.
  K 2 rows.
  2,3, under 4 8,9 under 7 k the row.
  K 2 rows.
  3,4 under 5 7,8 under 6 k the row.
  K 2 rows.
  4,5 under 6,7 k the row.
  K 2 rows.
  4,5 under 3 6,7 under 8 k the row.
  K 2 rows.
  3,4 under 2 7,8 under 9 k the row.
  K 2 rows.
  2,3, under 1 8,9 under 10 k the row.
  K 2 rows.
  1,2 under 3 9,10 under 8 k the row.
  K 2 rows.
  2,3 under 4 8,9 under 7 k the row.
  K 2 rows.
  3,4 under 5 8,9 under 6 k the row*.
  Rep from * to *.

Zigzag Cable

Pattern over 8 sts and 24 rows:
K 1 row.
  *1,2 under 3 k the row.
  K 1 row.
  2,3 under 4 k the row.
  K 1 row.
  3,4 under 5 k the row.
  K 1 row.
  4,5 under 6 k the row.
  K 1 row.
  5,6 under 7 k the row.
  K 1 row.
  6,7 under 8 k the row.
  Make bobble over 4,5,6 k the row.
  8,7 under 6 k the row.
  K 1 row.
  7,6 under 5 k the row.
  K 1 row.
  6,5 under 4 k the row.

K 1 row.
4,5 under 3 k the row.
K 1 row.
3,4 under 2 k the row.
K 1 row.
2,3 under 1 k the row.
Make bobble over 3,4,5 k the row*.
Rep from *to*.

Zigzag Bobble Cable.

Diamond and Bobble.

DECORATIVE CABLES

Lacy Cable

Pattern over 6 sts and 8 rows:
* K 6 rows.
Unthread the yarn from the carriage and set to slip the row. Move the carriage to the opposite side of the yarn. Starting from the right, knit manually until the cable stitches are reached. Bring N 6 forward until the yarn is behind the latch. Place the yarn in the hook of the N and push back to NWP rep until all cable stitches have been knitted back in this way. Knit manually to the end of the row. Rethread carriage and push needles to WP. 1, 2, 3 under 4, 5, 6. K the row*.
Rep from * to *.

Lacy Cable.

Wavy Cable

Pattern over 9 sts and 32 rows:
*K 15 rows.
  1, 2, 3 under 7,8,9 k the row.
  K 15 rows.
  1, 2, 3 under 7, 8, 9 k the row*.
  Rep from * to *.

Wavy Cable.

Rounded Linked Cable

Also known as Coin and Shell Cable.
Pattern over 8 sts and 6 rows:
*K 2 row.
  1 under 2,3,4   8 under 5, 6, 7   k the row.
  K 2 row.
  4 under 1,2,3   5 under 6, 7, 8 k the row*.
  Rep from *to*.

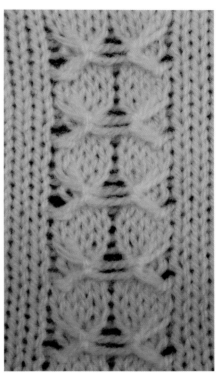

Rounded Linked Cable.

Chain Cable

This cable can be knitted singly, for example to add interest to a Fairisle stitch pattern, therefore mixing patterns together.

Pattern over 8 sts and 12 rows:
*K 4 rows.
   4 under 1,2,3   5 under 6,7,8   k the row.
   K 1 row.
   2,3,4 under 5,6,7   k the row.
   K 2 rows.
   2,3,4 under 5,6,7   k the row.
   K 1 row.
   1 under 2,3,4   8 under 5,6,7   k the row*.
   Rep from *to*.

Keyhole

Pattern over 7 sts and 6 rows:
*K 5 rows.
   5,6,7 under 1,2,3 k the row*.
   Rep from *to*.

This can be doubled up to create a chunky, wavy pattern as shown in the next variation.

Double Keyhole

Pattern over 15 sts and 12 rows:
*K 5 rows.
   5,6,7 under 1,2,3   k the row.
   K 5 rows.
   13,14,15 under 9,10,11   k the row*.
Rep from *to*.

Double Keyhole Cable.

Cable in a Cobweb

A beautiful, delicate, lacy cable that is very easy to knit.
Pattern over 11 sts and 4 rows:
*K 1 rows.
   Transfer st 5 and 7 on to 6   3,4 under 1,2   10,11 under 8,9   k the row.
   K 1 rows.
   Transfer 5 to 4 and 7 to 8   k the row*.
   Rep from *to*.

Chain Cable.

Keyhole Cable.

Cable in a Cobweb.

Diamond Rope Cable

Diamond Rope Cable.

Table 14.2: Pattern over 18 sts and 28 rows

Rows	Transfer Sts	Transfer Sts	Transfer Sts
1	knit		
2	8,9 under 10,11		
3	knit		
4	8,9 under 7	10,11 under 12	
5	knit		
6	7,8,under 6	11,12 under 13	
7	knit		
8	6,7,under 5	10,11 under 8,9	12,13 under 14
9	knit		
10	5,6 under 4	13,14 under 15	
11	knit		
12	4,5 under 3	10,11 under 8,9	14,15 under 16
13	knit		
14	3,4 under 2	15,16 under 17	
15	knit		
15	10,11 under 8,9		
17	knit		
18	2,3 under 4	16,17 under 15	
19	knit		
20	3,4 under 5	10,11 under 8,9	15,16 under 14
21	knit		
22	4,5 under 6	14,15 under 13	
23	knit		
24	5,6 under 7	10,11 under 8,9	13,14 under 12
25	knit		
26	6,7 under 8	12,13 under 11	
27	knit		
28	7,8 under 9	11,12 under 10	

Rep from row 1 as required.

Outlined Cable

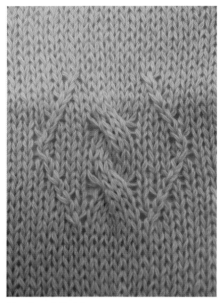

Outlined Cable.

Table 14.3: Pattern over 18 sts and 16 rows

Rows	Transfer Sts	Transfer Sts	Transfer Sts
1	knit		
2	6 under 5	13 under 14	
3	knit		
4	5 under 4	14 under 15	
5	knit		
6	4 under 3	7,8,9 under 10,11,12	15 under 16
7	knit		
8	3 under 2	16 under 17	
9	knit		
10	2 under 3	17 under 16	
11	knit		
12	3 under 4	7,8,9 under 10,11,12	16 under 15
13	knit		
14	4 under 5	15 under 14	
15	knit		
16	5 under 6	14 under 13	

Rep from row 1 as required.

Hour-Glass Cable

This is a progression from the outlined previous cable; it would be suitable to place another cable inside or to use as a base for embroidery.

Hour-Glass Cable.

Table 14.4: Pattern over 17 sts and 16 rows

Rows	Transfer Sts	Transfer Sts	Transfer Sts	Transfer Sts
1	*Knit			
2	5 under 4	8 under 7	10 under 11	13 under 14
3	knit			
4	4 under 3	7 under 6	11 under 12	14 under 15
5	knit			
6	3 under 2	6 under 5	12 under 13	15 under 16
7	Knit			
8	2 under 1	5 under 4	13 under 14	16 under 17
9	knit			
10	1 under 2	4 under 5	14 under 13	17 under 16
11	Knit			
12	2 under 3	5 under 6	13 under 12	16 under 15
13	Knit			
14	3 under 4	6 under 7	12 under 11	15 under 14
15	Knit			
16	4 under 5	7 under 8	11 under 10	14 under 13*

Repeat from *to*.

Spider Cable

A small, pretty cable.
Pattern over 3 sts and 8 rows:
*K 1 row.
 1 under 3 k the row.
 K 1 row.
 Transfer 2 to 3 to make an eyelet, k the row.
 K 1 row.
 1 under 3 k the row.
 K 1 row.
 2 to 1 to make an eyelet, k the row*.
 Rep from *to*.

Spider Cable.

Chain Link Knotted Cable

This is a textured stitch.
Pattern over 6 sts and 6 rows:
*K 5 rows.
 Twist sts 3,4 through 360 degrees and place back on to the needles. 5,6 under 1,2 k the row*.
 Rep from * to *.

Chain Link Knotted Cable.

Entwined Lozenges

An intricate cable that stands on its own as a motif or as part of a panel climbing up a garment.
Pattern over 12 sts and 11 rows:
*K 1 row.
 5,6, under 7,8 k the row.
 K 1 row.
 5,6 under 7,8 k the row.
 1,2 under 3   5,6 under 4   7,8 under 9   11,12 under 10 k the row.
 K 1 row.
 2,3 under 4,5   8,9 under 10,11 k the row.
 K 1 row.
 2,3 under 4,5   8,9 under 10,11 k the row.
 K 1 row.
 2,3 under 1   4,5 under 6   8,9 under 7   10,11 under 12 k the row*.
 Rep from * to *.

Entwined Lozenges.

Old Scottish Stitch

Pattern over 30 sts and approx. 39 rows.

There is one book that I have returned to all my knitting life; it is a wonderful source of fabulous stiches and one that has never been bettered – *Mary Thomas's Book of Knitting Patterns*, which was originally printed in July 1943. Although a hand knitting book, I have adapted many of the patterns for the knitting machine; the following pattern is adapted from an early seventeenth-century Scottish bonnet, and is suitable for an elaborate centre panel in a jumper.

This panel is basically three smaller panels combined to make a larger one. It is interesting to note that this sample is fairly faithful to the original, so the middle decorative cable is not centred.

To make a lacy hole a stitch is transferred from one needle to the adjacent needle, and the empty needle creates a hole when the row is knitted. This is expressed as 1 to 2, for example.

Table 14.5: Pattern for Old Scottish Stitch Bonnet

Rows	Transfer Sts	Transfer Sts		Transfer Sts
1	4,5 under 6,7			23,24 under 25,26
2	5 to 6	14,15,16 under 11,12,13		24 to 25
3	6 to 5			25 to 24
4	5 to 6			24 to 25
5	6 to 5			25 to 24
6	5 to 6			24 to 25
7	6 to 5	14,15,16 under 17,18,19		25 to 24
8	5 to 6			24 to 25
9	6 to 5			25 to 24
10	4,5 under 6,7			23,24 under 25,26
11		14,15,16 under 11,12,13		
12	5 to 6			24 to 25
13	6 to 5			25 to 24
14	5 to 6			24 to 25
15	6 to 5			25 to 24
16	5 to 6	14,15,16 under 17,18,19		24 to 25
17	6 to 5			25 to 24
18	5 to 6			24 to 25
19	6 to 5			25 to 24
20	4,5 under 6,7			23, 24 under 25,26
21		12 to 13	17 to 18	
22	5 to 6	13 to 12	18 to 17	24 to 25
23	6 to 5	12 to 13	17 to 18	25 to 24
24	5 to 6	13 to 12	18 to 17	24 to 25
25	6 to5	12 to 13	17 to 18	25 to 24
26	5 to 6	13 to 12	18 to 17	24 to 25
27	6 to 5	12 to 13	17 to 18	25 to 24
28	5 to 6	13 to 12	18 to 17	24 to 25
29	6 to 5	12 to 13	17 to 18	25 to 24
30	4,5 under 6,7	13 to 12	18 to 17	23,24 under 25,26
31		12 to 13	17 to 18	
32	5 to 6	13 to 12	18 to 17	24 to 25
33	6 to 5	12 to 13	17 to 18	25 to 24
34	5 to 6	13 to 12	18 to 17	24 to 25
35	6 to 5	12 to 13	17 to 18	25 to 24
36	5 to 6	13 to 12	18 to 17	24 to 25
37	6 to 5	12 to 13	17 to 18	25 to 24
38	5 to 6	13 to 12	18 to 17	24 to 25
39	6 to 5	12 to 13	17 to 18	25 to 24

Rep from row 1.

Old Scottish stitch.

CHAPTER 15

STITCH PATTERN DIRECTORY

It is always a useful exercise to look back at your previous patterns and designs. Viewing ideas from a distance can help us to revaluate, sometimes creating new possibilities and avenues to explore and develop. The joy of working with, and reassessing materials that are warm and soft to touch is second to none.

Try considering the finished article in a broader sense – here the important idea is not just about the product and the effect it has on the wearer, but also someone viewing the result. Material and colour choice will each trigger a reaction. A garment may be beautifully crafted and fit perfectly but the colour and materials used may be garish or substandard. Each person who views the item will have a different reaction, and the texture, colour, feel, weight and fit all play a part in the finished piece.

Colour choice is separate from yarn choice. There are many shades of blue – slate, grey, green-blue, international Klein, pale, sky, denim, marine and so on. The choice of yarn can be thick, thin, light, heavy, shiny, smooth, hairy, slubby and so on. With all these colour and texture options available before you even think about shape, it is vital to build up a visual catalogue, as this will increase your understanding of the feeling for the materials to be used in a haptic and visceral way. Certain

textures and colours will appeal to you more than others, so always consider what pleases you and what speaks to your own standards and perceptions.

Following fashion requires a certain amount of copying and this can lead to trite designs, but you can creatively use the nub of an idea from somewhere else and then creatively infuse it with your own design ideas, thus avoiding the trap of just slavishly copying someone else's ideas. The material chosen must work with the colour and pattern, as this is the heart of the design – without it there is no colour, stitch pattern, or tactile finished piece to trigger any emotion. Working with all the different yarns, absorbing their differences and understanding their characteristics, will make it easier for you to distinguish between all the different yarn types – synthetic fibres, regenerated fibres, silk, cotton, wool and even types of wool such as Donegal, Shetland, merino, alpaca, or cashmere. This character knowledge is vital when designing anything from a bag to a hat.

Constant experimentation and using new techniques is the keystone to creating dynamic work. Mastering techniques and breaking some rules opens the door to new and further experimentation, and this in turn creates a catalyst for yet more creative ideas. The process is an ongoing

journey which keeps the designs fresh, innovative and original.

The following stitch patterns are all designs that I have used, and my hope is that they will be used to inspire and encourage you to create further designs and experiments of your own.

FLORALS

Bluebell Variation

The outline of this clump of bluebells is naturalistic and impressionistic. With navy in Feeder 1 throughout, work seven rows green in Feeder 2, followed by seventeen rows in various shades of blue.

Bluebell naturalistic stitch pattern.

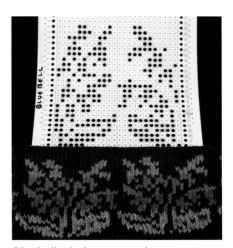

Bluebell stitch pattern chart.

Columbine

Columbine is also known as aquilegia, from the Latin word aquila, meaning eagle, due to the shape of the petals, which are supposed to be reminiscent of an eagle's claw. The motif here is a stylized version.

The border pattern is fluid and organic, which juxtaposes with the more stylized flower pattern. With a dark background and various shades of red and gold used in the border and floral pattern, the overall effect is rich

and intricate. Any floral repeat should be offset and the colour sequence changed. This pattern was originally designed to complement a Varuna wool fabric in a design for Liberty of London.

Columbine stitch pattern charts.

Table 15.1: Stitch Pattern and Colour Sequence for Columbine

Rows	Stitch Pattern	Pattern Setting	Feeder 1	Feeder 2
2	Border	Knit	Elderflower	
8	Border	Fairisle	Elderflower	Mustard
2	Border	Fairisle	Elderflower	Bright Red
2	Border	Fairisle	Brown	Bright Red
2	Border	Fairisle	Brown	Pink
2	Border	Fairisle	Brown	Red
2	Border	Fairisle	Brown	Dark Red
2	Border	Fairisle	Brown	Cerise
2	Border	Fairisle	Brown	Dark Red
2	Border	Fairisle	Brown	Mustard
6	Border	Fairisle	Elderflower	Mustard
2		Knit	Elderflower	
2		Knit	Denim	
2		Knit	Petrol Blue	
4		Knit	Navy	
6	Columbine 1	Fairisle	Navy	Dark Red
2	Columbine 1	Fairisle	Denim	Orange Red
8	Columbine 1	Fairisle	Blue mix	Orange Red
2	Columbine 1	Fairisle	Blue mix	Pink
2	Columbine 1	Fairisle	Turquoise	Pink
1	Columbine 1	Fairisle	Elderberry	Pink
7	Columbine 1	Fairisle	Elderberry	Dark Red
4	Columbine 1	Fairisle	Navy	Dark Red

Iris

The Iris dates back to Ancient Greece and takes its name from the Greek word for rainbow.

Two Iris patterns are shown here, each with a different character. The smaller Indian Iris is based on a fragment from an Indian block-printed muslin, and creates a stylized compact plant. The larger version is more naturalistic. Any repeat should be off set.

The colour changes occur on rows ten green, three cerise, one orange and four lavender in Feeder 2.

The large iris could be knitted using many more shades of purple and lavender, but I tried to keep this one simple, allowing the distinctive silhouette space to breathe.

Table 15.2: Stitch Pattern and Colour Sequence for Iris

Rows	Stitch Pattern	Pattern Setting	Feeder 1	Feeder 2
16	Large Iris	Fairisle	Black	Mid green
4	Large Iris	Fairisle	Black	Grass Green
10	Large Iris	Fairisle	Black	Purple
1	Large Iris	Fairisle	Black	Grey
6	Large Iris	Fairisle	Black	Mauve

Indian Iris stitch pattern chart.

Large Iris stitch pattern chart.

Desert Orchid

The desert orchid is an organic flower that blooms in the desert; it is used here for a summer design. The oat-coloured background was chosen to create the spirit of a desert.

Table 15.3: Stitch Pattern and Colour Sequence for Desert Orchid

Rows	Stitch Pattern	Pattern Setting	Feeder 1	Feeder 2
17	Desert Orchid	Fairisle	Oat	Green
4	Desert Orchid	Fairisle	Oat	Moss Green
4	Desert Orchid	Fairisle	Oat	Terracotta
2	Desert Orchid	Fairisle	Oat	Orange
4	Desert Orchid	Fairisle	Oat	Russet

Desert Orchid stitch pattern chart.

Gentian Flower

The intense shades of blue yet glorious open bell-shaped flowers are very distinctive in an alpine meadow.

Blue and white always look fresh and smart, and this large flower is knitted in shades of blue and silver. Although the border is unrelated to the shape of the flower, it does compliment the overall design. The gentian flower repeat is offset.

Table 15.4: Stitch Pattern and Colour Sequence for Gentian

Rows	Stitch Pattern	Pattern Setting	Feeder 1	Feeder 2
2		Knit	Cream	
3	Border	Fairisle	Cream	Blue
3	Border	Fairisle	Cream	Mid Blue
3	Border	Fairisle	Cream	Klein Blue
3	Border	Fairisle	Cream	Turquoise
2		Knit	Cream	
9	Gentian	Fairisle	Cream	Grey
13	Gentian	Fairisle	Cream	Pale Blue
8	Gentian	Fairisle	Cream	Blue
5	Gentian	Fairisle	Cream	Royal Blue
5	Gentian	Fairisle	Cream	Klein Blue
4	Gentian	Fairisle	Cream	Bright Blue
2		Knit	Cream	

Gentian stitch pattern chart.

The Gillyflower

The gillyflower is a carnation or dianthus flower with a wonderful scent of cloves and other spices, and is utterly gorgeous in the summer border.

Shades of blue on a cream background create a fresh and summery design.

The first small flower shows the stitch pattern without a dragonfly added, while the second flower shows one added to prevent long floats. The three plants were combined within one design, incorporating the more stylized and natural flowers together.

Table 15.5: Stitch Pattern and Colour Sequence for Gillyflower

Rows	Stitch Pattern	Pattern Setting	Feeder 1	Feeder 2
2		Knit	Cream	
2	Gillyflower 1	Fairisle	Cream	Navy
13	Gillyflower 1	Fairisle	Cream	Mid Blue
3	Gillyflower 1	Fairisle	Cream	Denim
5	Gillyflower 1	Fairisle	Cream	Bright Blue
6	Gillyflower 1	Fairisle	Cream	Dark Blue
3	Gillyflower 1	Fairisle	Cream	Mid Grey
2		Knit	Cream	
7	Gillyflower 2	Fairisle	Cream	Pale Blue
5	Gillyflower 2	Fairisle	Cream	Blue
1	Gillyflower 2	Knit	Cream	
1	Gillyflower 2	Fairisle	Cream	Navy
2		Knit	Cream	
8	Gillyflower 3	Fairisle	Cream	Grey
4	Gillyflower 3	Fairisle	Cream	Denim
5	Gillyflower 3	Fairisle	Cream	Bright Blue

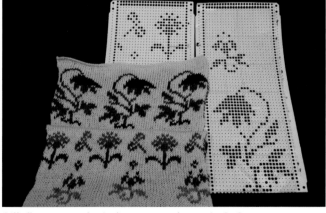

Gillyflowers and stitch pattern charts 1, 2, 3.

Polyanthus

An exuberant flower found in a variety of blazing colours. It is an English cottage garden classic and a close relative of the primrose. The design is embellished with Swiss Darning to the centre of the flower.

Table 15.6: Stitch Pattern and Colour Sequence for Polyanthus

Rows	Stitch Pattern	Pattern Setting	Feeder 1	Feeder 2
11	Polyanthus	Fairisle	Navy	Grass
9	Polyanthus	Fairisle	Navy	Red
4	Polyanthus	Fairisle	Navy	Mid Green
11	Polyanthus	Fairisle	Navy	Cerise

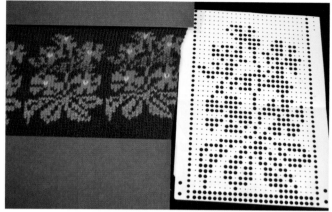

Polyanthus stitch pattern chart.

Primrose

The primrose has a distinctive silhouette and shines out amongst the dark damp bark and branches of a woodland. As one of the first flowers to appear in spring it is always a welcome sight after a cold dull winter. The leaves are wrinkly and slightly hairy, and so offset the perfect, delicate yellow flowers. Here embroidery is added to the centre of the flowers.

The MY in Feeder 1 remains navy but the colours in Feeder 2 change on rows six, lime green, seven bright green, and fifteen, yellow.

Primrose stitch pattern chart.

Nasturtium

The nasturtium is a bright lively plant that scrambles its way over the summer garden. Colour shades of red, yellow and orange are the most common, and create a happy space with their vibrancy.

The original pattern was designed to complement a Liberty fabric, where the nasturtium flower is anchored on to a striped background. Reverse the stitch pattern to work a repeat, and choose different colours within the same palette.

Table 15.7: Stitch Pattern and Colour Sequence for Nasturtium

Rows	Stitch Pattern	Pattern Setting	Feeder 1	Feeder 2
6		Knit	Grey	
4	Nasturtium	Fairisle	Grey	Olive
1	Nasturtium	Fairisle	Blue	Olive
6	Nasturtium	Fairisle	Navy	Olive
3	Nasturtium	Fairisle	Navy	Orange
2	Nasturtium	Fairisle	Navy	Gold
1	Nasturtium	Fairisle	Blue	Red Mix
1	Nasturtium	Fairisle	Grey	Red Mix
4	Nasturtium	Fairisle	Grey	Orange
6		Knit	Grey	

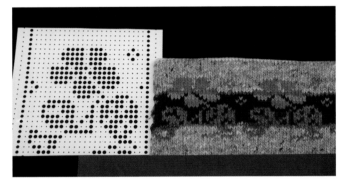

Nasturtium stitch pattern chart.

Pinks

Taken from an old English plant dictionary, this floral design is placed on a cream background and resembles an antique textile. Any repeat will benefit by being offset.

Table 15.8: Stitch Pattern and Colour Sequence for Pinks

Rows	Stitch Pattern	Pattern Setting	Feeder 1	Feeder 2
6		Knit	Cream	
8	Pinks	Fairisle	Cream	Dark Green
24	Pinks	Fairisle	Cream	Grass Green
7	Pinks	Fairisle	Cream	Maroon
4	Pinks	Fairisle	Cream	Dark Pink
5	Pinks	Fairisle	Cream	Pink

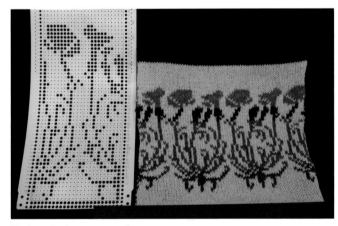

Pinks stitch pattern chart.

Tyrolean Carnation

Adapted from a cross-stitch pattern book, this stylized carnation is decorative and summery. The small border pattern can be used on its own, or mixed in with other more traditional Fairisle patterns.

Table 15.9: Stitch Pattern and Colour Sequence for Tyrolean Carnation

Rows	Stitch Pattern	Pattern Setting	Feeder 1	Feeder 2
5	Small	Fairisle	Cream	Lime
2	Small	Fairisle	Cream	Sugar Pink
3	Small	Fairisle	Cream	Pink
6	Large	Fairisle	Cream	Bright Green
5	Large	Fairisle	Cream	Lime
4	Large	Fairisle	Cream	Pink
6	Large	Fairisle	Cream	Sugar Pink
3	Large	Fairisle	Cream	Mid Green
5	Large	Fairisle	Cream	Red

Small and Large Tyrolean Carnation stitch pattern chart.

Rock Rose

A native of the Mediterranean region with large, tissue-paper petals. The scented flowers bloom and only last a day.

This stylized stitch pattern was designed to complement a Liberty fabric. A simple petal motif is transformed into a flower on a rich and varied background.

The design also works well when knitted in cotton and bright summery shades are used with fewer background changes.

Table 15.10: Stitch Pattern and Colour Sequence for Rock Rose

Rows	Stitch Pattern	Pattern Setting	Feeder 1	Feeder 2
2	Rock Rose	Fairisle	Black	Dark Red
4	Rock Rose	Fairisle	Black	Cranberry
3	Rock Rose	Fairisle	Black	Purple
2	Rock Rose	Fairisle	Black	Maroon
5	Rock Rose	Fairisle	Black	Dark Red
3	Rock Rose	Fairisle	Mauve	Red
4	Rock Rose	Fairisle	Teal	Red
2	Rock Rose	Fairisle	Teal	Pink
2	Rock Rose	Fairisle	Black	Pink
4	Rock Rose	Fairisle	Black	Cerise
2	Rock Rose	Fairisle	Grey	Cerise
2	Rock Rose	Fairisle	Elderberry	Cranberry
4	Rock Rose	Fairisle	Grey	Pale Cerise
2	Rock Rose	Fairisle	Black	Maroon
6	Rock Rose	Fairisle	Black	Dark Red
6	Rock Rose	Fairisle	Teal	Pink

Rep the colour sequence.

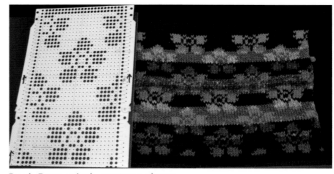

Rock Rose stitch pattern chart.

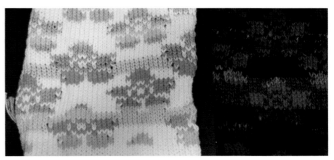

Rock Rose and summer variation.

Thistle

'Thistle' is the name given to a variety of plants whose characteristic sharp prickly leaves are to be avoided. This pretty thistle motif could be mixed with other Fairisle border patterns, or used with an all-over Plaid stitch pattern. Here it is worked with MY black in Feeder 1 throughout, while the colours change in Feeder 2: Olive on rows one to seven, three rows in Grass Green, and four rows in Cerise.

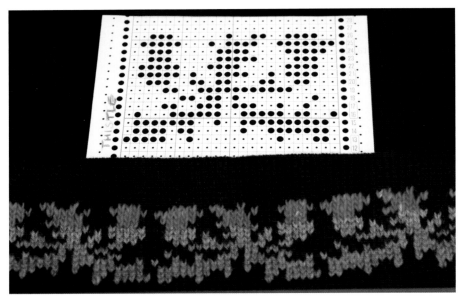

Thistle stitch pattern chart.

BERRIES AND FRUITS

Wild Strawberry

The strawberry plant is followed by the strawberry and flower stitch pattern, and repeated. The patterns could be used to design a panelled cardigan similar to the Violets design outlined in the chapter detailing panelled cardigans.

15.11: Stitch Pattern and Colour Sequence for Wild Strawberry

Rows	Stitch Pattern	Pattern Setting	Feeder 1	Feeder 2
2	Strawberry Plant	Fairisle	Elderberry	Red
2	Strawberry Plant	Fairisle	Elderberry	Cerise
4	Strawberry Plant	Fairisle	Elderberry	Red
2	Strawberry Plant	Fairisle	Elderberry	Pink
12	Strawberry Plant	Fairisle	Elderberry	Grass Green
14	Strawberry Plant	Fairisle	Elderberry	Mid Green
7	Strawberry Plant	Fairisle	Elderberry	Olive
6		Knit	Elderberry	
4	Strawberry	Fairisle	Elderberry	Red
2	Strawberry	Fairisle	Elderberry	Cerise
2	Strawberry	Fairisle	Elderberry	Maroon
2	Strawberry	Fairisle	Elderberry	Pink
2	Strawberry	Fairisle	Elderberry	Red Mix
3	Strawberry	Fairisle	Elderberry	Bright Green
5	Strawberry	Fairisle	Elderberry	Off White

Wild Strawberry stitch pattern chart.

Rose Hip

This design is a distinctive silhouette depicting a naturalistic rose hip. It is placed on a Navy background in Feeder 1, with colour changes in Feeder 2: eleven rows Red, eight rows Brown and eleven rows Olive.

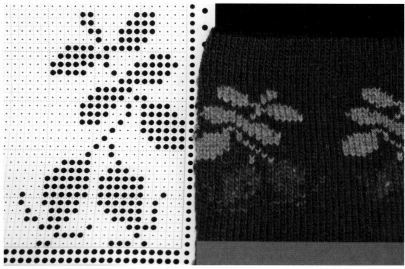

Rose Hip stitch pattern chart.

Bramble Pattern

The Bramble design consists of three stitch patterns: a small Checker pattern XX00XX00XX00 with the colours changing every two rows; a small Blackberry pattern with a bobble being hand worked (see instructions for Bobbles in the cable directory); and the main Blackberry and Leaf pattern.

Table 15.12: Checker Stitch Pattern and Colour Sequence

Rows	Stitch Pattern	Pattern Setting	Feeder 1	Feeder 2
2	Checker	Fairisle	Dark Green	Mauve
2	Checker	Fairisle	Purple	Mid Green
2	Checker	Fairisle	Grass	Charcoal
2	Checker	Fairisle	Dark Pink	Olive
2	Checker	Fairisle	Lavender	Mulberry
2	Checker	Fairisle	Dark Red	Elderberry
6		knit	Pepper	
2	Berry	Fairisle	Pepper	Mauve
5	Make Bobble	Over 3 sts	Elderberry	
1	Berry	Fairisle	Pepper	Mauve
3	Berry	Fairisle	Pepper	Dark Green
6		Knit	Pepper	
4	Blackberry 1	Fairisle	Pepper	Dark Red
2	Blackberry 1	Fairisle	Pepper	Purple
4	Blackberry 1	Fairisle	Pepper	Dark Purple
2	Blackberry 1	Fairisle	Pepper	Midnight
2	Blackberry 1	Fairisle	Pepper	Elderberry
2	Blackberry 1	Fairisle	Pepper	Roseberry
9	Blackberry 1	Fairisle	Pepper	Juniper Green
10	Blackberry 1	Fairisle	Pepper	Dark Green
6		Knit	Pepper	

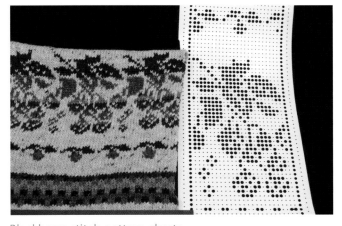

Blackberry stitch pattern charts.

Blackberry 2 can be worked by reversing the stitch pattern and using different colours or the same colours in a different sequence to create variety.

Shells

The Shells stitch patterns can be used for a summer sweater or as a border pattern. Use the Twigging pattern (found in the Painting with Yarn chapter) as seaweed.

Table 15.13: Shells Stitch Patterns and Colour Sequence

Rows	Stitch Pattern	Pattern Setting	Feeder 1	Feeder 2
4	Shell 1	Fairisle	Cream	Oat
2	Shell 1	Fairisle	Cream	Grey
2	Shell 1	Fairisle	Cream	Pale Blue
4	Shell 1	Fairisle	Cream	Grey
2	Shell 1	Fairisle	Cream	Pale Pink
2	Shell 1	Fairisle	Cream	Dark Pink
2	Shell 1	Fairisle	Cream	Pink
4	Shell 1	Fairisle	Cream	Pale Blue
2	Shell 2	Fairisle	Cream	Dark Pink
2	Shell 2	Fairisle	Cream	Pink
2	Shell 2	Fairisle	Cream	Red Mix
4	Shell 2	Fairisle	Cream	Pink
6	Shell 2	Fairisle	Cream	Red Mix
4	Shell 3	Fairisle	Cream	Pale Grey
2	Shell 3	Fairisle	Cream	Pale Blue
2	Shell 3	Fairisle	Cream	Blue
8	Shell 3	Fairisle	Cream	Dark Grey
2	Shell 4	Fairisle	Cream	Pink
2	Shell 4	Fairisle	Cream	Pale Pink
2	Shell 4	Fairisle	Cream	Pink
4	Shell 4	Fairisle	Cream	Dark Pink
3	Shell 4	Fairisle	Cream	Red mix
4	Shell 5	Fairisle	Cream	Grey
4	Shell 5	Fairisle	Cream	Pale Blue
6	Shell 5	Fairisle	Cream	Blue
6	Shell 5	Fairisle	Cream	Dark Grey

Sea Shell stitch pattern chart.

Look to Nature

Look to nature for design inspiration – the source is endless. The idea is not to imitate but to record an idea or emotion inspired by nature. Decide what it is in particular that inspires you and captures your interest, and what are the emotions that you feel when studying a particular aspect. Simplify and edit your thoughts, sketches and swatches so you get to the core of the catalyst, then work on the journey as to how you can best represent this – then present it as a piece of work.

GEOMETRICS

Antique Gingham

Subtle shades were used for this design with the colour in Feeder 1 remaining the same, while the colours in Feeder 2 change every three rows. It would work just as well using bright vibrant colours.

Harlequin

Several small patterns were used in this design, with each cardigan front and the sleeves being worked in a different stitch pattern. Each of these patterns will stand alone, while the zigzag pattern has been used to create hats in various colourways.

HARLEQUIN DIAMOND 1

The patterns above can also be mixed in with more traditional Fairisle patterns. The border Flag pattern reflects all the other patterns. The Diamond pattern is offset at each repeat and consists of colour changes in Feeder 2 on rows four and six. The bright-coloured middle fourth row creates an interest and texture change.

HARLEQUIN DIAMOND 2

The small border pattern is less striking than the previous border, and the diamond shape is more distinct; however, this can alter when the background colour is changed and subdued shades used. Any repeat should be offset to allow the diamond to swing back and forth across the fabric.

Squares

A design using squares can produce a vibrant and colourful pattern or a subtle nuanced fabric depending on colour choice.

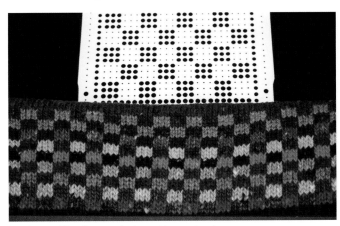

Antique Gingham stitch pattern chart.

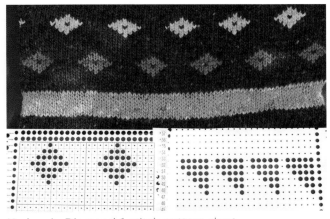

Harlequin Diamond 1 stitch pattern chart.

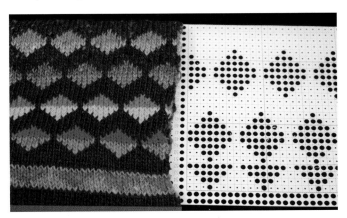

Harlequin Diamond 2 stitch pattern chart.

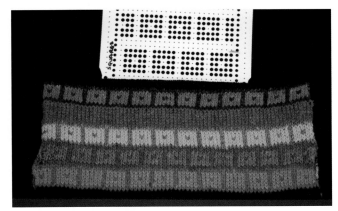

Squares stitch pattern chart.

Worcester Check

Worcester Check is a neat check stitch pattern. When knitted it appears to move and create optical illusions. Some of the squares appear to lean, while others recede. Working the pattern changing colour every four rows appears to enhance this effect.

JAPANESE-INFLUENCED STITCH PATTERNS

The following set of patterns was inspired by a small book published by Webb and Bower for the Victoria and Albert Museum. The patterns reproduced in the book came from the Victoria and Albert Museum collection

of Japanese stencils, and although many of the motifs are traditional and reach far back into Japanese history, the acquired stencils were from the nineteenth century.

In the Japanese designs intricate shapes are cut into stencil papers, which are then laid on a fabric of choice, and a rice paste applied to the fabric through the stencil shapes. During the dyeing process the areas covered with paste – the intricate stencil shapes – remain white while the remaining fabric is dyed blue.

I used elements of the Japanese designs, translated and simplified them, whilst acknowledging the integrity of my original sources.

Stencil Fish

The stencil fish uses shades of blue and turquoise to create movement in the water. The fish is knitted in white to emulate the original stencil design. Note that the shape of the fish tail was changed from the original jumper design by masking some holes in the punchcard and punching others.

Bamboo Forest

The four small borders are based on Japanese patterns. From bottom to top:
Border 1 is a small eight row border.
Border 2 is reminiscent of a Greek key pattern. Work nine Fairisle rows.
Border 3 was inspired by Japanese

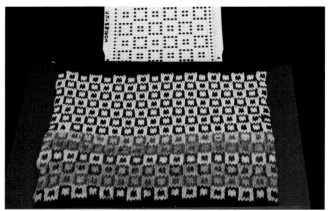

Worcester Check stitch pattern chart.

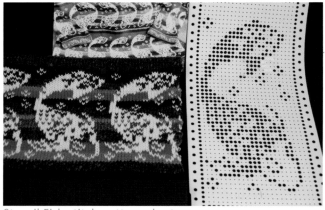

Stencil Fish stitch pattern chart.

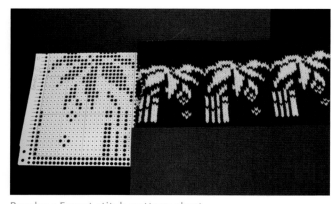

Bamboo Forest stitch pattern chart.

Japanese Border stitch pattern charts 1, 2, 3, 4.

fretwork designs.

Border 4 works twenty-one Fairisle rows. This bold pattern can be broken down into more colour changes for a completely different style.

Lotus Flower

These are relatively simple shapes, all of which can be separated and used singly. The oblong spiral border pattern anchors the lotus flower to a base. The small six-row Lotus pattern repeats could be used as an all-over design.

Prunus

The two Japanese border patterns and prunus have been coloured to create a strong lacquer design. The fretwork border worked using primary red colour has been given depth by adding the turquoise stripe in the middle row.

The border above, whilst being solid at the base, gives way to the impression of a lotus flower. The prunus, whose colours range from dark deep red to orange and gold, floats on the cream surface; the diamond shape picks up the floats on the back of the work, and appears to be falling blossom on a gentle breeze!

ETHNIC-INSPIRED PATTERNS

Many years ago I was looking at a cardigan that Simone De Beauvoir was wearing: I wanted to adapt the ethnic design into a knitted fabric, and the following stitch patterns are the result. I also worked a version with a pale background but this was not successful, so the dark variation is shown here. The motifs are strong and positive, and reflect some Mexican border patterns that I had seen.

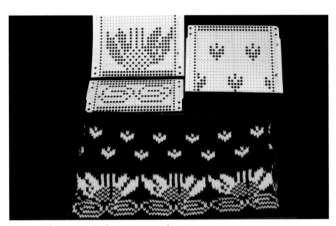

Lotus Flower stitch pattern charts.

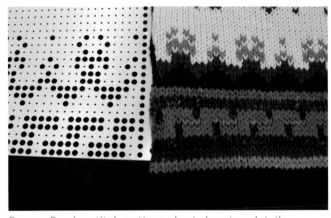

Prunus Border stitch pattern chart showing detail.

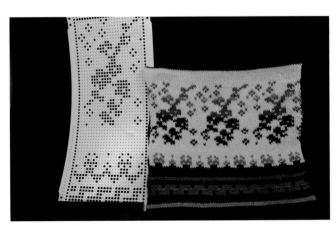

Prunus stitch pattern chart.

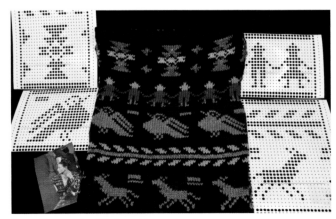

Four Beauvoir stitch pattern charts.

246/247

Navajo Inspiration

Based on a Navajo blanket the following designs explored three colours in a row using slip stitch. It does make a thick fabric with a few floats, but eye catching.

Navajo Blanket, Wave, Arrow and Diamond.

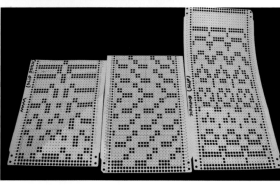

Navajo stitch pattern charts.

Table 15.15: Arrow Stitch Pattern and Colour Sequence

Rows	Stitch Pattern	Pattern Setting	Feeder 1
2	Arrow	Slip	Brown
4	Arrow	Slip	Gold
6	Arrow	Slip	Orange
Rep 3 x			
2	Arrow	Slip	Brown
2	Arrow	Slip	Orange
2	Arrow	Slip	Gold
Rep 2 x			

Table 15.16: Diamond Stitch Pattern and Colour Sequence

Rows	Stitch Pattern	Pattern Setting	Feeder 1
2	Diamond	Slip	Red
2	Diamond	Slip	Brown
2	Diamond	Slip	Red
2	Diamond	Slip	Brown
2	Diamond	Slip	Red
2	Diamond	Slip	Brown
2	Diamond	Slip	Ochre
2	Diamond	Slip	Red
2	Diamond	Slip	Brown
2	Diamond	Slip	Ochre
2	Diamond	Slip	Red
2	Diamond	Slip	Ochre
2	Diamond	Slip	Red
2	Diamond	Slip	Ochre
2	Diamond	Slip	Cream
2	Diamond	Slip	Red
2	Diamond	Slip	Ochre
2	Diamond	Slip	Red
2	Diamond	Slip	Brown
2	Diamond	Slip	Ochre
2	Diamond	Slip	Red
2	Diamond	Slip	Brown
2	Diamond	Slip	Ochre
2	Diamond	Slip	Red
2	Diamond	Slip	Brown
2	Diamond	Slip	Red
2	Diamond	Slip	Brown

Table 15.14: Wave Stitch Pattern and Colour Sequence

Rows	Stitch Pattern	Pattern Setting	Feeder 1
2	Wave	Slip	Ochre
2	Wave	Slip	Brown
2	Wave	Slip	Cream
2	Wave	Slip	Ochre
2	Wave	Slip	Brown
2	Wave	Slip	Cream
2	Wave	Slip	Ochre
2	Wave	Slip	Brown
2	Wave	Slip	Cream
2	Wave	Slip	Ochre
2	Wave	Slip	Brown
2	Wave	Slip	Cream
2	Wave	Slip	Ochre
2	Wave	Slip	Brown
2	Wave	Slip	Cream
2	Wave	Slip	Ochre
2	Wave	Slip	Brown
2	Wave	Slip	Ochre
2	Wave	Slip	Cream

Tropical Bird

The bird is stylized and works well within a band followed or preceded by a leaf design.

Tropical Bird and Leaf stitch pattern chart.

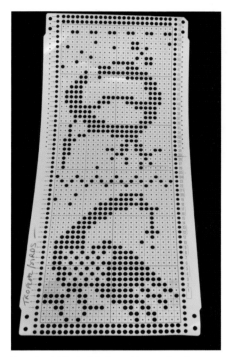

Tropical Bird stitch pattern chart.

ALL-OVER PATTERNS

Lollipop

This stitch pattern resembles a lollipop before colours are added. Choose a colour palette such as dark colours in Feeder 1 and bright colours in Feeder 2, and change colours in each feeder on every alternate four rows. If this stitch pattern is turned on its side it resembles a more compact version of the Reflected Blossom stitch pattern found on the Kimono Jacket.

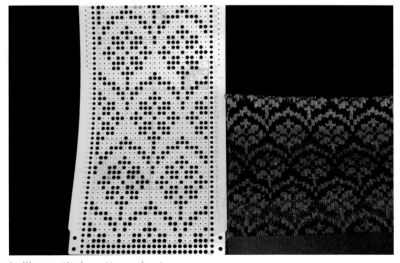

Lollipop stitch pattern chart.

Palmetto

The stylized image is based on a palmetto palm leaf formation. A natural leaf shape is taken and reimagined into a single motif. This can then be offset and overlapped to fit alongside the top of the first motif. This creates a definite diamond shape when knitted on a plain background. When using shades of grey, blue and beige in Feeder 1 and pinks and reds in Feeder 2, and changing colours in alternate feeders every four rows, the whole character changes and becomes more dynamic.

The Argyll stitch pattern below right shows that a border pattern can become an attractive all-over pattern. Change the colours on odd rows to create surprises.

Palmetto stitch pattern chart.

Argyll Fairisle pattern.

BORDER PATTERNS

The three border designs can be mixed with traditional Fairisle patterns. They are all delicate and light patterns. The Ribbon and Ribbon and Swag pattern add interest to the top of a sleeve when working on a floral design.

From bottom to top, Little Flower, Ribbon, Ribbon and Swag stitch pattern charts.

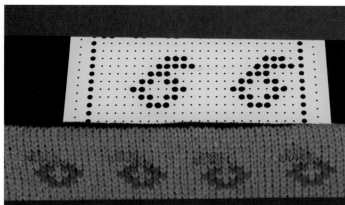

Small Boteh.

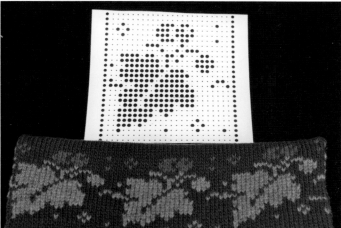

Figure of Eight border.

Leaf and Berry border.

Heraldic

I love knitting in strips and sewing them together to make a patchwork cardigan. They are always vibrant and allow for lots of colour combinations. These are the patterns that I used when making a heraldic-themed jacket. The panels are 40 sts wide and consist of two for each front and four on the back, working for 210 rows and neck shaping on RC 180 by casting off 5sts

three times, 2sts twice and 1 st on each alt row until 25 sts have dec in total.

The sleeves consist of three strips, the left and right worked by casting on 20sts and increasing evenly over 170 rows to 60sts. For the centre strip cast on 25 sts and inc evenly to 50sts. The hem, cuffs and button and neck band uses a stylized border stitch pattern.

Refer to the strip coats and cardigans in previous chapters for details.

All the stitch patterns are works in progress – each time they are used I usually alter a colour or a stitch or two. Some areas can be masked out with tape or redrawn and other stitches added and a completely new design emerges.

Heraldic Cardigan and stitch pattern charts.

Heraldic stitch pattern charts.

Designs and works in progress.

ADDRESS BOOK

MACHINES AND REPAIRS

Andee Knits: www.machine-knitting.co.uk

LINKERS AND SPARES

B Hague and Co Limited:
www.haguedirect.co.uk

YARNS

Black Isle Yarns:
www.blackisleyarns.co.uk
Blacker Yarns: www.blackeryarns.co.uk
British Wool: www.britishwool.org.uk
Cambrian Wool:
www.cambrianwool.co.uk
Daughter of a Shepherd:
www.daughterofashepherd.com
Eden Cottage Yarns:
www.edencottageyarns.co.uk
Gaddum Silk:
www.gaddumandgaddum.co.uk
Garthenor Organic:
www.garthenor.com
Ginger Twist Studio:
www.gingertwiststudio.com
J C Rennie: www.knitrennie.com
Jamieson's of Shetland:
www.jamiesonsofshetland.co.uk
Jon Arbon: www.jarbon.com
Kettle Yarn Co:
www.kettleyarnco.co.uk
King Cole: www.kingcole.com
Knoll Yarns Limited:
www.knollyarns.com
Laxtons Ltd: www.laxtons.com
Pitti Filati Trade Yarn Fair, Florence:
www.pittiimmagine.com
Robert Todd: www.roberttodds.com
Rowan: www.knitrowan.com
The Grey Sheep Co.:
www.thegreysheep.co.uk
The Knitting Goddess:
www.theknittinggoddess.com

Toft Alpacas:
www.toftalpacastud.com
Uist Wool: www.uistwool.com
West Yorkshire Spinner:
www.wyspinners.com
Yeomans Yarns: www.yeoman-yarns.co.uk
Z Hinchliffe: www.zhinchliffe.co.uk

HABERDASHERY

Dunelm for cushion pads:
www.dunelm.com
J H Crickmay for buttons:
2A Everton Road, Croydon, CR0 6LA
James Grove for buttons:
www.jamesgroveandsons.co.uk
Karadia for buttons:
www.karadia-trimmings.co.uk
Parkin Fabrics for millinery stiffening:
www.parkinfabrics.co.uk
Textile Garden for pins and buttons:
www.textilegarden.co.uk

MILLINERY SUPPLIES AND COURSES

Louise Pocock:
Studio, Dragon House, High Street,
Chipping Campden, Glos GL55 6AG
Email:
louise.pocock235@btinternet.com
Web site: www.louisepocock.com

USEFUL GROUPS

Anti Copying in Design (ACID):
www.acid.uk.com
Campaign for wool:
www.campaignforwool.org
Guild of Machine Knitters:
www.guild-mach-knit.org.uk

Knitting History:
www.knittinghistory.co.uk
Knitting International:
www.wtin.com
Knitting Trade Journal:
www.knittingtradejournal.com
Machine Knitting Monthly:
www.machineknittingmonthly.net
Missoni News Letter:
www.missoni.com
The Worshipful Company of Framework
Knitters:
www.frameworkknitters.co.uk
Vogue Knitting:
www.vogueknitting.com

DESIGN COLLECTIONS

Victoria and Albert Museum, London:
https://www.vam.ac.uk/
Fashion and Textile Museum, London:
https://www.ftmlondon.org/
Anna Wintour Costume Center at the
Metropolitan Museum of Art New York:
https://www.metmuseum.org/about-the-met/collection-areas/the-costume-institute
Musée de la Mode et du Textile, Paris:
https://www.fashionandtextilemuseums.com/musee-de-la-mode-et-du-textile/
Musée de al Mode Palais Galliera, Paris:
https://www.palaisgalliera.paris.fr/en/collections/collections
Kyoto Costume Institute, Tokyo:
https://www.kci.or.jp/en/
Museum of Royal Worcester:
https://www.museumofroyalworcester.org/
National Museum of Ireland:
https://www.museum.ie/en-ie/home

BIBLIOGRAPHY

Allwood, J.M., Laursen, S. E., Malvido de Rodríguez, C., & Bocken, N. M. P. (2006) *Well dressed? The present and future sustainability of clothing and textiles* (University of Cambridge).

Atterbury, P. (1990) *Art Deco Patterns* (Studio Editions).

Audsley, G., & Cutler, T. (1989) *The Grammar of Japanese Ornament* (Arch Cape Press).

Audsley, W. (1987) *Medieval Ornamental Styles: Thirty-Six Plates in Colours with General Introduction and Descriptive Letter Press* (Wordsworth Editions).

Bårdsgård, A. (2021) *Selbu Mittens* (Trafalgar Square).

Bårdsgård, A. (2021) *Selbu Patterns* (Trafalgar Square).

Barnes, L., & Lea-Greenwood, G. (2010) 'Fast fashion in the retail store environment' *International Journal of Retail & Distribution Management,* Vol 38 No. 10, pp. 760–772.

Beauclair, R. (1988) *Art Nouveau Patterns and Designs* (London: Bracken Books).

Broega, A. C. (2019) 'Sustainability in the Textiles and Clothing Fashion Industry: An Ongoing Study in Portugal' *Global Perspectives on Sustainable Fashion* (London: Bloomsbury Visual Arts, pp. 100–109).

Bye, E. (2020) 'Sustainability Must Drive Design' in *The Dangers of Fashion: Towards Ethical and Sustainable Solutions* (Bloomsbury Publishing USA pp. 19–34).

Calloway, S. (1988) *Art Deco: Interior and Panel Designs* (London: Bracken Books).

Cao, H. (2020) 'Fibers and Materials: What is Fashion Made of?' in *The Dangers of Fashion: Towards Ethical and Sustainable Solutions* (Bloomsbury Publishing USA pp. 53–69).

Carrington, M.J., Neville, B.A. & Whitwell, G.J. (2010) 'Why ethical consumers don't walk their talk: towards a framework for understanding the gap between the ethical purchase intentions and actual buying behaviour of ethically minded consumers' *Journal of Business Ethics,* 97, pp. 139–58.

Cook, G. (2001) *Handbook of Textile Fibres: Man-Made Fibres* (Cambridge UK: Woodhead Publishing)

Defra (2011) 'Sustainable clothing roadmap progress report' (London: Defra). Available online at: https://www.gov.uk/government/upl oads/system/uploads/attachment_da ta/file/69299/pb13461-clothing-actionplan-110518.pdf

Don, S. (1979) *Fair Isle Knitting: A Practical Handbook of Traditional Designs* (London: Mills and Boon).

Dresser, C. (1988) *Studies in Design* (Studio Editions).

Dupernex, A. (2020) *Machine Knitting: Designing with Colour* (Marlborough: The Crowood Press Ltd).

Eckhardt, G.M., Belk, R. & Devinney, T.M. (2010) 'Why don't consumers consume ethically?' *Journal of Consumer Behaviour,* 9, pp. 426–36.

Fair Trade Foundation (2021) 'What is fair trade?' Available online at: https://www.fairtrade.org.uk/what-is-fairtrade/

Faulkner, R. & Victoria and Albert Museum (1988) *Japanese Stencils* (Exeter: Webb & Bower).

Fiedler, J., Ackermann, U., & Feierabend, P. (eds) (1999) *Bauhaus* (Konemann).

Fletcher, K. (2008). *Sustainable Fashion and Textiles: Design Journeys* (London: Earthscan).

Gernes, P., Luckow, D., Deichtorhallen Hamburg, & Malmö Konsthall (2010); Poul Gernes: [retrospective; Deichtorhallen Hamburg 8. Oktober 2010-16. Januar 2011 ; Malmö Konsthall und Lunds Konsthall 20. Mai – 21. August 2011] (Köln Snoeck).

Gillow, J. (2016) *African Textiles* (Thames and Hudson).

Gillow, N. (1988) *William Morris: Designs and Patterns* (London: Bracken Books).

Goworeka, H., Fisher. T., Cooper, T., Woodward, S., & Hiller, A. (2012) 'The sustainable clothing market: an evaluation of potential strategies for UK retailers' *International Journal of Retail & Distribution Management,* 40(12), pp. 935–955.

Goworeka, H., Oxborrow, L., Claxton, S., McLaren, A., Cooper, T., & Hill, H. (2018) 'Managing sustainability in the fashion business: Challenges in product development for clothing longevity in the UK' *Journal of Business Research,* 117, pp. 629–641.

Grasset, E. (1988) *Art Nouveau Floral Designs* (London: Bracken Books).

Hardy, A-R. (2003) *Art Deco Textiles: The French Designers* (Thames and Hudson).

Hedlund, A., L. & Glueck, G. (2010) *Gloria F. Ross & Modern Tapestry* (New Haven: Yale University Press, 2010).

Henry, B., Laitala, K., & Klepp, I.G. (2019) 'Microfibres from apparel and home textiles: Prospects for including microplastics in environmental sustainability assessment' *Science of* the Total Environment 652 pp. 483–494.

Hiller Connell, K. Y., & LeHew, M. L. A. (2020) 'Fashion: An Unrecognized Contributor to Climate Change' in *The Dangers of Fashion: Towards Ethical and Sustainable Solutions* (Bloomsbury Publishing USA pp. 71–85).

Jones, O. (1986) *The Grammar of Ornament* (Omega Books).

Jones, O. (1987) *The Grammar of Chinese Ornament* (London: Studio Editions).

Klein, B. (1965) *Eye for Colour* (London: Collins).

Klein, B. (1976) *Design Matters* (London: Secker and Warburg).

Laitala, K., Klepp, I.G. & Henry, B. (2018) 'Does use matter? Comparison of environmental impacts of clothing based on fiber type' *Sustainability*, 10(7) 2524.

Loughman, E. F. (2016) 'An Evaluation of Environmental Impact Data Collection Methods Used in the Apparel Industry' *Doctoral Thesis* (University of California, Los Angeles).

Morris, W. (1988) *William Morris Full-Color Patterns and Designs* (New York: Dover Publications).

Mucklestone, M. J. (2011) *200 Fair Isle Designs: Knitting Charts, Combination Designs and Colour Variations* (Tunbridge Wells: Search Press).

National Trust for Scotland (ed.) (1981) *Traditional Fair Isle Knitting Pattern* (Hat, V-neck Slip-on, Scarf) (National Trust for Scotland).

Niinimäki, K. (2012) 'Proactive fashion design for sustainable consumption' *The Nordic Textile Journal*, 1, pp. 60–69.

Racinet, A. (1988) *The Encyclopedia of Ornament* (Studio Editions).

Rae, J. (1987) *The Quilts of the British Isles* (E. P. Dutton).

Raeburn, M. & Feiler, P. (2018) *Paul Feiler: 1918–2013* (London: Lund Humphries).

Rana, S., Pichandi, S., Parveen, S. & Fangueiro, R. (2014) *Natural Plant Fibers: Production, Processing, Properties and Their Sustainability Parameters* (Springer Singapore Pte).

Reilly, V. (1989) *Paisley Patterns: a Design Source Book* (London: Studio Editions).

Rutter, C., Armstrong, K., & Blazquez Cano, M. (2017) in 'Sustainability in fashion: A cradle to upcycle approach' pp. 11–30 (London: Palgrave Macmillan).

Samuels, C. (2008) *Art Deco Textiles* (V & A Publications).

Seguy, E., A. (1988) *Abstract and Floral Designs* (London: Bracken Books)

Serena, R. (1998) *Embroideries & Patterns of Nineteenth-century Vienna from the Nowotny Collection* (Antique Collector's Club).

Shepherd, N. (1977) *The Living Mountain* (Canongate).

Stocks, C., & Lewin, A. (2019) *The Book of Pebbles: from Prehistory to the Pet Shop Boys* (Norwich: Random Spectacular).

Stravinsky, I. (1970) *Poetics of Music in the Form of Six Lessons*. Cambridge, Mass. (Harvard University Press).

Sundbø, A. (2001) *Setesdal sweaters: the History of the Norwegian Lice Pattern* (Kristiansand Torridal Tweed)

Thomas, M. (1934) *Mary Thomas's Knitting Book* (London: Hodder and Stoughton).

Thomas, M. (1943) *Mary Thomas's Book of Knitting Patterns* (London: Hodder and Stoughton).

Triossi, A., & Mascetti, D. (2007) *Bulgari* (London: Abbeville Press).

United Nations (1987) 'Report of the World Commission on Environment and Development – Our Common Future' (United Nations).

van der Velden, N. M., Patel, M. K., & Vogtländer, J. G. (2013) 'LCA benchmarking study on textiles made of cotton, polyester, nylon, acryl, or elastane' *International Journal of Life Cycle Assessment*, 19, pp. 331–356.

Van Lemman, H. (1988) *Decorative Tiles Throughout the Ages* (London: Bracken Books).

Verneuil, A., & Calloway, S. (1988) *Abstract Art: Patterns and Designs* (London: Bracken Books).

Victor Vasarely, V., Orosz, M., Imre, G., & Museo Thyssen-Bornemisza (2018) *Victor Vasarely: The Birth of Op Art* (Madrid: Fundación Colección Thyssen-Bornemisza).

Victory Vasarely *The Birth of Op Art*. *Vogue Knitting Magazine* (Conde Nast Publishing. Available online at: https://www.vogueknitting.com/).

Vogue (2021) 'Sustainability' (Conde Nast Publishing. Available online at: https://www.vogue.com/tag/misc/eco-friendly).

Volker, A. (1994) *Textiles of the Wiener Werkstatte 1910–1932* (Thames and Hudson).

INDEX